Gifts from the foot of the Cross

by Gary Robert Villani

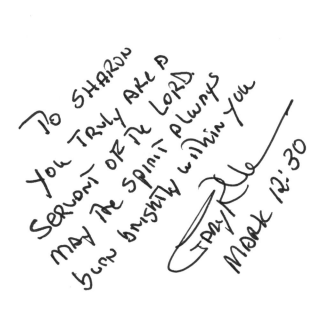

To Sharon
You TRuly ARe A
Servant of The LoRD
MAy The SpiRit plUNTs
buRN bRightly wiThiN you
Gary Villani
MARk 12:30

DORRANCE
PUBLISHING CO
EST. 1920
PITTSBURGH, PENNSYLVANIA 15238

The contents of this work, including, but not limited to, the accuracy of events, people, and places depicted; opinions expressed; permission to use previously published materials included; and any advice given or actions advocated are solely the responsibility of the author, who assumes all liability for said work and indemnifies the publisher against any claims stemming from publication of the work.

Dorrance Publishing Co
585 Alpha Drive
Pittsburgh, PA 15238
Visit our website at www.dorrancebookstore.com

ISBN: 978-1-4809-5316-1
eISBN: 978-1-4809-5292-8

An Opening Blessing

We have all read or heard about people who are of outstanding character. They are people of faith, truth, joy, integrity, and so on. They are the kind of person you wished you knew personally. They are the kind of person that if they asked, you would follow them anywhere because you trust them and knew that it was right. Gary Villani is such a person to me. His joy and enthusiasm comes from a deep and committed relationship with God as made known in the teaching and life of Jesus Christ. Gary has taught Sunday school at St. Thomas for over twenty years, and people come to his class no matter what the topic or format. These people are lovingly and proudly called 'Garyites.' They love to hear his Garyisms, which fill the pages of this book. The Garyisms are offered not in the sense of pride as in, 'look what I came up with,' but with a sense of joy as in, 'look what God gave me to share with you.' These pages are notes from the classes he has taught and they give a sense of Gary's humility, excitement, and gratitude for God's gift to him of faith and joy. The reading of this book is not a task to be accomplished, but a joy to be experienced, like a good wine, a beautiful sunset, a child's smile, or a Belgian Ale. Each to be fully considered on its own merits and the lessons it might teach us. Linger over the teaching and the insight and see what God will share with you. You won't be disappointed. May God richly bless you as He has blessed Gary with faith, hope, and love.

The Rev. Chuck Woehler

Forgiveness
Faith
Charity
Love
Truth
Caring
Honesty

JUST A FEW OF THE MANY 'NUGGETS' OF LIFE LEFT
AT THE FOOT OF THE CROSS FOR GOD'S PEOPLE

Salvation
Prayer
Bible
Gifts
Belief
Repentance
Worship
Eternity
Trust
Life
Passion
Righteous
Heart
Spirit
Humility gratitude
Generosity

Contents

Chapter One:

God and You

Do We Play God?

As strange as this title might sound, I sometimes feel that there may be people out there who believe they have either been blessed with 'the power' to make things happen or with 'below zero' patience. I'm not referring to anything satanic or evil; I'm referring to good old everyday garden variety dilemmas we face almost daily. Don't believe me; take a moment to reflect on the following majestic displays of power.

You're at a traffic light, its red. You continually inch your car forward knowing that by doing so; you will make the light change faster than it's normally scheduled to change. Those cars sitting around you have no earthly idea of the power you possess and how you and you alone will quietly but very deliberately and very dramatically reduce the wait time at the light. You are truly awesome. You have either done this yourself or have witnessed someone accomplish this mighty task. Is it a matter of Power or Patience?

You're at the elevator. I hear you laughing already. Someone has already pushed the call button and it's illuminated, meaning the car will arrive fairly soon. You, however, have the power, that mighty juice running through your veins; you walk over and push the call button again. Why, because you know deep in the inner chambers of your heart this action will make the elevator car arrive much sooner than it would have from the original call. Is it a matter of Power or Patience?

Something is broken and you boldly announce, 'Give it to me, I can fix anything.' Sadly, you're probably the only one in the room that actually believes that you can fix almost anything and surprisingly without the aid of someone else, instructions or divine intervention. So, what just happened here, was it another in a long line of declarations that you can leap tall buildings with a single bound? I'm told that the 'S' on your t-shirt confirms your inner wonderfulness. Well, Power Ranger, you did not say, 'Let me see if I can repair the item,' you chose to make the ultimate statement; it will be fixed by your mighty hands, end of discussion. Is it a matter of Power or Patience?

And finally my favorite; you're at your PC or laptop and you are sitting there repeatedly tapping on the enter key as this will ensure a rapid response from your computer. Well, we all know that is wrong, all it does is make the darn thing even slower. Is it a matter of Power or Patience?

While all of the above was harmless enough, I'm sure many folks read the above examples and most probably proclaimed; 'That's me all right.'

Well, whether you choose 'the power' or 'the patience,' I'm going to build a case on why both selections can sometimes be the wrong choice.

Let's begin with the 'power' selection. Power in the wrong hands can be a very scary and dangerous proposition if we are not adequately and spiritually grounded to handle it, and even then it still comes with a modicum of danger attached to it. Remember a then-famous evangelist by the name of Jim Baker. He allegedly was a spiritual man, yet he was overcome by the power he and many of his followers believed he possessed. This false sense of power caused a mighty 'Praise and Worship' organization to crumble, all in the name of power.

When we allow ourselves to become power mongers and we truly believe that we have achieved a Kingly or even a Godly level of power, that, my friend, is when the dominoes begin to fall. Why? Because we need to exercise that power as a confirmation to ourselves that we indeed wield the big stick and everyone better step up and take notice. There is a very simple explanation for this type of self-absorption; it's called 'Drunk' with power. To those of us that may have experienced this state of power inebriation, we know that it is a force greater than ours and it takes over rational thought, impairing our normal ability to think clearly and consequently, we make some incredibly dumb decisions. The frightening difference between just being drunk as opposed to being drunk with power is very simplistic; after a night of overindulging, we become ill and swear we will never drink again. After a night power flexing, we become falsely energized. We reflect back to its satisfying intent; we just issued a command and our underlings jumped either out of fear or a sense of duty to make the command an instant reality. It reminds me of *The Wizard of Oz*; remember 'The Great and Powerful Oz'?

Let's take a look at Jesus for a moment; he surely could have become a power broker, he had the juice, he could make anything he wanted a reality and this all occurred while He was in a human state of mind and being. He knew all too well the power that was bestowed upon Him by His Father, yet he also had the spiritual presence of mind to exercise that power when it served the will of His Father.

The Lord knows our hearts and minds, and He will only give us what we can handle, no more and no less. What we do with the blessings that have freely been given to us, defines who we really are and more importantly what we will become. Occasionally, the best of our intentions can fall prey to the easy way out; we must guard against this practice and seek repentance and direction to get back on a spiritual track. Remember what happened to Pharaoh when he allowed his hate for Moses and a misguided belief that he was more powerful than the God of Moses? Pharaoh not only lost his only son but his entire army as well. Truly I say to you, use your gifts wisely, the playing field between God and Man is only level at the foot of the cross, and I believe that was by divine design.

A controlled Power must exist in any society if for no other reason than self-preservation. We can have a powerful military, someone can be a powerful speaker, and our Pastor can give us a powerful sermon. Properly used, power can serve man both physically and spiritually very well. Like everything in life, power was created by our Lord and He does not make junk.

Now, one of my favorite areas of study both scripturally and worldly, the absolute bane of mankind: patience. How do we pray for patience? 'Dear Lord, I would like patience and I want it NOW.' How about this gem: 'Lord please grant me patience while I await patience.' I believe I share the same theory regarding patience as most people; be very careful on what you ask for, especially when asking the Lord for patience.

My personal belief is that we all live in a plethora of patient perplexities; I can't wait until it's Christmas, I can't wait until the kids go to bed, I can't wait until our vacation starts, and so it goes. How about long lines, we would rather walk away than stand in line for a freebee if we believed the wait would be 'forever.' We seemingly live on fast food, we fly on fast jets, we have microwave ovens because they cook our food much faster and we always wind up in the fast lane on the highway.

Why do we get so caught up in this patience thing anyway? I think there is a very simple and clear answer; we are running on worldly time as opposed to spiritual time. We live in the I want it now generation. The problem as I see it is self-serving, we really don't want an answer in His time, we want it in our time. If we know what the answer should be, why make us wait? Do we believe our timetables are significantly better than His? I'm not even going to touch that line.

We have all heard the saying 'Patience is a Virtue.' Is it really a virtue? I believe that once we have truly mastered the art of patience, when we no longer look at our watches but look toward heaven, we are becoming the Poster of Patience. When you know in your heart that, whatever it is you're waiting upon, you are sincerely content, discard your old timepiece and trust in His, your life has taken on a new meaning and a new purpose. Who better than our Lord to know what we need and when we need it. You may have heard me say this on numerous occasions but it still rings true: 'The best punishment the Lord can give us is to let us have our own way, to give us what we want and when we want it.' Does this phenomenon exist because it feeds on our impatience or are we simply spiritually deprived?

Okay, it's time to join together these two mighty forces: power and patience. When these virtues co-exist and are skillfully exercised by those whom are spiritually grounded, they can and will produce very positive results. If you still need convincing, re-read the Book of Job. Here was a man who was unquestionably faithful to God, even after his family and every possession he amassed in his time on earth were abruptly taken from him. Through his plight, he remained strong in his faith and truly believed that his God had a plan for him. Now that's what I call intense spiritual power. He did not whine or complain; instead he used his inner strength to calm his anxieties and patiently accepted the path his Lord had chosen for him. Job's power and patience were rewarded as the Lord's blessings made him richer and more powerful than he ever dreamed possible. Throughout Job's ordeal, his Family and Friends ridiculed his patience and saw him as a weak, powerless, and broken man. The beautiful irony of this story is that the naysayers who mockingly cast aspersions upon Job would never come to understand how rich he truly was; he possessed a spirit-filled richness that went well beyond their limited and biased comprehension. The Lord chose Job for his steadfast and unshakable faith, a faith like no other and he stood tall in the face of an adversity that would bring most men to their knees in defeat. When Job went to his knees, it was for fervent prayer, accepting and thanking God for His Blessings, for he knew deep in his spirit-filled soul two undeniable truths; the first being God is the friend who walks in when the whole world walks out and if God brought him to it, God would bring him through it. Amen!

The power of this spiritual equation is the power of three, The Father, Son, and Holy Spirit. Successful men know that work begun in prayer will end in power and they also know that patience is a tree whose root is bitter but fruit is sweet. Simply put, Eve, put down that apple.

Job 1:8 'Then the Lord said to Satan, "Have you considered my servant Job. There is no one on earth like him; he is blameless and upright, a man who fears God and shuns evil."'

Deuteronomy 8: 'You may say to yourself, "My power and the strength of my hands have produced this wealth for me." But remember the Lord your God, for it is he who gives you the ability to produce wealth, and so confirms his covenant, which he swore to your forefathers, as it is today.'

Like Father, Like Son

How many times have we heard that statement? Usually, it's most commonly heard when depicting a negative action or trait. Another common saying is 'the apple does not fall far from the tree.' With that in mind, here is a little something for all of us to think about.

A child is not likely to find something of a father in God unless they find something of God in their father. Did that get your attention, it certainly got mine. One of the toughest things for parents to realize is that our children take our example far more seriously than our advice. The 'do as I say and not do as I do' is completely passé and today's youth are far too savvy to accept that lame excuse.

When I was a young child, my parents (God Bless their Souls) never told me why, just that I had to go to church on Sundays. While they were both believers, I guess they were hoping that someone else would fill in the blanks on their behalf. Consequently, I never really learned or understood why I was there and Sundays just became a day of dread for me. Parents always take an active role with their children when picking out a school or college, so who not take that same active role with their spiritual education?

Have you ever heard anything similar to these statements before? 'What do you mean I can't drink? You drink!' 'What do you mean I have to go to Sunday school? You don't!' Okay, so how do you make sure you're on the right spiritual track? If you want to show your children what Jesus will do for them, show them what Jesus has done for you. Below are a few questions you might want to think about.

Do you tell others, beside your children, what God has done for you?

Do you give all glory to God or are you a self-made person?

Do you show your children what's right, or do you tell them what's right?

Do you pray together and worship together?

Do your children ever see you read the Bible?

Do your children have their own Bible?

Proverbs 17:6 'Children's children are a crown to the aged, and parents are the pride of their children.'

Ephesians 6:1–4 'Children, obey your parents in the Lord, for this is right. Honor your father and mother, which is the first commandment with a promise; that it may go well with you and that you may enjoy long life on the earth. Fathers, do not exasperate your children, instead bring them up in the training and instruction of the Lord.'

If you really want to show your children the measure of how close you are to God, show them how quickly you can get to your knees in prayer. Let them see you Thank God, Praise God, and in everything, seek His Guidance. We have already established that whatever you do, it will set an example, so why not set the right example? Put them in touch with Jesus, because Jesus, your children, and you will all be glad you did.

What's Filling Your Cup?

Whenever we need to be nourished, there always seem to be two cups available for that purpose. While both are uniquely different, there is a very important choice to be made. Do we want to drink from the 'Cup of Salvation' or that other cup, the 'Cup of Doubt'?

The Cup of Doubt, you know whose handiwork that is. The questions seem too mind-boggling to answer: what shall I do, should I accept the new job offer, should we move into a bigger house, did I say the right thing at the right time? The list goes on and on. Satan loves confusion because while he's got you bogged down in this messy mire of doubt, chances are you will make the wrong decision and put another dent into your Christian armor.

The Cup of Salvation, a cup that, while we are not always deserving of it, is always available to us. When drinking from this cup, we experience strong flavors of faith, a rich sense of choice, the warm feeling of spiritual satisfaction and the smooth finish of conviction. Now, doesn't that sound like a better cup than that other one? Order one for a friend while you're at it.

Choose your cup wisely; it's far too easy to second guess your decisions, especially the ones you have made on your own. You cannot expect the Lord to bless plans that He has not been consulted on. You need answers; pray, read your Bible, talk to fellow Christians—you will feel so much better.

Matthew 21:21 'Jesus replied; I tell you the truth, if you have faith and do not doubt, not only can do whatever was done to the fig tree, but you can also say to this mountain, go throw yourself into the sea and it will be done.'

James 1:6–7 'But when he asks, he must believe and not doubt, because he who doubts is like a wave of the sea, blown and tossed by the wind. That man should not think he will receive anything from the Lord; he is a double-minded man, unstable in all he does.'

I would guess that 'doubt' is one of Satan's favorite tools, because once he can introduce doubts into your life, he knows there is a chance to get you to doubt almost anything, even your faith.

You really want to know what God wants you to do . . . Ask Him!

So You Say You're a Christian

One of the scariest moments of my spiritual life was when someone came up to me one day and said, 'I didn't know you were a Christian!' Wow, that knocked the holy wind out of me. My mind raced. I'm a good Christian, why would they ask that, don't they know I go to church? I lead a Sunday school class!

The more I thought about it, the more things swirled in my head. What was I doing or not doing that could have evoked this comment? One thing immediately jumped into my mind: I don't know how or when it happened but for some unknown reason, I stopped saying 'grace' before a meal when I was in a restaurant. Could that be it? How's my driving, I have really been trying not to be an aggressive motorist on the road? Was it a stupid joke I told? Did I walk by someone in need and not realize it or worse yet, did I realize it and fail to render help? It must be my focus; I'm losing my spiritual focus.

Well, as more often than not, my humanness got in the way. I was sure I could crack this case wide open on my own. Duh!

It took a while but I eventually realized that, as much as I would like to be, I'm not perfect. Does that make it okay to do something wrong or cause someone else to stumble? The answer is a resounding 'no' if it is done intentionally or with malice. And the second and most important thing I forgot to do was go directly to the Lord for direction and correction.

I was really stressing out over this, but then I remembered something very important: the Lord knows my heart. Sometimes people who are not of Christian faith seem to take enjoyment in watching a Christian stumble and that is usually followed by the line: 'And you call yourself a Christian.' I wonder if this validates their guilt for not being a part of a Christian world. (This is all conjecture on my part.) The second life tenet which is something that only Christians have and this really eased my pain is 'Christians are not perfect, just forgiven.'

So, with that last thought in mind, I went to the Lord first to seek His forgiveness if indeed I was not measuring up as a solid Christian.

2 Samuel 22:33 'It is God who arms me with strength and makes my way perfect.'

Psalm 28:7 'The Lord is my strength and my shield; my hearts trusts in him and I am helped.'

1 Peter 4:16 'However, if you suffer as a Christian, do not be ashamed, but praise God that you bear that name.'

Okay, now that I'm feeling better, it doesn't take away from my need to correct my actions if indeed there is a real problem out there or if I'm doing something that is being misconstrued. It is my greatest wish and desire that I do not intentionally or even unintentionally cause a fellow Christian to stumble. So, I will still ask the Lord to help me become a better Christian and a much better servant. 'Seek, Serve, and be Saved.'

Now that I have said all this, may I ask a favor of you? Should you one day run into me at a restaurant and it is very noticeable that I have forgotten to say grace before my dining experience, please feel free to come over to my table and say 'May we pray first?'

Are You an Empty Vessel?

Truly each one of us is a vessel, a vessel of the Lord. I like to think of myself as the *S.S. Gary*, I have been Christened (ships get Christened, right?), I have been baptized with 'Living Water' (some vessels get baptized under fire), and I have the best crew: The Father, Son, and the Holy Spirit.

Skilled sailors were not made on smooth seas, and our Lord does not bring us into rough seas to drown us but to cleanse us and to make us better sailors of our vessels.

So now let me ask you a few questions about your vessel.

Are you indeed the captain of your ship?

Who is steering your ship?

What cargo are you allowing on board your ship?

Is your ship in shape?

Are you the love boat or the show boat?

If your ship is not sailing in the right direction and you are beginning to feel as though you're on the *Titanic*, may I offer some recommendations on a new crew?

Captain of the ship – Jesus Christ

Steering the ship – The Holy Spirit

Cargo on the ship – Bible, Faith, Repentance, Joy, and Hope

Ship shape – Spiritual food, church fellowships, sermons, and prayer

Love boat or show boat – Humility

Once you make the new crew changes, while I cannot guarantee smooth seas, I can guarantee it will be a heavenly cruise.

Psalm 48:14 'For this God is our God forever and ever; He will be our guide even to the end.'

Psalm 73:24 'You guide me with your counsel, and afterward you will take me into glory.'

John 16:13 'But when He, the Spirit of truth, comes, He will guide you into all truth.'

So, keep those vessels filled with His spirit and His grace, read your Bible daily, stay in the Living Word, and enjoy the journey. It was designed especially for you.

One final thought on a full vessel, Jesus allows no one to go away empty except those who are full of themselves. Amen!

So I Asked the Lord for a Sign

Signs, signs, signs, they are everywhere you go. Can you think of a place where there are no signs? Remember when we enjoyed all those billboards around town that had those great messages from God: 'Do I need to come down there,' 'Behave or I will make rush hour an hour longer,' and so many others that always seemed to make our day. Signs, the 'Billboards of Life,' can provide aid for us, amuse us, and certainly they are there to direct us.

I needed direction one day and was at a loss for what to do on a relatively important decision that needed to be made. So, I did what any good upstanding Christian would do; once I figured out I couldn't handle the decision on my own. I went to the Lord for help. I said, 'Lord, please give me a sign on what I need to do.' I wanted to be sure I made the right choice.

After a day or so and still no sign, I went back to the Lord and said: 'Lord, I guess I need a much bigger sign because I seem to be missing the little one.' Well, I'm here to tell you that; A) I got a very big sign and B) I will never ask for a big sign again.

Well, the reason I was missing the many signs I'm sure the Lord was giving me was because I had asked for a sign, but in my heart I had already made a decision. No wonder I couldn't see all the signs. I was guilty of 'Lord I need help and here's what you need to do.' Well, it doesn't work that way. When you ask for a sign, you need to take a cue from a railroad sign: 'Stop, Look, and Listen.'

Stop: Stop and pray, stop and watch carefully with an open heart and an open and unbiased mind. When you seek his help, it is essentially an exchange of wills; His will for your will.

Look: Look for the sign you asked for and don't ignore the signs that are contrary to what you want. Look in the Bible, it's loaded with answers. Trust in the Lord.

Listen: Listen for the voices of the Lord, His signs come in many forms and one of the ways He talks to us is through those around us.

Don't play the asked and answered game with the Lord, ask for the direction you need and leave the prayerful request right there at His feet. He doesn't need or require a detailed explanation or helpful hints. If you think about it for just a moment, He knew about this little issue of yours hundreds of years before you were born. Do you still think He needs your help? (Remember, be careful what you wish for.)

Isaiah 7:14 'Therefore the Lord Himself will give you a sign.'

Isaiah 40:26 'Lift your eyes and look to the heavens.'

Proverbs 1:5 'Let the wise listen and add to their learning.'

Beware of the Terrible D's!

So, you're having a bad day, things are not going your way, everything you touch seems to turn ugly and you're thinking, 'What else could go wrong?' As all these woes pile up around you, you become the perfect target for the Evil One's 6D attack offense.

Discouragement – you start to 'doubt' your spirituality and your abilities.

Despair – you begin to feel all hope is lost.

Deceit – you begin to think of non-spiritual solutions to your problems.

Distrust – you can no longer discern who to trust, everyone is out to get you.

Disconnection – you disconnect from your beliefs, your family, and your friends.

And the ultimate terrible 'D'

Defeat – you accept that there is 'no one' and 'no way' out of your problems.

When you allow these unsavory thoughts into your life, you don't slide; you plunge into a dark, isolated, and lonely existence. Sadly, it is at this point that Satan will attempt to secure his claws into your vulnerable soul. There is only darkness at the end of this tunnel and it will go on forever if you succumb to it. Allow Jesus to be the light that brings you out of this despair and back into the ranks of the spiritually healthy. Just as Christ Jesus would never abandon you and I, we must never abandon one in need.

Someone once told me that to be enslaved to one's self is the heaviest of all servitudes. Take heart, fellow believers, through the grace of God the cross has provided the undeniable relief from anything life can throw your way; hope comes in the name of Jesus Christ. The Lord can have anything He wants and all He wants is you, sitting at His side for eternity.

If you know of someone who may be suffering at any level of an attack by Satan, get them medical and spiritual help immediately. Pray for them and with them, get them on a prayer list and use all your spiritual goodness to aid Christ in bringing them back into His loving protection. You and I have been given the great responsibility of bringing others along with us, on our pursuit of a heavenly home. We should never be content to take this trip alone.

Psalm 42:5 'Why are you downcast, O my soul, why so disturbed within me. Put your hope in God.'

Psalm 62:5–6 'Find rest, O my soul, in God alone, my hope comes from Him, He alone is my rock and my salvation; He is my fortress, I will not be shaken.'

Romans 15:13 'May the God of hope fill you with all joy and peace as you trust in Him, so that you may overflow with hope by the power of the Holy Spirit.'

The Blood of Christ makes us safe.

The Word of God makes us sure.

So the next time it seems like everything is going wrong and you feel completely abandoned, turn to Jesus, because the Lord walks in when everyone else walks out. He loves you far too much to leave you alone.

So how do we spell hope . . . JESUS! Because you can never fall below the love of God, no matter how far you think you fell. Amen.

Trouble Sleeping . . .

When people tell me that they have trouble sleeping, my advice is always the same; 'Instead of counting sheep, talk to the shepherd.' **Gary: 24:7:365**

We are all guilty of sleep walking through our spiritual lives some-times, we get a little lazy, we're too tired, and my personal favorite, I'll do it tomorrow. All too often, many of life's tomorrows never come to pass. What's the old saying? 'Out of sight, out of mind'?

The truth of the matter is that you cannot walk with God unless you talk with God. Maybe the reason you're having a problem sleeping is because your mind is centered on a mass of worldly issues—i.e. how will we ever afford college, we can't survive on this income, where will my next meal come from—instead of laying all the issues of the day at His feet. Someone once blessed me with a quick and easy resolve to life's problems: 'The shortest distance between a problem and the resolution of that problem is the distance between your knees and the floor.' Amen to that, my friends.

John 6:35 'I am the bread of life. He who comes to me will never go hungry, and he who believes in me will never be thirsty.'

Want more proof? In every story in the Bible, everyone who had ever approached Jesus with a humble servant's heart, a true believer in knowing that through Him all things were possible, always benefited from His grace, His mercy, and His compassion.

John 4 – Jesus heals the Official's Son

John 5 – The Healing at the Pool

John 9 – Jesus heals a man born blind.

When you retire for the evening and your mind is racing out of control on the events of the day and the events yet to come, sleep will surely evade you. Change your post-sleep routine to begin with prayer and thanksgiving. Next, try switching your thoughts to those of God, recall to mind the many blessings He has bestowed upon you, His abundant love for you, and before you know it, a very peaceful slumber will engulf you and your heavenly thoughts. When you are communing with God, He will not let the outside world interrupt your relationship with Him, He knows what you need and He is there to help you achieve it.

So, the next time that you are stumbling around in spiritual insomnia, try talking with the Shepherd, you will be absolutely amazed by His attention, His love, and how much better you will feel knowing that He has taken on your burdens as His own. Who else do you know that would do all that for you? And if you're still having problems sleeping, try reading the Good Book. The Bible is the only book you will ever read where the author is with you the entire time that you are reading it. Now that thought surely has got to make you feel warm, safe, and comfortable.

Good Night and Sweet Dreams.

Who Do You Trust?

Trust; while it may seem to be a relatively small word, it requires a huge amount of responsibility and the need for solid moral conviction. The dictionary defines trust as having faith in an outcome, a strong belief, and the confidence in knowing an anticipated outcome. Trust means you can rely on an action or count on a specific result.

You may be familiar with the trust exercise, whereby an individual standing on an elevated platform must fall backwards, trusting the folks standing below the platform will catch you, especially before the first painful bounce off the floor. Trust plays a huge part in our daily living. When we go to bed at night, we trust or anticipate that we will wake up in the morning, as children, we trust in the fact that our parents will protect us from the vulgarities that permeate every nook and cranny of becoming a responsible adult. We trust family and friends who stake claim to our heart and soul by their offering of three simple words: I love you. We trust the ability to immediately drive through an intersection when the light turns green, trusting that the cars coming from opposite directions will stop on their respective red signal.

By our very nature we would like to believe that for the most part we are a trusting group of people until someone or something gives us a reason to either be suspicious or withdraw our trust from the entity that has caused us to doubt.

So, all this brings me to the million-dollar question: Who do you trust? Our money has the slogan printed right on it for the entire world to see: 'In God we Trust.' Or do we? How often do we rely on our own wiles to direct an outcome? Why not God? Is the slogan 'In God we Trust' only applicable to those times when we really need Him, or do we trust God with even the smallest details of our lives? There is no sliding scale on trust; you are either fully committed to trust or you are fully committed to your own self-conceived and self-proclaimed special powers.

A note of clarification must be inserted at this point. When you put your trust in God, you have to be fully committed to Him and the path He has chosen for you. A false and dangerous trust is when you weigh God's response against what you personally desire and then choose your own resolution. Whether you care to believe this fact or not, when you place your wisdom above God's, you have just unknowingly demoted Him to second place and elevated your wisdom above His. God does not endorse spiritual arbitration; when you go to Him, you go in complete and total trust and you must surrender whatever thoughts you have as an answer or resolution to your problem. Trust me when I tell you these are not decisions that will lavish spiritual joy upon you. There is an old saying that is very relevant here; 'let go and let God.'

Psalm 9:10 'Those who know your name will trust in you, for you, Lord, have never forsaken those who seek you.'

Proverbs 3:5–6 'Trust in the Lord withal your heart and lean not on your own understanding; in all ways acknowledge him, and he will make your paths straight.'

Romans 10:11 'As the scripture says, 'Anyone who trusts in him will never be put to shame.'

Jeremiah 17:7 'But blessed is the man who trusts in the Lord, whose confidence is in him.'

Isaiah 26:3–4 'You will keep in perfect peace whose mind is steadfast, because he trusts in you. Trust in the Lord forever, the Lord, is the Rock eternal.'

Worldly trust is not always 100 percent faithful but Godly trust is 100 percent faithful and true. Strive to keep your spiritual trust centered on God and the worldly trusts will become easier to discern and those that are trustworthy will be illuminated by His guiding light.

The next time someone asks, 'Who do you trust?' boldly announce that you put your trust in the Lord.

God in a Box

Another favorite Bible verse of mine is **John 20:2** 'They have taken the Lord out of the tomb, and we don't know where they have put him.'

If I can be so presumptuous, I know where He is: He's in a box neatly tucked away in the top of my closet. No, I haven't lost my mind nor am I being disrespectful; I'm being honest. Tell me if this scenario sounds familiar.

You're faced with a major problem and you need the help of the Lord. It must be a big problem because all of the other problems we faced on a daily basis, we were able to solve ourselves, without His help. So okay, it's big and we need help. Now where have I put Him? I remember, He's in the box on the top shelf of my closet. So, I get Him down, I open both my heart and the box and when He's out, I pray that He will help me through this rough patch I've gotten myself into. *Voila*, life is good again. So, what do I do? I carefully and neatly put Him back in the box and back on the top shelf.

Okay, that was a little off beat for most, but let's translate that story into something that hits closer to home. During times of war, they have a neat little slogan for that story; it's called the Fox Hole Prayer. It goes something like this, "Lord, if you get me out of this I promise I'll go to church every Sunday; I'll be a good person etc. etc. etc."

As humans, we think we can handle the majority of everything that life throws at us; after all, it's in our nature, right? Well, the Lord wants all of our problems, not only the catastrophic, but even the little issues that in our minds seem very trivial.

While we may think we have God tucked away neatly in a box on the shelf, that may be our own misguided perception of how we view God. You can take this next statement to your spiritual bank; God was never in the box, He was always right there with you, right by your side through thick and thin, every moment and during every event in your life. He loves you far too much to ever leave you out on that limb by yourself, even when we have not asked for His help. Like the story about the footprints in the sand, it is during times of adversity that He is actually carrying us as opposed to you and I believing that we wangled out of a tight one on our own. Unfortunately, we get so good at handling life's calamities; we are prone to developing a false sense of security, believing we have the juice to handle the majority of what life throws our way. We become self-absorbed in believing we only need God when all else fails; we enter into the dangerous waters of 'don't call me, I'll call you, I can handle this.' The irony of this whole scenario is that by the time we really call on God, I often wonder if he was thinking, 'My wonderful child, why didn't you let me help you from the very beginning, it hurts to see you suffer needlessly.'

As I have become more spiritually mature, I can't imagine going anywhere or doing anything without inviting God to come along. While I know He is always with me, it's comforting to me in believing how pleased He may be that I was thinking about Him and at the invitation to join me. While my parents were alive, it was always enjoyable for me to pay a visit as often as I could but those visits always became significantly more enjoyable when either Mom or Dad would call saying; 'Hey, son, I really miss you, why don't you come for a visit.'

Psalm 46:1 'God is our refuge and strength, an ever-present help in trouble.'

Psalm 33:20 'We wait in hope for the Lord; he is our help and our shield.'

Check your closets, I've checked mine!

I Fired Myself

For many more years than I care to relate or remember, I was not in total wellness or total peace with myself or the direction that was my life moving in. My marriage was wonderful, I had a wonderful and beautiful wife and two awesome children, but something was missing. I felt a void I could not put my finger on.

I read somewhere an axiom that said, 'If your life is not abundant, maybe you should fire the guy running it.' So, I fired myself. In looking back at years gone by, it was the one of the best decisions I had ever made.

So, there I sat, fired, still no answers, not feeling a whole bunch better yet and wondering what happens next. What happened next was easy; I went to my go-to person, my wife, Cathy, a woman of great wisdom and whose heart always seems to be in the right place, God-centered. After sharing my feelings of an unexplainable emptiness, she looked me straight in the eyes and said, 'I know exactly what you need, it's time for some religion.' So, here's the thumbnail version of where she led me. First, I began going to church on a regular basis; next, she had me attending Sunday school classes, which in turn led to a seven-year stretch of BSF (Bible Study Fellowship) and culminating with seventeen years of personally leading Sunday school classes for both children and adults. Whew.

Yes, Virginia, the unexplainable void in my life was filled, and it wasn't Santa Claus, it was Jesus. My life took on a new direction and meaning, I felt a peace I did not have before, and my favorite book became the Word of God, the Bible. I sometimes regret having lost so many years of not being grounded in the Word, yet I am also very thankful that the Lord opened my eyes and had Cathy available to usher me through.

I can now understand and appreciate all the blessing of my life and truly enjoy serving the Lord as an ambassador of His Word and to the world.

So, on to the new me and a short sampling of what I have I learned since becoming closer to God? I have come to understand that it's good to be content with what you have but not with whom you are. I compare myself to the glass of water analogy, whether the glass is half full or half empty. Either way you look at the glass, it still is only a half a glass and there is room for so much more. I guess the best way to explain it was that my void was now being filled by the Holy Spirit, a dormant resident within me who was now actively participating in my life.

I learned that it was so much better to serve others than to serve myself. I thoroughly enjoy leading Sunday school classes, sharing the word and my faith and doing what God expects of me.

My faith developed from believing that God can to a more mature faith in knowing that God will. My mornings have progressed from 'Good Lord, it's morning' to a more spiritually directed 'Good Morning, Lord,' as I start each day with an exchange of wills, His will for my will.

Proverbs 1:1–5 'For attaining wisdom and discipline; for understanding words of insight; for acquiring a disciplined and prudent life, doing what is right, just and fair; for giving prudence to the simple, knowledge and direction to the young. Let the wise listen and add to their learning and let the discerning get guidance.'

Ephesians 4:2–6 'Be completely humble and gentle; be patient, bearing with one and another in love. Make every effort to keep the unity of the Spirit through the bond of peace. There is one body and one Spirit. Just as you were called to one hope when you were called, one Lord, one faith, one baptism, one God and Father of all, who is over all and through all and in all.'

Proverbs 8:35 'For whoever finds me finds life and receives favor from the Lord.'

I started out by telling you I had fired myself and now I pleased to let you know that I have applied for a job with the Lord and he said absolutely, you're hired! I love my new job; the benefits are awesome, eternal life, peace, understanding, humility and love. The hours are also great; my boss works 24/7/365 but allows me some time off to smell the roses and enjoy His creation like never before.

He also wants me to let you know that He has an eternity of openings for whoever would like to join in, no references needed and no previous experience is required.

Lord . . . I'm Very Angry with You

Is it truly okay to be angry with God?

I recently had the wonderful opportunity to see the movie *The Shack*, which is based on the bestselling novel of two years ago. Whether your struggle with anger issues or the inability to forgive, I cannot stress how important this movie will be to your soul. If it's out of the theaters by the time you read this, then I urge you to rent it. And when you do procure it, bring your family and friends together for a truly awesome spiritual experience.

The question of can you be angry with God is yes, but the anger should be a righteous anger and preferably not of the worldly variety. Heinous and unthinkable acts, especially when we own a close relationship with the victims, can sometimes bring out the very worst in us. These feelings are not a depiction of our inner spiritual self, but rather a knee jerk reaction of our humanness. Sometimes we can find ourselves looking toward heaven and saying or thinking, *Lord, how could you have let this happen?*

The Lord gave all mankind free will, and sometimes this free will is grossly misused due to a variety of reasons, many of which I am not medically qualified to comment on. Even when the unthinkable happens, we need to remember that the perpetrator of the act is still one of God's children, even though this person may still be a work in progress. God does not orchestrate ill deeds nor does God stop every person from using their free will, albeit good bad or indifferent. Our Lord loves all His children and wants them to be saved, even the ones that we believe should be given a nonstop ticket to hell. But then we would be judging others and that's not our job. It's hard for us to accept that a loving God can allow evil to happen, but when it does, I can guarantee you that the first one on the scene is God, with a love and compassion in His heart far greater than anything our human hearts and minds can even begin to comprehend. The safe and perfect world we all long for is not under our collective feet, that slice of paradise is waiting for us in a place called heaven.

When the unexpected and unwanted hurts barnstorm into our lives, we can sometimes have the tendency to say, 'Why me, Lord?' and 'Why did this have to happen?' I would like to offer a modicum of caution here, be very careful in calling God to account as He owes us no explanations. Remember, your attitude and mind during times of prosperity will determine your destiny during times of calamity. It is during moments of tragedy that you must allow your heavenly Father to give you what your earthly family cannot, an inner strength and peace that can only be found through the Lord. It's hard to accept this point while in the throes of despair, but many a life that is marred by accident is really being shaped by providence.

Okay, so we addressed the anger issues; the next protocol is even harder to deal with, and that is forgiveness. When someone wrongs us even in a simple way, we can become cold and distant to that individual, but when the crime is of a horrific nature, our minds and our hearts are in a tremendous conflict with one another. What is so devastating here is that unless we let go of that hate, it will take over our entire being and we will be consumed with ill thoughts and unsavory feelings forever. But one must ask, how can I forgive someone who has hurt me or a loved one so badly? There is only way to accomplish this feat, and it is in conjunction with God; you need to summon up the Holy Spirit within you, pray for strength and for a forgiving and discerning heart and know that God is with you every step of this difficult journey. This healing process will not happen immediately or overnight; deep and hurtful wounds can take a while to heal, but without God, your wound will fester and bleed for the rest of your days on earth. Only God can provide the healing power to bring closure to even the most gaping wound but He must be invited into your heart with great faith and reverence.

Exodus 34:6 'The Lord, the lord, the compassionate and gracious God; slow to anger, abounding in love and faithfulness to thousands and forgiving wickedness, rebellion and sin.'

James 1:20 'For man's anger does not bring about the righteous life that God desires.'

Hebrews 8:12 'For I will forgive their wickedness and remember their sins no more.'

Mark 11:25 'And when you stand praying, if you hold anything against anyone, forgive him, so that your Father in heaven may forgive your sins.'

Daniel 9:9 'The Lord our God is merciful and forgiving, even though we have rebelled against him.'

Consider, if you will, a tube of toothpaste being completely emptied of its contents. Now consider what you would do if someone said, "Okay, now put all that toothpaste back into the tube.' 'Impossible,' you say. Angry words are just like the toothpaste tube; once they are levied against someone, they cannot be taken back no matter how hard we try.

Is there someone in your life that would benefit from a forgiving word or perhaps an offer of an olive branch? May the peace of the Lord be always with you.

Did I Forget to Say Thank You Lord . . . Again!

I was having my morning coffee with my friend and coworker Willie Nichols, when he looked across the table in the airport food court and asked, 'When was it you first became a writer?'

Like I sometimes do, I immediately put on my thinking cap when I should have immediately donned my spiritual cap and went as far back as high school. After a few moments of self-deliberation, I determined it was not high school, it must have been college. However, this little trip down memory lane only served to remind me of my less-than-stellar report card grades in English class, both in high school and college. I also sadly recall my parents saying when reviewing my report cards saying, 'I'm paying for this?'

In hindsight I can see the Lord looking down at me and saying, 'This one still needs more work, I love the guy but sometimes he can be so unaware, even when I put things right under his nose; LOL.'

Well, once again I'm sure that I have missed the numerous opportunities the Lord provided for me so that I might listen and learn, so like any good cowpoke, I rode off into the sunset thinking it must have been a hereditary talent. Go ahead and laugh, but just remember we all have those special little moments when we are waiting at the bus depot for our train to come in. You can't fib about this because you know you were there.

As we know, our Lord does work in mysterious ways and according to his own timeline and not ours, which ultimately led to His tapping me on the shoulder months later and saying, 'Great News, I have another Sunday school for you to lead and it's entitled "The Story" and I know you're going to love it.'

Well eighteen weeks into the study, it's a thirty-week program, I came upon the story of Daniel. As I am reading the passages about this young man who has been exiled from his homeland and is being led into a strange new land with even stranger customs, values, and a place fraught with idolatry, the answer to my dilemma is starting to unfold before my eyes and in my heart. As I was being led to the service of leading Christian Education classes, I—like Daniel—needed the gifts from above to accomplish the task the Lord had set before me. In looking back, I should have immediately realized that our Lord always equips those He calls. I now know for sure when I was blessed with the gift of writing, it was eighteen years ago, my first day of entering into a spiritual teaching role.

The Lord, knowing Daniel's heart and what he will be faced with, provides him with the gift or knowledge and wisdom, tools, and skills he will most certainly need to survive in this hostile environment.

Throughout Daniel's ordeal, he remained true to his Lord and repeatedly offered prayers of praise for the attributes of the Lord his God and for the blessings so graciously bestowed upon him.

So, all of the above leads me right back to the title of this missive, have I accepted, used, and thanked my Lord for blessing me with the desire and ability to write. I have but most probably not enough. And while I'm at it, I need to thank Him for each morning that He opens my eyes to the beauty of His creation.

In our sometimes self-serving humanness, we exercise our God-given right to classify many blessings as an entitlement, such as 'I will wake up each morning, I will see the beautiful flowers, I will see my beautiful family, I will drive to work in the beautiful car you blessed me with' and the list goes on and on. Does this mean that God just gave us free will to use however it bests suits us? Do you think our Lord and Savior would like a thank you that is either scheduled or coerced, or a thank you that is timely and heartfelt?

So, when does the 'Thank You Lord' portion of our existence kick in? Well, sometimes on Sundays when I'm feeling particularly thankful, I'll offer up some kudos to the Lord while I'm sitting in my pew. Does that now cover me for a week's worth of blessings? What if I miss church one Sunday, am I now two weeks behind in my thanksgivings?

Like any great parent, I'm sure our Lord would like to hear 'I know I don't do this enough, Lord, and I'm equally as sure I truly do not deserve all that you provide, but thank you so very much for all the blessings of this life.' Okay, was that so difficult to do. Now if you really want to how to be thankful, listen to a child offer an open and honest dialogue with God. Thank you, God, for my friend Jimmy, he's the best. Thank you, God, for my great backyard, did you see us playing out there yesterday? Thank you for my Mom and my Dad and for my puppy, Rascal.

When was the last time you thanked the Lord for your family, your home, your friends, and relatives?

I have heard people say that they are very thankful but there so busy that they sometimes forget to offer up a simple thank you. The only way I can answer this is by simply saying, what if our Lord forgot or was too busy to listen to our petitions and thank offerings? Remember that time when you helped your brother-in-law out of a jam and how put out you were that he didn't even say thank you. Hmmmmm!

Now for the ultimate *AH-HA*; a total stranger opens a door for you and without the blink of an eye, we offer a thank you. Don't get me wrong, that's the right thing to do. So, here is the irony; why then is it so easy to thank a complete stranger and yet it seems so hard at times to thank the Lord who has given us eternity, a God who can't wait until he sees us again and who is building a special place in heaven for each and everyone one of his beloved children?

Now, as a very busy person myself, I am fully aware how time can quickly slip by, but I also know that every day has a 'free moment' compliments of our Lord, that nirvana moment, where we can seemingly hold the passing of time captive, however brief it may be. That's the moment you stop and look up or drop to your knees and from the deepest recesses of your heart, say Thank you, Lord.

Let's jump back to our friend Daniel and his three companions who were being exiled to a strange land. Their faith was unshakable and they would not take anything that would bring shame upon themselves in the eyes of their God. Conversely, even while being led into a foreign land and with not even a glimmer of hope for their fate, they offered thanks to God for yet another day. And here is the blessing that Daniel and his three faithful companions received.

Daniel 1:17 'To these four young men, God gave knowledge and understanding of all kinds of literature and learning. And Daniel could understand visions and dreams of all kinds.'

Colossians 3:17 'And whatever you do, whether in word or deed, do it all in the name of the Lord Jesus, giving thanks to God the father through Him.'

2 Corinthians 9:15 'Thanks be to God for His indescribable gift.'

1 Thessalonians 5: 16–17 'Be joyful always, pray continuously, give thanks in all circumstances for this is God's will for you in Christ Jesus.'

'Thank you, Jesus' is one of the most powerful phrases in your spiritual arsenal, a small phrase that serves to build an eternal relationship. Amen!

Fear the Lord
Over the years I've struggled with the passages similar to these:

Deuteronomy 6:13 'Fear the Lord your God, serve him only and take your oaths in His name.'

Psalm 33:8 'Let all the earth fear the Lord, let all the people of the world revere him.'

If the Lord is a loving and forgiving God, why then should I fear Him? If there are any Biblical Scholars out there who may be reading this and are about to form a lynch mob and have me excommunicated for heresy, please let me convey my personal feelings on this matter first.

Fear can take on many different faces and meanings but the dictionary describes fear as 'An unpleasant feeling of anxiety, or apprehension caused by the presence or anticipation of danger.'

How many of us remember this little ditty: 'Just wait until your Father comes home.' Definitely Fear! 'You're in trouble now, mister.' Definitely Fear! Fear can also lurk in the 'unknown'; will I get the job, where will we get the money we need and I'm afraid they will not like me,' are just a few of the many faces of secular fear. Fear can take over our very lives, as evidenced by the hundreds of bona fide phobias out there, traumatizing so many people. So here I am, fear is trying to put a strangle hold on me, my dad will be home soon and he can't help but notice the rather large dent I put on the fender of his car. I'm dead meat! He was indeed mad, but while I thought he would kill me, I have been spared to relate this tale. Like most, I thought the worst, the end was near and my life was just about to come to a horrible end. My fear was so great I considered running away from home, but that was equally as fearful to me as facing potential death at the hands of my father. Yes, I got an ear full, I was grounded for many weeks, but most fortunately, his love for me was much stronger than the steel fender on the car. He taught me right from wrong when I needed it, he disciplined me when I needed it and yes, it did not matter how stupid I could sometimes be, he loved me very much.

Spiritual fear takes on a slightly different complexion. When we define fear from the Old Testament and with a tongue in cheek perspective, we need to understand that death was sometimes characterized as 'Incoming' and what was left was a burnt mark on the ground. Some scholars feel that God needed to teach and ready the world for the upcoming transition of His Son, so death was sometimes harsh. With the advent of Jesus on the cross, a loving sacrifice by God whereby we can now seek forgiveness and death no longer has a hold on us, we see God in a different light. We see a God who loves us so much he sacrificed His only son, we see a God who says I forgive you and you will never fall from my grasp.

What led us to believe that the actions of God in the Old Testament were so vastly different than today's God?

In the Old Testament, we see a strong and spiritually sound soul named Moses, who was asked by God to lead tens of thousands of Israelites across the desert to a land of milk and honey. The logistics of such a journey and the accompanying responsibility would have struck fear in the strongest of leaders, yet Moses accepted the task. During this Exodus from Egypt, many great difficulties were encountered, but faithful Moses stayed true to his God given assignment. What a guy, right? So why then, when he made one little slip up, allowing the consistent complaining of the Israelites to induce his anger and frustration and in a godlike fashion he declared to the multitudes, 'You need water, watch this, I'll tap on this rock with my trusty staff and out will flow all the fresh water you could possibly hope for'? God was not particularly happy with this little stunt by Moses and immediately revoked his free pass into the Promised Land. Wait, you say, after all he did, God pulled his pass for a little mistake, something that could equate to a typo? Remember, we were still in the learning process being shaped for the times to come. And I know God still loved Moses very much, but there was no room for 'mistakes' back then. Biblical historians can also recall the thousands upon thousands that were killed by the righteous. What about Sodom and Gomorrah; completely wiped out as there were only four righteous citizens in the entire city? While all these events of the past do conjure up sentiments that God was a strict disciplinarian, it is like anything else in life, we learn from the past and have faith in the future. I have a favorite phrase I like to use when talking about the Old Testament punishment, and it goes like this; 'Mess up and beware of an incoming lightning bolt; you're now going to become a spot on the ground.'

I'm not saying that I can do whatever I desire, but 'fear' has now taken on a different meaning for me. While I still have a God that wants me to be strong both spiritually and morally, once He broke the chains of eternal death through the sacrifice of Jesus, my view of the New Testament God is now as a loving parent, someone who cares about every aspect of my life, a God that I can have a relationship with and most of all a God with whom I can share the most intimate details and secrets of my life. When I fall into sin, I know my loving Lord wants me to seek forgiveness, and while He may be upset with some of the bone head things I say and do, His greatest desire is for me to repent and become a humble servant and we are both looking forward to a time when He brings me to the eternal home He has lovingly prepared for me.

So yes, my friends, do fear your Lord, but not as someone who can't wait to punish you and make you sorry for any misdeeds, but rather fear Him as the Loving father who will always be there for you and whose loving hand will provide the spiritual discipline you need to re-shape you down here so you will fit perfectly up there. Amen, Brothers and Sisters.

Hi, Dad, It's Me!

Remember our teenage and pre-adult years and all those 'life-defining decisions' that loomed on our horizons like a mounting storm, those seemingly impossible dilemmas that we instinctively knew would be the bitter end, we were in fact doomed? Our last vestige of hope was quickly fading away, and Superman was unfortunately not available to save the day. Just when it seemed all was lost, that little voice in our heads would say, 'Hey, dummy, call home.' Whenever we were faced with a big decision or problem, we speed dialed Mom or Dad for guidance and/or financial assistance, as they were that all important life-preserver we knew would always at the ready to pull us from the clutches of disaster. You know the calls I'm talking about; 'Dad, I'm a little short on rent this month' or how about 'Mom, can I come over to do my laundry and maybe have a hot meal' and finally, 'Dad, there is a slight dent in the car and it wasn't even my fault.' We could always rely on the fact that while the decision rendered by our parents may not have been what we wanted at the time, the advice was always sound and ultimately made us feel better about the direction and choices we were about to make. We also knew that Mom and Dad would be behind us every step of the way until our crisis was over. When you think about it, even

E.T. had to 'phone home' even though it seemed that he could make things better simply by touching it.

Call home—what a great concept. We have a Heavenly Father who wants to hear from us and He wants all of our problems, all of the time, placed directly at His feet. This being the case, why does prayer seem like a difficult and solemn task for some of us? I think that one reason might be that we are not comfortable with the specific order of prayer; Praise and Thanksgivings always come first, followed by our personal supplications. Perhaps another reason may be we never know what 'holy' words we are supposed to use when offering up a prayer.

While there is a suggested 'style' or order for prayer, I think our Heavenly Father would be thrilled to hear from us, even if our 'style' was not in a perfect order. I learned this lesson from my daughter Breanna. During her early years, I would join her for prayers before she retired for the night. As we knelt next to her bed, I was poised and ready to walk her through the proper 'order' of prayer. Hah, it was Breanna that walked me through what prayer was all about. Her prayers were a conversation with her best friend. Still to this day, a warm glow shines in my heart when I think about these wonderful dialogues. I can still hear her say, 'Lord, today I played over at Caitlyn's house and we had so much fun, we made mud pies and they looked kind of yucky, but it was still fun. Oh, then her mom gave us ice cream, it was real good, you would have liked it. My dad is with me and he likes to talk to you to, right, Dad?' It took a moment for me to answer because I was thinking about how wonderful it must be to have such a loving relationship with the Lord. I could almost see our Father smiling from ear to ear as she related the days stories and adventures, talking about how much He would have enjoyed being a part of it all.

What's the saying, 'out of the mouths of babes'? All these years I would try to make my prayers sound like a benediction of some sort, when in truth all I needed to do was develop that' same style of 'loving relationship,' that same level of trust and then I could get over the semantics that were always making me stumble and fumble through my prayer life. I simply needed to call home; I simply needed to talk to my Heavenly Father, my Friend.

Well, I'm happy to report that my prayers became much easier from that point on and a funny thing happened along the way. I can't tell you exactly when or how, but one day I found my prayers were in the 'order' that had once been my prayer nemesis. I believe the Holy Spirit said, 'Now you've got it' and graciously got me back on the right spiritual track. I now fully understand that I need to offer praise to a Lord that truly loves me no matter what, a Lord that always has time for me and will never turn away from me even when the demands of a hectic life (that is self-imposed and a self-diagnosis, or a clinical way of making an excuse) start to pull me away from Him. I also understand that I need to thank my Lord for the many blessings He has bestowed upon me, much of which I truly have not earned or deserve.

I am an acronym nut, so I will offer you the simple 'ABC's to prayer.

A = About. It's all about our Lord and Savior, not us. Praise Him as the Most Holy of Holies, Praise Him as the Great Physician and the Great I am, Praise Him as the King of Kings, the Lord of Lords.

B = Blessings. Thank Him for all the blessings in your life, for His Grace, His patience with us, His unceasing forgiveness of our sins and especially for all the things that we take for granted. Thank Him for your family, your job, a sunrise, a sunset and for yet another day to enjoy the life and the blessings He has so graciously bestowed upon us.

C = Communication. Open up your heart, tell Him what's troubling in your life, tell Him about the person who needs to feel the presence of the Lord in their life, tell Him about the weaknesses you struggle with and tell Him how much you need Him in your life. We have a Lord who wants every one of His children to one day be at His side in the heavenly home He has already prepared for us.

And remember, under no circumstances underestimate the power of prayer. I look back on many of the trials and tribulations of my life and I simply cannot begin to imagine how I would have been able to face the issues head-on no less get through them without the presence and guidance of the Lord. We would never step onto a football field without the proper protection, nor would we drive our cars without a seatbelt, so why would we ever consider attempting to step onto the field of life without the full armor of God? The armor is free, it has already been paid in full through the blood of Christ, and as a direct result of a committed prayer life, our armor becomes stronger and stronger.

One final note on prayer and this is an important one to remember. When seeking guidance from the Lord, avoid saying; 'Lord this is my problem and this is what it will take to fix it.' Never put limitations on the Lord and never go to prayer with pre-conceived solutions, because you will most certainly miss the message and direction our Father has for you. When offering prayer requests, don't tell your Lord how big your problem is, tell your problem how big your Lord is. A good point to ponder is if the Lord did not love us so very much, He would indeed let us have our own way.

So, if you're one of those individuals who still feels a little bit uncomfortable with prayer, try the Breanna method, talk to your best friend and you will be amazed how much you have to share. Now, for heaven's sake, please Call Home, your heavenly Father is anxiously waiting to hear from you.

P.S . . . The line is open and available 24/7/365

Lord's Telephone Number:

Jeremiah 33:3 'Call to me and I will answer you and tell you great and unsearchable things you do not know.'

I'm Still in Charge!

During the past two months, I have been going through a rough patch, so to speak. My company recently participated in a bid regarding the majority of services we provide at the airport. Unfortunately, the bid did not go our way and I will lose approximately ninety employees. I am very concerned about what will happen to these ninety souls. Will the new company hire them on? What if they don't, what will these folks do? What can I do to help them? And finally, what about my job, which is a completely secondary concern; the welfare of my employees is first and foremost, then we will talk about me.

Yes, the questions kept swirling around in my head. I think I did a very good job in trying to stay spiritually strong, knowing the Lord would provide and work this dilemma out, so my focus was always directed at keeping the faith and equally as important, sharing the faith by example. Of course, every now and again, a shadow of doubt and worry would begin to flicker deep within my soul and I would catch myself and say, 'Sorry, Lord, my humanness is getting in the way again' and I would immediately offer up prayers and petitions for strength of character and spirit. Alas, what seemed like a few measly minutes later, the worries were back again and more Tums to the rescue. I think I was becoming a Tums-aholic, if there is such a thing. Unfortunately, in my prayers, I foolishly gave the Lord a timetable that needed to be followed. Honestly, folks, I really do know better and I should have remembered that 'emotion without devotion leads to commotion.'

It seemed that the majority of the time I was able to control my worries, or so I thought, as evidenced by the Tums popping described above. I started to believe that between a combination of prayer and Tums Smoothies, life would be good again. I'm ashamed to say that after a few hollow victories and a bottle of Tums later, I began to believe that I had this puppy under control. Well, we all know the answer to that . . . NOT!

Most unfortunately, the Tums were going down faster and more frequently than my knees to the floor. Just when I thought my inner brilliance, better known in this case as Tums, had led me astray, I started to compliment myself for getting all the issues at hand under complete control. I had an awesome plan in place, even if I say so myself. I guess the Lord had about all the nonsense He was going to put up from me and yanked the rug right out from under my brilliant prospectus. It was like the magician that pulls the table cloth out from under the dinnerware without breaking a single item and we all go 'wow.' Well, in my case the dinnerware went away with the table cloth and what I felt was not a 'wow' but a spiritual ouch.

Well, like any good stumbling smarty pants, I began planning my pity party; it seemed like it was not only necessary, but the right thing to do. While deep into my self-imposed funk, my wife, Cathy, asked me to take out the garbage. This was not a monumental task; I've taken it out to the garbage container along the side of the house probably five hundred times since we've moved here. However, on this particular occasion, the Lord had something He wanted to tell me. As I proceeded to the side gate, I typically never look up or around, I simply open the gate, empty the trash, done deal. Well, this time, it was different than ever before. The Lord lovingly took his hand and lifted my head up toward heaven. Directly above my house was a perfectly formed cross in the sky. Now, most folks would say that it was just two aircraft contrails that crossed over each other. Perhaps, but I would like to believe it was a two-part message from the Lord directly to me.

It was as if He was saying to me, 'Gary, why do you think I formed this cross above you?' First, my child, it's to help keep your heart calm and your spirit strong, I want you to physically see that I will always be with you.' Okay, that set me back on my heels almost immediately; pangs of guilt began to rack my entire spiritual existence. Was I was putting more faith into a bottle of stupid Tums, instead of into my Lord and Savior? Shame on me! I truly do know better, but sometimes when we fail or forget to go to the Lord for help and we become righteously arrogant about who is best equipped to fix the problem and it is usually at that very moment when we get our socks pulled up real fast, or as like to call it, a much-needed attitude adjustment.

The second part of His message was equally as dramatic as the first and certainly more painfully direct. I felt Him telling me with a paternally strong but with loving admonishment, 'That cross above you, and the key words here are "above you," was put there by me to remind you that *I'm still in charge.*'

Matthew 6: 25, 27 'Therefore I tell you, do not worry about your life, what you will eat or drink or about your body, what you will wear. Is life not more important than food and the body more important than clothes? Who of you by worrying can add a single hour to his life?

Romans 8:8 'Those controlled by the sinful nature, cannot please God.'

Philippians 2:5 'Your attitude should be the same as that of Christ Jesus.'

I know there are many wonderful medications out there that come in a bottle and are designed to help heal many of life's maladies and there is absolutely nothing wrong in partaking of these medically prescribed and legal ointments. The great care we must exercise occurs when we put the majority of our trust in something man has made as opposed to seeking a strong dose of spiritual guidance. Need more justification, even with insurance, the majority of over the counter meds come with a price. Our spiritual guidance and direction is completely free; as Christ has already paid the ultimate price tag, He surrendered his life so that each and every one of us would have unlimited and eternal blessings. Amen!

How Precious is Our Life?

Have you ever stopped to think about how precious and how fragile our lives are? The Lord gave us a most beautiful gift, the ability to temporarily walk this big marble called earth? If all that was not great enough, He also promised us eternity by His side in a beautiful home that He has prepared just for you and I. So, the big question then becomes 'are we enjoying the gifts of this life or are we blindly sleepwalking as we stumble and trample through these precious moments, never smelling the roses?'

During the past thirty days, I have been in the midst of some of the vulgarities of life: death, sorrow, and brutality. My wife's stepsister passed, a week later my wife's stepfather passed, then one of God's beautiful creatures, a cardinal, flew into a window next to where I was standing and broke its neck, and finally one of my employees sent me a picture of her broken face after being brutally attacked by her ex-husband.

During this thirty-day period, I watched and listened to the sorrow and the heart-wrenching tears of my wife, Cathy, and my mother in-law Joy, as they mourned the loss of those so very close to them. Later, when I was sharing the story of the Cardinal that flew into our window, my wife, Cathy, shared with me that Cardinals mate for life. I know I'm going to sound like some sappy tree hugger, but for the next two days I listened to the mate of that Cardinal calling constantly for her now missing companion, and yes, all of the sorrow and pain, including the Cardinal brought tears to my eyes.

As He always does, the Holy Spirit within me said, 'Okay, Gary, let's sit at your desk, open your laptop and Bible, and let me show you what I'm thinking about life.

Deuteronomy 30:19–20 'This day I call heaven and earth as witnesses against you that I have set before you life and death, blessings and curses. Now choose life, so that you and your children may live and that you may love the Lord your God, listen to His voice, and hold fast to Him. For the Lord is your life, and He will give you many years in the land, He swore to give your fathers, Abraham, Isaac and Jacob.'

Our Lord is telling us that He is your life. When you choose the Lord, you choose life, so make your life full, rich, and productive as your Lord created it to be. Truly I tell you, it's a simple choice to make, so please do not make it complicated or seem out of reach. Start that relationship, start each day on your knees, asking your Lord for daily direction, thank Him for all your blessings and the blessing of this life and know that during every single moment of the day, He is right there with you. I don't know about you, but I can't think about going anywhere or doing anything without the comfort and knowledge that my Lord is with me through the good times, the sorrow, and the learning opportunities for my personal growth.

Like the passing of my relatives and the cardinal, we never really know when our time is at end, when our Lord and Savior says' my dear child, it's time to come back home to me.'

As in the Deuteronomy passage above, we have been given choices and in most cases, many years to live, learn and love. How many times have we either said or have heard someone say, I can't believe how fast time is flying by. It can't be Christmas already, it seems like we just put all the decorations away.

If we know that time is indeed moving much faster than we would like, why not make our lives rich, full, and productive as our Lord wishes it to be.

Live: Enjoy each and every moment, savor the beauty around you, inhale the fragrance of life and look with awe of the splendor of His creation. Satan would love nothing better than to hang that anchor of doubt and despair around your neck, so learn from adversity and look to a future of great spiritual and physical enrichment. The Lord has painted a tapestry of life unlike any other, and He wants us to fully experience and appreciate His creation, while He is preparing a place for us in for His heavenly home.

Learn: If our heavenly father brings you to it, He will most certainly bring you through it. Take each step in life forward and not backwards. He is calling to you; listen to the spirit within you. When faced with difficult situations, ask God for direction, protection, and the strength to understand and grow from the experience at hand and then be sure to thank Him for the blessing of knowledge so that you may be a blessing to someone else in need. If every step we took in life was easy, safe, and uneventful, while that may sound great, would we truly learn anything? Would we truly appreciate anything?

Love: Love your God with all your heart, Love your family, friends and neighbors as our Father has requested us to do. If there are broken relationships, fix them; if irreparable, pray for guidance and direction; old feuds still in effect, patch them with love; any grudges still taking up space in your heart, release them and move on. Love is a word we sometimes take for granted; 'of course I love you even though I don't always say it.' My thought is, why can't we always say it? There is no cost involved, there is much to be gained by saying it and it takes little effort and no calories are expended. What could be easier than that? Want to learn a lot about Love, open your Bible.

Live, Learn, and **Love** are the essentials of our earthy existence, of our mortal souls, as we are being shaped down here by our Lord, so that we fit perfectly up there.

In this seemingly short jaunt through life, we can be bogged down by many obstacles intended to keep us from our appointed path; heaven. In my heart, I do not believe our Father intends or wishes for us to be tied to unrelenting grief, unhappiness, sadness, or misfortune. He has given us the power of the Holy Spirit to exercise our free will to navigate around and through these anomalies of life and in the end, become a much stronger and wiser Christian. When we are happy our Father in Heaven is happy as He truly shares in our fears, tears, sad moments, and joyful moments.

If any of this has made you hungry for life, remember what our Lord has told us;

John 6:40 'I am the bread that came down from heaven.'

Psalm 8:3–5 'When I consider your heavens, the work of your fingers, the moon and the stars, which you have set in place, what is man that you are mindful of him.'

Not knowing her fate, an employee of mine once said to me, 'Had I'd known I was going to live this long, I would have taken better care of myself.' Three hours later, her plane crashed in the Virgin Islands and she died.

Our Lord has blessed us with temporary wings, like the Cardinal in the beginning of this story, to soar to great heights, to see wondrous things, to enjoy the majesty of life to its fullest. Do we really want our epitaph to read, 'I knew I would go one day but just not this soon, there was so much I wanted to do and see.'

Spread those wings and accept the blessings of life; live, learn, and love until your cup over flows, because before we know it, we will be trading in those temporary wings for a beautiful set of eternal wings called your heavenly home. All the instructions you will ever need are found in your Bible, and remember, God is your co-pilot.

Wake up and smell the Roses . . .

Wake up to His glory . . . .

Wake up to the Father who gave you life . . . .

Wake up!

Man and God

God, a Man, a Woman, a Serpent, an Apple, Death, a Birth, a Tree, the Holy Spirit, and Eternal Salvation. As diverse as the names are in the above succession of people and events may be, the theme of this relationship will forever will be known as a story of love. A thumbnail sketch from creation to the very moment you are reading this and beyond.

Man and God, a match most certainly made in heaven. We know that this relationship originated in the Garden of Eden, and we also know how much God enjoyed spending time walking in the cool air of the garden with His creation, Man. We also know that a serpent tempted Eve, Adam's mate provided by God, to eat fruit from the Tree of Knowledge, thereby ignoring the one command God gave them; don't eat from this tree. Eve in turn tempted Adam to eat the apple as well, and as the story goes, the Man and Woman were driven out of the garden. No longer protected within the garden because of an ill-advised choice in fruit, mankind has now come under the grasp of death. Since Adam and Eve were naked and in need of clothing, it was necessary for God to slay an animal to provide clothing for the couple, thus being the first indication in the Bible of death.

Man's creational relationship with God no longer existed once He departed the safety of the garden. In today's environment, a breach of policy can usually be rectified with an apology or a consequence of minor proportions. However, when you disobey God and enter a world inhabited by sin, the apology process is not so simple. Despite being sent out of the garden, God still loved His creation of man and woman very much and now He would have to make a supreme sacrifice to fix man's folly and save him from deaths beckoning. God sent His only son, whom He loved, to sinful us, to be hung on a tree where He would die for our sins, removing death from our doorstep and guaranteeing eternal salvation. This all culminates in the two specific events below;

The birth of Christ brought God back to man but it took the cross of Christ to bring man back to God. How great is His love for us? God spilled His own blood rather than our blood. A sacrifice beyond our human fragility and one we could never conceive on our own and one where we can only imagine the pain associated with the flogging, the beatings and the horrible spikes that pieced his body as He was hung from that tree. No greater love exists than the agape love of our Lord for His children. Thanks be to God!

Prior to His death, Jesus promised us the gift of the Holy Spirit, a gift from His Father, and it was from that moment that man was blessed with an internal intercessor, the Spirit of God within us, a beacon for right and wrong, someone to help guide us to our heavenly home. Now that we have been freed from deaths mortal grasp, the doors of heaven have swung back open, with a huge spiritual sign stating; this way home.

The sacrifice of Christ has given us the ability to seek forgiveness of our sins, enabled us to have meaningful dialogue through prayer with our Savior and has guaranteed to those who believe, a seat at the table in heaven.

Genesis 2:16–17 'And the Lord God commanded the man, 'You are free to eat from any tree in the garden; but you must not eat from the tree of the knowledge of good and evil, for when you eat of it you will surely die.'

Genesis 3:13 'Then the Lord God said to the woman, 'What is this you have done'? The woman said, 'The serpent deceived me and I ate.'

Genesis 3:21 'The Lord made garments of skin for Adam and his wife and clothed them.'

Genesis 3:23 'So the Lord God banished him from the Garden of Eden to work the ground from which he had been taken.'

Matthew 1:21 'She will give birth to a son and you are to give him the name Jesus, because he will save his people from their sins.'

John 14:15–17 'If you love me, you will obey what I command. And I will ask the Father and he will give you another counselor, to be with you forever, the Spirit of truth.'

John 19:16 'Finally Pilate handed him over to them to be crucified.'

John 19:30 'When He had finished the drink, Jesus said, 'It is finished' With that he bowed his head and gave up his spirit.'

Romans 2:7 'To those who by persistence in doing good seek glory, honor and immortality, he will give eternal life.'

Perhaps the best summation to this to this story can be 'the ultimate destination in your journey is not the end, it's the new beginning.' Hallelujah!

Conflicting Schedules

To my way of thinking, there are two very real and distinct schedule conflicts in life, our personal schedules, which serve to please us, and God's schedule, where we should be doing work that is pleasing to God. Whether we choose to acknowledge it or not, each one of us, at one time or another, will be faced with a scheduling conflict: God or me?

I'm quite certain our hearts do not arbitrarily put God behind our own desires, but as living, breathing, walking, talking members of this world we call home, on occasion we seem to put creature comfort ahead of spiritual necessity. Need a few examples?

I really wish I could go to church on Sunday, but that's the day I play on a league baseball team. The questions that immediately pop into my mind; are there other services you can attend on Sunday, or does your church celebrate a service on days other than Sunday? Have you even checked, or was it because you didn't want to know the answer?

I can't help down at the soup kitchen because I have a new car and I'm very concerned about parking it in that part of town. My next questions are who blessed you with that new car to begin with and why can't you take an Uber ride? It's certainly cheap enough. Hmmm, didn't think of that either?

How is it then, when we need God's help, we don't want any excuses, we want His help immediately. What if God said, 'Hey, Gary, I'd really love to help but I can't seem to find my GPS for directions to you.' Certainly not the answer we were looking for, was it? So, the critical question becomes; do we only serve God when it is convenient for us to do so? God wants us to do the things we like, to experience joy and happiness in our lives but it's also a two-way street, we need to be mindful of the things He has set before us.

We all live very busy and hectic lives and I'm sure our life schedules are bursting at the seams from time to time, yet when there is something we really want to do, we somehow find or make the time. If indeed we only serve God at our convenience, we must accept the fact that we are only serving ourselves and not God.

Think back over the past year or two, was there any event that was more important than God? I can hear you saying; absolutely not as one would have to be out of their mind to say otherwise. Then what's the deal, why is it so hard to serve God when He needs us most? I don't believe I need to remind you that it is the Evil One who helps us prioritize the order of events if we allow him to do so. And it goes without saying where he will put God's work on your list of priorities.

Another soul-searching question we need to ask ourselves: 'Does my schedule reflect my desire to get to know God?'

In a previous book, I wrote something that bears repeating; No God, No Peace; Know God, Know Peace. Our relationship with God must be the most important one of our lives, we need to be in regular communication with Him and always seek an exchange of wills, His will for our will.

Deuteronomy 10:12 'And now O Israel, what does the Lord your God ask of you but to fear the Lord your God, to walk in all his ways, to love him, to serve the Lord your God with all your heart and with all your soul.'

Matthew 6:24 'No one can serve two masters. Either he will hate the one and love the other, or he will be devoted to the one and despise the other.'

Hebrews 9:14 'How much more, then, will the blood of Christ, who through the eternal spirit offered himself unblemished to God, cleanse our consciences from acts that lead to death, so that we may serve the living God.'

Ephesians 6:7 'Serve wholeheartedly, as if you were serving the Lord, not men.'

Be very mindful not to serve God leftovers; your time and money, etc. God should always be your first and foremost priority, the first fruits of life, in all that you do and in all that you say.

I'm positive that you will be far more satisfied in serving God than in serving yourself. As a final note, the only thing in your life that should be 'self-serve' is the ice cream machine at your favorite restaurant.

The Key to Life

If you have ever struggled with what is the secret to life, I can unequivocally tell you that it would be a great waste of time to climb a mountain to consult a guru as the Apostle Paul has already defined this for us in his letter to the Colossians.

Colossians 2:2–5 'My purpose is that they may be encouraged in heart and united in love, so that they may have the full riches of complete understanding, in order that they may know the mystery of God, namely, Christ, in whom are hidden all the treasures of wisdom and knowledge. I tell you this so that no one will deceive you by fine sounding arguments. For though I am absent from you in body, I am present with you in spirit and delight to see how orderly you are and how firm your faith in Christ is.'

When we need answers or are struggling with life in general, there is absolutely no need to go any further than the nearest Bible. As the Apostle Paul has so eloquently stated, all that we will ever need for spiritual enrichment, wisdom, and knowledge can be found on the pages of our Bibles.

While I understand and acknowledge there are many other vehicles for worldly wisdom and knowledge available to those who desire to seek these treasures, I am addressing those of a spiritual and Christian nature, as once we become spiritually grounded in the Word, everything else takes on a proper perspective.

There are some people that require absolute and undeniable proof before any hypothesis or life tenet can be stamped as an absolute truth. While this may provide a modicum of contentment for some, using this type of philosophy for solving the great mysteries of life completely negates the need for even the slightest bit of faith. If it cannot be proven, it is not an accepted fact of life.

If I may, I would like to pose a simple question to those that subscribe to the 'prove it' philosophy. When you go to sleep at night, you do so with the expectation that you will awaken the next morning? Has anyone come up with a scientific equation that proves this event? Since there is no mathematical hypothesis that I'm aware of that explains this phenomenon, could it be an exercise of faith?

Some things in life will always remain a mystery, that is the nature of life and until such time our Lord brings us into His light, we need to accept His word and His promises to us as the gospel truth. If this were not the case, would we be dismissing the need for heavenly intervention on the premise that anything that cannot be proven simply does not exist?

I shudder to even begin to think of a world without faith and without God. We may think we're pretty hot stuff, smart as a whip and totally self-sufficient, but when the proverbial stuff hits the fan and none of the self-proclaimed sages and gurus can come up with a tangible answer, we immediately turn our thoughts and prayers to our Heavenly Father.

Knowledge is a wonderful attribute and technology certainly serves to make our lives much easier with each new discovery, and for that I'm very thankful. But conversely, I must say that I truly do not want to know what the scientific reasoning is as to why I awaken each morning. I'm very content in my faith and belief that Jesus is watching over me as I sleep and brings me into each new day and into His service, and for that I am eternally thankful.

In closing, I would like to state in my humble opinion that I do not believe the Lord gave us a set of keys to his creation, planet Earth. What He did give us is a gift beyond our greatest expectations and one that we certainly did not deserve: eternal salvation.

God entrusted only one person with the keys to life, and it was His Son, Jesus, and we should all get down on our knees daily in thanks for that bit of wisdom. Amen!

Genesis 2:7 'The Lord God formed the man from the dust of the ground and breathed into his nostrils the breath of life, and the man became a living being.'

Romans 8:38 'For I am convinced that neither death of life, neither angels nor demons, neither the present nor the future, nor any powers, neither height nor depth, nor anything else in all creation, will be able to separate us from the love of God, that is in Christ Jesus our Lord.'

John 14:6 'Jesus answered, 'I am the way and the truth and the life.'

Proverbs 19:3 'A man's own folly ruins his life, yet his heart rages against the Lord.'

John 6:47–48 'I tell you the truth, he who believes has everlasting life. I am the bread of life.'

Deuteronomy 30:20 'and that you may love the Lord your God, listen to his voice and hold fast to him, for the Lord is your life and he will give you many years in the land he swore to give your fathers, Abraham, Isaac and Jacob.'

Chapter Two:

Worship

Some Thoughts about Worship

The birth of Christ brought God to man, but it took the cross of Christ to bring man to God. Wow, what a powerful statement of love. Now the question becomes, how do we repay that love? Well, you guessed right, I have a few thoughts on that.

Do not lean on your own understanding, lean on God's word.

Never put a question mark where God puts a period.

God will give His best to those who leave the choice with Him.

Real faith is man's weakness leaning on God's faith.

His glory shines and is revealed through our service.

We repay Jesus by being a blessing to others on this earth.

Each of us can be as close to God as we choose to be. The question becomes do we hold Him at arm's length or do we embrace Him with the same reverent love He has for us? We were each chosen by God's grace to be here. We also need to be very cognizant of how fortunate we are that we can openly worship God and not face persecution or even death as in other parts of the world.

Worshipping God is also an act of love, an act of the will, treating others as God has treated us. Our obedience then becomes the measure of our love for Jesus. Once we belong to Christ, we cannot be separated. And it must be added here, how fortunate and blessed are we, knowing that we will never fall from His grasp. The scarlet thread of redemption that runs through each of our lives then becomes very clear; we are not holding on to Him, He is holding on to us.

Someone once told me that knowing God is more important than knowing about God. At the time, I didn't fully understand what they were trying to tell me, but when I opened my heart to that message, I realized the answer was very simple; keep my focus on Christ, ask Jesus to make me more mature and more secure, as God reveals Himself to those who earnestly seek Him.

Take a simple worship test. Start each day with an exchange of wills, His will for your will. Begin your mornings with a prayerful conversation with God, open your Bible and just read a few verses with your morning coffee. You will be absolutely amazed at the new peace and comfort you will begin to enjoy. Who knows, you might even change from the person who wakes up and proclaims 'Good Lord it's morning' to your newfound greeting 'Good Morning, Lord.' And don't forget about Sundays, worshipping God with fellow Christians is an awesome experience, as you grow both individually and as a member of a church family.

Now that I have you in church, give some thought to attending a Sunday school class, a time of Christian fellowship that will most definitely feed your soul and bring great peace and joy into your life and the lives of those around you. Studying the Word with fellow Christians is perhaps one of the most rewarding classes you will ever attend. What I personally like about Sunday school is the fact that no biblical experience or knowledge is required to attend; just show up with an open heart and open mind, Christ will take care of the rest.

Psalm 95:6–7 'Come, let us bow down in worship, let us kneel before the Lord our maker, for He is our God and we are the people of His pasture, the flock under His care.'

Psalm 100:2–3 'Worship the Lord with gladness; come before Him with joyful songs. Know that the Lord is God. It is He who made us and we are His, we are His people, the sheep of His pasture.'

A final point to ponder, the man who knows God, worships God. The man who does not know God will find other things to worship.

Hey, Whose House is This Anyway?

In previous discussions you have heard me talk about how important the church is, how important our church family is to our spiritual wellness. Additionally, the word 'church' and the word 'family' both have six letters, representing a true oneness. The church is the Lord's House, and we are His Family. Having now said this, I need to ask the burning question that is at least on my mind. Why does Satan do his best work in the Lord's House, our church? Who invited him in anyway; did he follow someone right through the front door?

Inside almost every church we can see Satan's handiwork. Folks whispering (did you see what so and so did or did not do), jealousies (who got to do what, who didn't get to do it), and small groups of folks who seem to stir the pot in the name of Christianity. Each time one of these little green monster types rears its ugly head in our church, make no mistake about it, it's a huge victory for the Evil One. Our church then becomes a marketplace for Satan to sell his wares.

John 2: 13–16 'So he made a whip out of cords, and drove all from the temple area, both sheep and cattle, he scattered the coins of the moneychangers and overturned their tables. To those who sold doves he said, "Get these out of here! How dare you turn my Father's house into a market?"'

Matthew 21:13 '"It is written" he said to them, "My house will be called a house of prayer, but you are making it a den of robbers."'

Wait, we're not selling sheep or cattle in church, what's the big deal? We are indeed a marketplace, and what we are selling is perhaps even worse. We're selling gossip, we're exchanging juicy stories about someone, we're selling someone's good name down the drain, and all in the name of a day's work or under the guise of what needs to be done.

I'm sure that most churches, like mine, have numerous ministries that offer services within the church community as well as ministries that reach outside the physical boundaries of the building. Additionally, there are many very solid Christian people who devote much of their time in support of these ministries. How tragic would it be if some ill-placed 'sellers of sin' besmirched our church name and family members for unsavory reasons? The sweat, tears, toil, and joy of so many volunteers stand to become victims of someone's own selfish desires.

If you need to whisper something or form a small lynch mob, it's not work; it's just plain old everyday garden variety gossip. If you need to besmirch someone's character, it's not forgiveness, its revenge. If it's jealousy, look in a mirror and count your own blessing before you ask God to account for what He has given someone else. If it's some bizarre power struggle, remember there is only one person in this house that has absolute power over everything, and the sooner you learn it's not you, the better you will be and the better our church will be.

We should all be truly saddened if we allow our church, a gift from our Father Almighty, a gift to His children, to become a marketplace of deceit and a place for the Evil One to do some of his very best work. Stand guard, Faithful Christian; protect your Father's House.

I don't know about you, but from now on when I enter our church, I'm looking back over my shoulder to make sure I'm not the one letting Satan into my Father's House!

Psalm 122:1 'I rejoice with those who said to me, Let's go to the house of the Lord.'

Nehemiah 10:39 'We will not neglect the house of our God.'

Regarding Worship

When researching the meaning of worship either on the web or in a dictionary, you will find the same qualifying attributes of worship: adoration, love, reverence, respect, devotion, adulation, and veneration. A quick soul-searching question, if I may. When in prayer or while attending church on Sunday, how many of the seven attributes listed above, do we bring with us?

There are many different types and styles of worship in our world, but there is one style we most certainly want to be wary of; emotion without devotion is nothing more than commotion. Putting that into layman's terms, it boils down to 'all thrust and no throttle.' We can include all of the theatrics and gyrations we want, but God will know if our heart is true or whether we are simply working on an Oscar-winning performance.

Take a journey back to years past, specifically reflecting on your relationship with God. How many times have we actually worshipped God in our prayers as opposed to how often was our worship centered on the things we wanted or the help we needed. Do not get me wrong, God wants us to seek His help with every aspect of our lives; my point is that we need to remember that thanksgiving and praise are also very important and necessary components of our dialogue with God. We need to let our Heavenly Father know how grateful we are for His blessings and His presence in our lives. What's the spiritual saying? 'There by the grace of God go I.'

Throughout the Bible we see story after story of people praising and thanking God for His love and attention to their needs. These same people knew that if it was not for His intervention into their plight, all would have been lost. Even when the Israelites strayed from God, once they came to their collective senses and returned to the fold, they praised and thanked Him for taking them back into his loving grace.

Let's accomplish a quick overview of our Sunday worship service. In all that we profess from our pews, in word or in song, it centers on praise and thanksgiving to the Lord, plain and simple. We collectively stop our busy lives for sixty to seventy minutes to let God know how much we love Him and how much we appreciate all that He does within our lives. We also cannot take for granted the body and blood sacrament we share, a true reminder of the price that was paid on our behalf, His blood, not ours. If nothing else, that deserves our complete attention and our very best praise and thanksgiving.

So, the next time you're in church or in prayer, don't forget to give credit where credit is due and thank your Heavenly Father for allowing you to come to His house (the Church) yet one more time and for the loving relationship that you share.

Now, let's take a look at what the Bible tells us about worship.

1 Chronicles 16:29 'Ascribe to the Lord the glory due his name. Bring an offering and come before him; worship the Lord in the splendor of his holiness.'

Psalm 95:6 'Come, let us bow down in worship, let us kneel before the Lord our maker.'

Psalm 100:2 'Worship the Lord with gladness; come before him with joyful songs.'

Romans 12:1 'Therefore, I urge you, brothers in view of God's mercy, to offer your bodies as living sacrifices, holy and pleasing to God, this is your spiritual act of worship.'

Worshipping God is as individual as your fingerprints; it is a relationship that is solely between you and your savior, developed over time and sealed by the Holy Spirit to be a unique love story, a Father and His Child sharing a common goal: Love and Forgiveness.

So next Sunday, when it's time to open the hymnal, even if you sing as bad as I do, make a joyful noise so that your Father in heaven knows that you are offering, to the best of your God given ability, praise and thanksgiving to His most holy name.

P.S. Don't worry about throwing the people in the next few pews off key; chances are they may be significantly worse singers than you. (If that's even possible.)

Repetition: Friend or Foe?

Repetitive actions can be very helpful and can sometimes pose the opposite effect; we begin to take the action for granted. Let's suppose you work on an assembly line of some sort. Typically, this job requires similar movements that must be accomplished quickly and repeatedly. The more repetitive the work becomes, the more skilled you become as an operator or employee.

Let's take a look at spiritual repetitiveness. During church on Sunday, at some point you will proceed to the altar to receive Holy Communion, partaking in the symbolic body and blood of Jesus Christ. If your church is like mine, this offering is available every single Sunday without fail, a repetitive event. Since this is a weekly event; a minimum of fifty-two times per year, do we become an unknowing victim or product of a repetitive event? Each time we go to the communion rail, is it because it's what we do every Sunday, or is our mind and our heart filled with humility and thankfulness for the sacrifice Christ made on our behalf? Repetition: is it friend or for?

Speaking of church, do we always sit in the same location, perhaps even the same pew? This becomes another repetitive action, which limits our ability to expand fellowship and friendship opportunities with others who are sitting outside of our comfort zone. Repetition: is it friend or foe?

When we recite the Lord's Prayer either in church, or elsewhere, do we present it as a meaningful offering in thankfulness to God or it is just words that we have memorized and spew them out when called upon to do so? Repetition: is it friend or foe?

I think you're getting the picture by now, don't allow repetitive or routine actions and/or events cause complacency in your spiritual life, keep these moments as true and heartfelt as humanly possible. Let your inner Spirit feel the conviction of your words and the humility of your soul as you profess your gratitude and love for your Lord and Savior. Make these moments special events in your life, not simply another 'here we go again' routine.

What is that old adage? 'It's not what you say, but how you say it.' Let your words and your actions become a window into your heart and soul, whereby others may see and feel the very presence of God working in your life.

Spiritual Wi-Fi

The electronic age, the birth of the techno child, programming a VCR or a new TV, the intricacies of owning and operating an iPhone or super computer; what ever happened to the basic and easy to operate simple communication devices we once knew? My skeptical self wonders whether today's technology is actual progress or a master plan designed to suck dollars out of our pockets and bank accounts. If you're a Baby Boomer such as me, you're remembering how simple life once was; you could easily make and receive a phone call without help and your television had two functions, channel changing and volume controls. If you're a millennial, like my children, they're thinking how inept and electronically illiterate we have become.

Well, I have some good news, despite all of the technological advances in today's world, prayer is still the best wireless communication known to mankind. It's extremely efficient, it's very easy to operate and unlike today's toys, a higher power greater than a CEO's profit sheets is listening to every single entry or offering. And best of all, it's free. Sorry Dell, IBM, and Microsoft, you will never be able to match the infinite power of prayer. Another awesome fact about this spiritual Wi-Fi is that it never goes down, it doesn't crash, and it's not affected by sun spots or weather, it's open 24/7/365.

I would like to provide a few personal observations and thoughts about prayer. When you use one of today's devices, it's all about taking and sharing pictures, texting, and becoming the cool person, as the device is designed to give you immediate and gratifying results. However, with prayer, it's not about getting what you want, it's about becoming what God wants. No device, no matter how advanced or how expensive, can or will ever be able to make that claim.

What about the internet, it's loaded with exciting and fascinating information. I fully agree with this fact and do use the internet on numerous occasions; however, while this information highway is given to us for information, prayer and the Bible are given to us for transformation. I bet your Dell super-duper processor can't do that.

Someone once told me that we cheat ourselves through prayerlessness or misguided prayer requests. A simple guide to avoid this pitfall is to pray first for prayer preparation, as we sometimes have the tendency to jump first and then find ourselves having to prepare an explanatory or prayer revision later. You know what I'm referring to, it goes something like; 'what

I really meant Lord was . . . ' It's the old ready, fire, and aim syndrome as opposed to the much safer and controlled ready, aim, fire.

Another tough question to ponder before you send up some spiritual Wi-Fi is what exactly is the purpose of prayer? Is the purpose of prayer for God to hear us or for us to hear God? I'll help on this one; I believe there are several answers to this question. Our loving and caring Heavenly Father most certainly wants our prayers and petitions, He desires to carry our burdens and that we may each to seek to grow through His divine guidance. Conversely, the only way we grow through adversity is to listen and learn. In our humanness, we have the propensity to ask and answer when offering prayers. Lord I really need your financial help and five thousand dollars would do me just fine. When this happens and we have a preconceived fix to our problem, we sometimes fail to see and hear the direction the Lord has given us. Are we that desperate that we feel the Lord cannot handle our problems without our intervention?

Another possible answer to the purpose of prayer is quite simply for us to hear God. God does not need to be instructed to hear us, He hears every prayer and petition of every single person because of who He is and because He loves us so very much.

Psalm 6:9 'The Lord has heard my cry for mercy; the Lord accepts my prayer.'

Psalm 4:1 'Answer me when I call to you, O my righteous God. Give me relief from my distress, be merciful to me and hear my prayer.'

Philippians 4:6–7 'Do not be anxious about anything, but in everything, by prayer and petition, with thanksgiving, present your requests to God. And the peace of God which transcends all understanding will guard your hearts and your minds in Christ Jesus.'

1 Peter 3:12 'For the eyes of the Lord are on the righteous and His ears are attentive to their prayers.'

Now that we know the best Wi-Fi is prayer, use this free service liberally, frequently, and with great humility. Surf the spiritual web, your Bible, and pray for understanding, guidance, and compassion.

Allow your Heavenly Father to give you what your earthly family cannot and never doubt or underestimate the Power of Prayer; it's your personal direct line to your Lord and Savior!

The Bible

And now for a few words on the most important book you will ever own and one that should be very well known, your Bible.

- To read the Bible prayerfully is like sitting at God's feet and being fed.

   What book can make this claim? When you open the book and prayerfully read chapter and verse, you can feel the Spirit within you, as each verse on each page begins to speak directly to you and then allow yourself to be drawn into the living word. I have to tell you, this is a far better experience than reading time with my third-grade teacher Mrs. Cranky, who would whack me over the knuckles with a ruler for pulling Mary's pigtails.

- Books are given to us for information; the Bible is given to us for transformation.

   Books take their readers into great adventures, provide an infinitesimal amount of useful information, and fill our quiet moments with an enjoyable serenity, all of which are an important part of our lives. While all of this is good, books cannot claim to be the inerrant word of God, only our Bibles can make that claim. The Bible prepares us for our spiritual journey, it tells the story of God and creation, but most important of all it transforms or clothes us with the righteousness of God and paves the way to salvation. The Bible is another of God's gifts to mankind.

- One Bible known is far better than many owned.

   He who owns the most Bibles has not secured a place in heaven, only a place in the Guinness Book of World Records. It's wonderful to own many Bibles, but unless they are well used and their contents well known, they only represent a false sense of spiritual security. If you have extra Bibles, why not share or offer them to those in need of God's word? Do your children own a Bible? If you own the world's greatest collection of written masterpieces, timeless classics, and have never opened a page, then perhaps they own you. Start each day by opening your Bible and just read a few verses from any chapter, I guarantee you will have a much better day and before you know it, you too are becoming a Biblical Expert.

- The Bible will keep you from sin or sin will keep you from the Bible.

This key point is a simple yet very profound statement on the value of your Bible. It is extremely hard if not impossible to be in sin when you are either on your knees in prayer or reading your Bible. The Bible outlines in great detail what our Lord expects of us, how we need to live our lives and how we can best serve the Lord and others in need. Open your Bibles and see for yourself the new joy and difference in your life.

- Why study the Bible? Because God has spoken and we better listen. I don't know about you, but when God speaks I listen. I seriously do not want to appear in front of the Lord on judgment day feebly attempting to explain why I ignored His call. God gave us this great gift because He loves us so very much and we return our love by obeying His wishes and commands. You only have two choices in life, you can listen to the Lord or you can listen to the Evil One, choose wisely my friends.

- The Bible is the only book you will ever own where the author is present with you the entire time you are reading it.

When you open a book by your favorite author, does the price of the book also guarantee that the author will be sitting right next to you while you read his work? Better yet, do you feel the presence of the author? Easy questions, the answer to both are a resounding 'no.' Want spiritual peace and oneness with God, and then allow the Holy Spirit to open your heart to the verses and pages in your Bible and enjoy the blessing of His presence. When you're finished reading, be sure to turn to Him and say 'Thanks' for this awesome gift and for being with me.

- One of my favorite acronyms for the Bible is 'Basic Instructions Before Leaving Earth.'

  While this witty catch phrase can draw a smile, it also presents a great and mindful truth. Everything you will ever need to know to enter the gates of heaven is contained in this one book, the Bible. Consider it as your passport to heaven, a step by step book of instructions that will take you on the most incredible journey of your life, a ticket to eternity.

I would also like to add a special note here; the instructions in the Bible are far less complicated than the ones that tell you how to program a VCR. Amen!

If these six bullet points have not stirred your heart, have not kindled a desire to locate and dust off your Good Book, then drop to your knees in prayer and ask our Heavenly Father to open your heart and mind to His word and grant you the desire to become grounded in the truths of His word. To those who own a dustless and well used Bible may I offer a 'well done, good and faithful servant'?

Chapter Three:

Gifts

So What's in Your Closet?

During one of his sermons, my pastor posed a question to the congregation. He asked, 'What would Jesus say if He entered your closet?' Seemed like a simple enough question at the time, but as the sermon went on, guilt started to get the better of me and that simple question was now becoming a huge giant in my life.

I couldn't wait for church to be over so I could get home and into my closet to rectify whatever was pulling on my heart strings. Now, a little background information is important here. I used to play in many golf tournaments; it was a wonderful perk of my job. As such, I either won or received many—and I do mean many—very nice and very expensive golf shirts. I am embarrassed to say how many I had hanging in my closet, but there were certainly more than I could ever wear or need. My plethora of golf shirts was a classic case of my hoarding items that would benefit others in need. Deep in my heart, I knew Jesus would not be happy with this terrible display of hoarding, but I was into myself and not others and I desperately needed His help if I was to get through this debacle.

59

I was in that darn closet for hours, agonizing over which shirts I needed to give up, as there were so many shirts that I knew I would probably never wear and worse yet, I was denying these shirts to someone who truly had a legitimate need. After numerous times of taking a shirt off the hanger and then putting it back on the hanger, it became apparent that I was hoarding 'stuff.' I was being selfish with blessings that were afforded to me and selfish horns should have begun to grow out of my head. I finally said, 'Lord, I need help.' He answered very quickly. The spirit moved my arms as they grabbed an entire section of shirts, perhaps about forty, and pulled them all out of the closet. I no longer played the game of 'I like this one, I can't give this one up,' and I was finally able to bundle the shirts for delivery to those in need. This truly was not one of my more stellar or shining moments and as embarrassing as it is to share this now, I offer it up as an example of what not to do.

Very shortly after the closet episode, friends of ours stopped over to our house to visit my wife and me and the conversation eventually led us to believe that our dear friends had fallen on some tight times. Then, as if on eue, one of the topics we discussed that evening was the rising cost of clothing and more specifically, how her husband had so few clothes, especially . . . (you guessed it) . . . shirts! I'm not the fastest gun in the west when it comes to picking up on nuances in conversation, but this little gem hit my heart and my soul like a rush of spiritual wind.

I jumped up from my chair, bolted down the hall to the garage, and retrieved the bundle of new, never-been-worn shirts, and with an enormous amount of joy presented them to our friends. They were speechless at first and then tears of joy slowly crept their way into everyone's eyes. It truly is better to give than receive.

I am willing to bet that if we took a stroll around our homes and through our closets, we may find an abundance of items never been used, rarely used and duplicates of the same items, some may even have collected a bit of dust from the amount of time they resided in their secret hiding places. Don't wait for an embarrassing moment like mine, do yourself and someone in need a favor, box up those forgotten treasures and donate them to your favorite charity. I promise you that you will never miss the items but you will always cherish the thought on the part you played in making someone's day.

Matthew 10:8 'Freely you have received, freely give.'

Proverbs 31:20 'She opens her arms to the poor and extends her hands to the needy.'

Jeremiah 22:16 'He defended the cause of the poor and needy, and so all went well. Is that not what it means to know me, declares the Lord.'

As for myself, I don't know what's better, the way our friend looks in those shirts or the way I feel every time I see him in one.

So my friends, what would Jesus say if he entered your closet?

Lord, I've Got a Problem, and It's *Me!*

Problems, problems, we face them each and every day, and like the dutiful firefighters we are, we extinguish problem fires at the office, at home, on the road, or where ever they may exist at the time. Why are we so good at putting out fires? Because we have the experience, right? Wrong. We may think we are good, but once again we have elected to take credit for the many spiritual blessing and talents from above.

I must sadly report that in my life there are sometimes two very distinct trinities—The Father, Son, and Holy Spirit and Me, Myself, and I. So, let me ask a few simple questions:

Why do we so often insist on being first or at the head of the line?

Why do we feel we are smarter than the other person?

Why do we feel that we can do things without instructions or go places without the use of maps? (That's more of a guy thing).

Why do we think we can leap tall buildings with a single bound?

Why do we never ask for God's help until we have made such a mess of things that even He must be thinking, okay, this is going to be a challenge.

And better yet . . .

Why do we tell the Lord our problems and then tell Him what it will take to fix the problems? Do we think He will fail? Do we think our solution is far better than anything He might come up with?

When we go to the Lord for help, it's not an arbitration or bargaining agreement, it's 'let go and let God.' While we may not agree or recognize it at the time because we are being blinded by our own self-serving nature, God's answers and solutions always turn out to be significantly better than ours in the final analysis. How many times, as a child or even young adult did we stop and think 'I should have listened to Dad.' Hopefully our stubborn ways are only a childhood affliction, but if not, get out your Bible and get on your knees in prayer, you need some quality time with your Heavenly Father.

If you've been in one of my Sunday school classes, you have heard me repeatedly say 'the best punishment the Lord can give us is to let us have our own way.'

Sadly, we have become so good at dowsing fires that we believe we can handle almost anything. At work, we get financial bonuses and 'atta boys' for being so good at handling problems. Got a tough problem, turn it over to Gary, he can handle anything. After a while, you start to believe you can handle anything by yourself and believe that all credit should be given to you. These are very dangerous waters to survive in, when you believe all credit and perhaps even all glory belongs to you and only you.

While it may be a difficult concept for some, we need to get out of our own way at times; it's not always all about us. The notion of 'it's my way or the highway' only serves one person, you. Trust me on this; you will be far more satisfied in serving God than serving yourself.

John 15:5 'I am the vine, you are the branches. If a man remains in me and I in him, he will bear much fruit, apart from me you can do nothing.'

Ephesians 6:7 'Serve wholeheartedly, as if you were serving the Lord, not men.'

Galatians 5:13 'You, my brothers, were called to be free. But do not use your freedom to indulge the sinful nature; rather serve, one another in love.'

1 Peter 4:10 'Each one should use whatever gift he has received to serve others, faithfully administering God's grace in various forms.'

We need to take the word ME and turn the letter M upside down so it becomes the letter –W- then, instead of me, it now becomes WE, the Lord and I. So the next time a problem rears its ugly head, don't tell God how big your problem is; tell your problem how big your God is! 'Nuff Said!'

Change Direction. North is much better than South

There is a saying out there that if you do not pass Satan on your way to work in the morning, then perhaps you're both headed in the same direction.

One of the most disturbing Bible verses to me is **JOB 1:7**. The Lord said to Satan, 'Where have you come from?' Satan answered the Lord, 'From roaming through the earth and going back and forth in it.' I don't know about you, but that passage sends chills up and down my spiritual spine. The Evil One is traversing back and forth across the earth, looking for his next victims, strategically placing his temptations where they will serve him well. We should never go anywhere without the full armor of God guiding and protecting our paths.

Sometimes when I'm driving, I revert back to what my wife, Cathy, calls my 'New York Driving Mode.' As a New Yorker, I drove very aggressively, because that's how you survived in that environment, or at least that's what I told myself. When I look back on how I drove, it was suicidal and rude. Well, every now and then, that old mode attempts to sneak its way back into my Texas driving experiences. Don't laugh; you know the situations I'm talking about.

'That bozo thinks when the light changes he's going to beat me off the line.'

'There's no way in heck I'm letting that guy cut in front of me.'

'Look at this clown, we're all patiently waiting in the line and he drives right to the front of the line and some darn fool will probably let him in.'

'I'll cling so close to his back bumper it will look like he's towing me, maybe then he'll get out of my way.'

Yup, I'm pretty sure Satan was not only going the same direction as I was, he probably was even riding in my car. So today, when those little urges sneak in, if I do something dumb, I immediately do the 'apology wave.' You know the one I'm referring too, it's where you shrug your shoulders along with the wave of a hand, which is supposed to give you absolution from your dumb move, or I offer an apology to the Lord on behalf of my stupidity. And then I proceed to tell you know who to get the H-E-Double-Hockey-Sticks out of my car. A quick arrow (prayer) aimed upwards will usually get me back on track and moving in the right direction, away from the evil backseat driver.

Prayer, common courtesy, and some helpful direction from my wife, Cathy, (LOL) afforded me the ability to affect a much-needed change in my attitude in life and most noteworthy, my driving skills. I can honestly say that I now enjoy driving more than ever before.

Now when I'm out there negotiating the local roads, instead of plugging in to Satan's ploys to get me crazy, I think positive thoughts. Hey, the guy out there trying to cut in might be rushing to a hospital or to a legitimate emergency, and the Christian thing to do is to help him, let him cut in. But wait, what if he's not going to an emergency and he's being dumb like I used to be? This is where Satan is trying to get back into my car. Then he'll have to answer to a higher power than my four cylinders.

Proverbs 12:16 'A fool shows his annoyance at once, but a prudent man overlooks an insult.'

Proverbs 14:16 'A wise man fears the Lord and shuns evil, but a fool is hot headed and reckless.'

Ephesians 4:32 'Be kind and compassionate to one another, forgiving each other, just as in Christ God forgave you.'

1 Thessalonians 5:15 'Make sure that nobody pays back wrong for wrong, but always try to be kind to each other and to everyone else.'

What's that Sound I'm Hearing?

There is this silent noise I hear frequently. At first, I was completely clueless to what it could be, so sometimes I took the easy way out; if I ignored it, hopefully it would go away. Guess what, it never did, and am I eternally grateful to God that He did not let it go away.

We were each given a very special gift; it is the Gift of the Holy Spirit. This gift came with one simple requirement; feed the Spirit within you, which by the way is a relatively easy and most rewarding task. Spiritual food can be found in your Bible, on Sundays in your church pew, and through prayer. Like you and me, we require nourishment for growth, the Spirit within us grows stronger and stronger as we feed on the living word of God.

1 John 3:24 'Those who obey his commands live in him, and He in them. And this is how we know He lives in us. We know it by the Spirit He gave us.'

2 Corinthians 1:22 'Set his seal of ownership upon us, as put his Spirit in our hearts as a deposit, guaranteeing what is to come.'

Romans 8:26–27 'In the same way, the Spirit helps us in our weakness. We do not know what we ought to pray for, but the Spirit intercedes for us with groans and words that cannot express. And he who searches our hearts knows the mind of the Spirit, because the Spirit intercedes for the saints in accordance with God's will.'

If you have not already done so, this is probably a good time to remind ourselves that while it's always fun to receive a gift, it's also important to thank the giver of the gift.

The Holy Spirit—the Great Counselor and Comforter, sent to us by God, at the request of Jesus. God indwells all those who accept and receive Jesus Christ as their Lord and Savior. The Holy Spirit comes to assist us; He comes as an encourager, an advocate, a sustainer of strength, and prepares us to do the work God has given us to do. So, what does this do for us? It makes us neither hopeless nor helpless, as the God of Heaven resides in each of us. I cannot think of one thing that is more comforting or encouraging than knowing the Spirit of God is always with me.

The Holy Spirit is with us each and every day, our constant and eternal companion, helping us through the day to day trials and tribulations, that little voice in the back of our heads that helps us discern right from wrong, the emotion that stirs our compassion, our love, and our forgiveness. Without an active Spirit within us, we would most probably be wondering why nothing seems to be going right in our lives. You know the feeling I'm talking about, when everything you say or do always seems to alienate the life situation you're facing, rather than soothe it. When this happens, reach into your inner Spirit and pray for guidance and discernment; I'm sure you will both find it to be a rewarding experience.

As Christians and being indwelled with the Holy Spirit, we were given only one requirement for this gift, to keep filling ourselves with the Spirit of God. When we feel our relationship with God getting distant, we need to ask ourselves, who moved? Am I moving away from God or am I pushing God away from me?

So why do I need to constantly keep spiritually nourishing the Spirit within me? The answer is quite simple, remember the silent noise I kept hearing; it's because I leak!

Selfish

Have you ever noticed that those with the most toys are hardly ever satisfied; they always seem to want more? Have you ever noticed that the people with the least amount of personal resources, time, and money always seem to give the most? Could it be they recognize the true value of helping those in need?

Tough questions but also thought-provoking questions which should have struck a chord somewhere within our souls which leads us to wonder, did I leave a proper tip for the waitress or did I feel the extra few dollars are better served in my own pocket? Do I really need three thingamabobs or should I at the very least give one to someone in need? Nah, I should keep them as backup. Now therein resides the definition of being selfish with the gifts that our Lord has blessed us with. Can we truly use multiple items at the same time? I'm thinking no, unless you're an octopus.

When my daughters Genese and Breanna entered the daycare environment, one of the first lessons they learned and were very proud to share with my wife and I, was the slogan 'share share at daycare.' That was the moment my daughters embarked on a lifelong philosophy: We need to share our gifts with those in need or with those who may be less fortunate than ourselves. I'm very happy to say that they have continued down this giving path right up through their adult years. Thank you, Lord!

What is the rationale behind our believing we actually need multiple items of a same or similar nature? Are we designating or elevating ourselves to the status of a bona fide collector or are we becoming a self-absorbed hoarder?

Just prior to my younger brother's passing, at his request I became the sole inheritor of all his worldly possessions, the majority of which were hand and power tools of every shape and description. After unloading this newfound cache of super tools into my workshop, I found myself thinking, 'Look at all my cool tools.' I literally had doubles, triples, and quadruples of the same tools. I'm happy to say it didn't take too long before the Lord brought me back to my senses and the stark realization of 'Okay, how many of these tools do I actually need and can actually use at any given moment?' Oh my goodness, was I becoming an out of control, an over-the-top selfish individual? Apparently, I was, although the moment was brief and quickly reconciled; I still felt those guilty-as-charged twinges. Fortunately for me, I answered the call of the Holy Spirit within me and began making toolboxes filled with many useful items for some of my friends who I knew were in need of some quality tools. And guess what happened next? Nothing. I didn't miss one item that I gifted away to my friends, but I did enjoy a warm feeling inside me each time I made the presentation of a toolbox.

Psalm 119:35–37 'Direct me in the path of your commands, for there I find delight. Turn my heart toward your statues and not toward selfish gain. Turn my eyes away from worthless things; preserve my life according to your word.'

Philippians 2:3–4 'Do nothing out of selfish ambition or vain conceit, in humility consider others better than yourselves. Each of you should look not only to your own interests, but also to the interests of others.'

James 3:14–16 'But if you harbor bitter envy and selfish ambition in your hearts, do not boast about it or deny the truth. Such wisdom does not come down from heaven but is earthly, unspiritual, of the devil. For where you have envy and selfish ambition, there you find disorder and every evil practice.'

Ecclesiastes 5:10–11 'Whoever loves money never has money enough; whoever loves wealth is never satisfied with his income. This too is meaningless. As goods increase, so do those who consume them, and what benefit are they to the owner, except to feast his eyes on them.'

So as a final thought, if I may slightly change my daughters' daycare mantra: 'Share, share what is fair.' I'm sure you will be glad you did, and I'm equally as sure that you will feel the warm glow of giving emanating from your inner Spirit.

It Can be an Ear-Opening Experience

Ask most parents how well their children listen. Remember back to our early school days when the teachers would square off with us, eye to eye, and offer up those all too familiar pleas? 'Please put your listening ears on.' How many times, even in our adult lives, have we heard someone say, 'Are you listening to me?'

Some people claim that proper listening skills are rapidly becoming a lost art. While I'm not an expert on the fine art of auditory listening skills, I would, however, like to talk about another kind of listening skill, specifically; spiritual listening.

We might all agree that when we do not listen at home or at work, there can be consequences involved and the majority of the time these failures can produce some level of chastisement and thankfully it is not life threatening. When we fail to listen to the Holy Spirit that resides in each and every one of us, the chastisement can have a devastating eternal effect, a fall from God's grace.

The Spirit within helps and guides us through every thought and every action we experience, every moment of the day. While God granted us 'free will' to choose between what is right and what is wrong, He also knew that as humans, we were not perfect and we would sometimes struggle with making sound decisions. Knowing we would need strong spiritual assistance from time to time, God gave us the gift of the Holy Spirit, a great comforter and counselor as a spiritual guide.

When faced with temptations or choices that would not be pleasing to God, our Spirit is whispering deep within our heart and mind, 'This is not a good choice, let's find another option.' And all this time you thought it was those two little imps on each shoulder. During those times when we are either not completely comfortable with a particular choice or completely clueless on what you should do; pray to your Heavenly Father for guidance and then listen as He speaks to you through the indwelling of the Holy Spirit.

The Spirit speaks to us 24/7/365 and doesn't miss a beat. The problem is always on our end, we don't listen because we usually are too pre-occupied with our own impeccable bravado at handling things and miss the all-important message from God through the Spirit. If you are hesitant about that last statement, then ponder this thought. When things in our lives are going smoothly and blessings abound, are you so bold that you believe all the wonderfulness you are experiencing is a direct result of your own abilities? Or could it be that you have a very well spiritually fed and active spirit operating within you? Could it be that when the spirit speaks; you actually listen?

1 John 4:6 'We are from God, and whoever knows God listens to us; but whoever is not from God does not listen to us. This is how we recognize the Spirit, of truth and the spirit of falsehood.'

Galatians 3:3 'Are you, so foolish? After beginning with the spirit, are you now trying to attain your goal by human effort?'

2 Corinthians 1:22 'Set his seal of ownership upon us, and put his spirit in our hearts as a deposit, guaranteeing what is to come.'

1 Corinthians 2:14 'The man without the spirit does not accept the things that come from the spirit of God, for they are foolishness to him and he cannot understand them, because they are spiritually discerned.'

While I may fail to listen to worldly communication from time to time (my wife will second this statement), I will make every effort to ensure I am listening to the Holy Spirit and hopefully avoid the static and interference of my ego that blocks His loving message and direction for my life.

Truth or Consequences

Our lives are filled with many truths, a smattering of falsehoods and unfortunately, consequences for poor choices. This all leads me to wonder, what is life's big question? The answer should be 'why I am here and what is my role in life?' Now, if you're a solid Christian, you already know the answer to that question; it is to honor God. But what about your friends and family members who cannot comfortably or confidently answer that question?

If there is any doubt about the answer to the question above, I have a few truths that you can share with those who may need a little extra spiritual confidence.

Truth 1 – God came down to us because we could never reach Him.

Truth 2 – Human achievement can never substitute for divine accomplishment.

Truth 3 – The blood of Christ makes us safe,

The word of God makes us sure.

Truth 4 – The Bible will still transcend truth when all of its critics are dust.

Truth 5 – When you pick up a Bible, you hold in your hands the very words of Almighty God.

Truth 6 – We are the people for whom Christ died.

Truth 7 – God did not say, 'I'll die for you when you deserve it.'

Truth 8 – The Bible is the only book you will ever read where the author is with you from cover to cover.

Truth 9 – You will find God's will when you go God's way.

Truth 10 – The word of God is like a spotlight, it reveals' our sin.

John 3:16–18 'For God so loved the world, that He gave His one and only Son, that whoever believes in Him, shall not perish but have eternal life. For God did not send His Son into the world to condemn the world, but to save the world through Him. Whoever believes in Him is not condemned, but whoever does not believe stands condemned already because he has not believed in the name of God's one and only Son.'

Our challenge is to reach out to those that need to hear the truth. The next time we need to provide a gift, what about giving the gift of life itself, the Living Word, a Bible. Perhaps we should show them what's right instead of telling them what's right; invite them to your church or to a Sunday school class. You'll both be glad you did.

I Gave at the Office

'He who dies with the most toys wins' We have all seen that little gem before. The word 'Mine' has become a staple in our lives. 'That's mine, leave it alone'; or 'All this is mine, isn't it wonderful.' Are we becoming obsessive-compulsive regarding our 'stuff'? This next question is for us Texans; is your garage so full of stuff that you can't even get your car in the garage? Better yet, do you even have an inkling of what is in all the boxes that are falling apart and are disintegrating from the effects of time?

Is giving really that important? After all, I have worked hard for all that I have. Well, to begin with, we own nothing; everything that we have is on loan, a gift from the Lord, so let's ponder a few thoughts together.

'Will I be judged on what I kept or what I gave?'

'Do I give what's right or what's left?'

'Giving is Grace, not giving is Disgrace!'

'The Lord gave me the greatest gift of all, Salvation. What have I given back?'

2 Corinthians 9:6–7 'Remember this: Whoever sows sparingly, will also reap sparingly, and whoever sows generously will also reap generously.

Each man should give what he has decided in his heart to give, not reluctantly or under compulsion.'

Luke 21:3–4 'I tell you the truth He said, 'this poor widow has put in more than all the others. All these people gave their gifts out of their wealth; but she out of her poverty put in all that she had to live on.'

Giving is not easy, especially when we have so many other financial hurdles on our horizons—there is our entertainment allowance, we go out for dinner and a movie several times a month, we have been thinking about buying a new car, we have that cruise coming up this winter. Okay, these are not bad things, but they can become barriers in our giving decision process. When we are tasked with giving, it encompasses our finances, our time and yes, some of that 'stuff' we have been hoarding, that even the Lord knows we will never use.

We know what we are supposed to do, we have the tools do to what we are supposed to do, and all we need is the spiritual push to do it.

Ask yourself these questions during the next giving dilemma:

'When God dwells in my heart, does He feel at home?'

'Am I a closet Christian; do I talk the talk, but stumble on the walk?'

Tough questions are always answered easily when you have the Spirit within you. Open your Bible, you'll find what you're looking for; it's just another one of the many gifts the Lord has given us. And speaking of the Bible, I wonder how long our Savior had to ponder over the decision as to whether or not He could afford to give us that great gift?

Happy Feet

Some of you may be thinking how is he going to turn the topic of feet into a spiritual message? Fear not, Christian solider, I have it covered.

Our Bibles tell us of a 'Happy Meal'; the offering of the Eucharistic body and blood of our Lord which had been shed for many for the forgiveness of sin. Now it's time to relate another happy story, one of 'Happy Feet.'

One of my favorites sounds in my home is the pitter patter of our Shih Tzu Heidi's feet when she is running toward me. One can almost hear the excitement in her prance. She is definitely a candidate for happy feet, but we're not there yet.

Another equally happy sound is the footsteps of my daughters walking into our home after an evening out; ah, now I can finally get a good night's sleep. (Parents, you know the feeling.) No, we're still not there yet.

On many occasions, I get what I like to call 'happy feet'; it's when I'm rushing off to the airport to pick up my wife, Cathy, who has been out of town for a week or two. Okay, we're almost there.

Romans 10:15 'How beautiful are the feet of those who bring good news!'

Okay, we're here! How beautiful are the feet that come out of the maternity ward and proclaim; congratulations, it's a boy! The approaching feet of the surgeon who tells you the operation was a complete success!

Isaiah 52:7 'How beautiful on the mountains are the feet of those who bring good news., who proclaim peace, who bring good tidings, who proclaim salvation, who say to Zion, 'your God Reigns.'

And now for the greatest news of all.

Luke 2:10 'But the angel said to them, 'Do not be afraid' I bring you good news of great joy that will be for all the people. Today in the town of David a Savior has been born to you, he is Christ the Lord.'

If that news doesn't get your feet doing the happy dance, then I will pray for you.

Our Bibles are full of good news that could and should be delivered daily. Open the book and read a few passages of good news and perhaps yours will be the next set of feet that deliver good news to someone. Here's a hint, start with the message of salvation.

Not unlike the postman's footsteps coming up your front walk delivering that long-awaited card or package from a loved one, are the footsteps or happy feet of the many authors of the Bible. From the very beginning to the very end of the Bible, they bring you the good news of Jesus Christ.

Yes, I do understand that our world is not all sugar plums and candy; however, I do understand the importance of sharing my faith, a good news passage, an olive branch to those in need.

In this lifetime, when offering the good news of salvation to someone in need, maybe, just maybe, they might one day recall my footsteps approaching them, my happy feet, before I said, 'Hello, my brother, if you're willing, do I have some great news to share with you.'

So, dust off those spiritual sneakers, those angelic wing tipped shoes, those high heeled helpers and get your happy feet out there, delivering the good news of Jesus Christ. Oh, by the way, all shoes that contain 'happy feet' are guaranteed a 'free shine' from above.

Please don't fret about where and when you will find someone to help. Our Heavenly father will provide those opportunities, just pray for discernment and the boldness to answer His call. Remember, He also has 'Happy Feet' and they are with you always.

The Sun Will Come Out Tomorrow . . .

And yes, the Son will also come out tomorrow. Thanks to our Lord Jesus, we will enjoy day after day of glorious blessings, because He is out there minute after minute, hour after hour and day after day, showering each one of us with His blessings. Having said this, when was the last time you woke up in the morning and said thank you Lord for yet another day?

We have become so accustomed to His blessings, that we automatically assume that when we go to bed at night, not only will we rise the next day but so will the sun. And of course it will, it has done so for every day of our lives, and surely we're not expected to say thank you Lord every day? Why not?

Repetition is not a bad thing. Each of us likes to know what's at the end of the rainbow, but repetition can also lead to complacency; ho hum, another sunrise. I personally think it's very cool that while I'm sleeping the night away, Jesus is preparing another sunrise for me. I also believe He knows our humanness and knows that we are not ungrateful, we're just victims of 'abundant blessings' and sometimes we forget to be thankful. That's why, every now and then, he gives us a sunrise that will knock the socks off even the most jaded individual, just to remind us who is behind the start of our day.

Do we need to offer a litany of thanks for every blessing He provides? Of course not, but it certainly would be nice if we offer a heartfelt thank you for the many blessings we enjoy day after day after day. Have you ever accomplished something really cool at work or at home and secretly couldn't wait for someone to recognize the cool achievement and the very cool author of that achievement, and yes, I'm talking about us! I'm not saying the Lord is looking for accolades, but I do know He is longing to hear from you and to know how much you enjoyed your vacation in the mountains, your trip to the Caribbean, and yes, even the clear sky at night which is laced with millions of sparkling diamonds.

When man builds something spectacular, we are quick to acknowledge its beauty or functionality. Yes, Frank Lloyd Wright certainly did build magnificent homes in his time. We know that Mr. Wright did in fact design the object of our attention and we graciously offer an acknowledgement of his fine talents. We also know that God, not man, painted the heavens and sky above us and we marvel at the majesty of it all. Can anyone explain to me why we praise Mr. Wright and not Jesus? Could it be that Mr. Wright only built a handful of homes around the country and Jesus gave us blessings too numerous to count? Complacency!

We, by our very nature, take some things for granted; when I inhale, air will rush into my lungs and keep me alive. If I leave work after 5:00 P.M., traffic will be ugly! We are definitely creatures of habit and rarely stop to smell the roses or, for that matter, thank the creator of the roses. Like air, roses are abundant, so what's the big deal? The big deal is without air, there would be no one around to be thankful for the beautiful roses and the symbol of love they portray.

Do we take the love of a spouse or of our children for granted or do we tell them repeatedly how much we love them? I sincerely hope it's the latter. My daughters compare me to an old worn out record: 'We know, Dad; you love us.'

Sometimes we try to justify our shortcomings by confusing reality with spirituality. Reality is something we can touch, see and from which we get immediate physical and visual gratification. Spirituality is accepting with your whole heart and soul in what you cannot see or touch, an undeniable faith and if you listen carefully you can hear your inner being saying, 'I feel the Love.'

Sometimes you have to be the group initiator of thankfulness. My wife and I were flying to Phoenix, and on our final approach to the airport, our aircraft got caught up in what we later learned to be a monsoon-type weather event. The wind shear was so fierce, it literally threw our aircraft onto the runway with such force the pilots lost control of the landing. Based on all witness observations, we should have crashed, but Jesus placed His loving hand on our plane and lifted us back up into the safety of the air. The interior of the aircraft was dead silent with the exception of one lone voice proclaiming boldly, 'Thank you, Jesus, Thank you, Jesus.' You guessed it, it was my wife, Cathy. It's okay to help others be thankful by your example.

So next time you're driving in your car and you see some of God's beauty and blessings, shoot an arrow of thanksgiving up, He prepared that glorious site just for you. The next time you're on your knees in prayer, don't be shy, rattle off a few of the things that caught your attention over the past days and let Him know how much those moments meant to you. You'll both be glad you did!

Lock this piece of truth in your heart and throw away the key: Everything we know, have, see, love, and touch is all provided by the grace of God.

Proverbs 1:32 'For the waywardness of the simple will kill them, and the complacency of fools will destroy them.'

2 Corinthians 2:14 'Thanks be to God for His indescribable gift.'

Psalm 95:2–6 'Let us come before Him with thanksgiving and extol Him with music and song. For the Lord is the great God, the great king above all God's. In His hands are the depths of the earth, and the mountain peaks belong to Him. The sea is His for he made it and His hands formed the dry land. Come let us bow down in worship, let us kneel before the Lord our maker.'

The Gift and the Gift Giver

We have all heard someone say, 'It's much better to give than receive.' To those who have experienced the wonderful sensation of being a gift giver, you know and have felt the 'magic' of the moment.

And then there are those who believe they are the living breathing epitome of Gift Givers until that fateful day when your gifting goes awry. You remember the day I'm talking about, you present what you think is the gift of all gifts to a friend or family member and you later learn that your gift was either re-gifted or never used. Oh, the horror of it all. What's the first thought that immediately pops into our minds? You guessed it, 'That's it, I'll never give them another gift,' and this is usually followed by 'I can't believe how ungrateful they were.' A gift should be an unconditional offering; it is not a loan nor is it a contract. Immediately upon presentation, it now becomes the sole ownership of the recipient and gift of giving has been completed in full.

So, I was wondering, when we present a gift, should it come with a Hallmark Card that has numerous boxes that you can check off, outlining the restrictions that are attached to the gift? These restrictions probably go something like this.

Check all that apply

[ ] Gift can never be re-gifted
[ ] Everyone must know the gift was from me
[ ] Gift must be displayed in a prominent area for all to see
[ ] . . . and so on and so on . . .

I was always under the impression that when you gave a gift to someone, there are no strings attached; it was not a required action but rather a gift from one heart to another. My friend Willie said it best, 'When I give a gift, I'm giving it to the Lord.'

The final and ultimate gift blemish occurs when we present a gift and we are expecting something back in return. When this happens, what we are now presenting no longer represents something from your heart; it has now taken on the role of a bargaining chip. It's no longer about the gift; it now becomes all about you.

If I may contradict myself for a moment, my sister and brother-in-law taught me that there can be an exempted condition when giving. Their family is financially sound, so when my daughters were college bound, at a cost that my wife and I could not easily afford, my in-laws called, stating, 'We're going to send you a check to help defray some of the cost of the girl's college tuition.' The only stipulation was that their generous gift must never be revealed to our children, as the best gift should always be from the parents. I'm sure our Lord would approve of that condition. This gift of love also taught me that I do not need recognition for what I give; I simply need to be thankful the Lord has blessed me with the resources and the wisdom to help others.

Now that we have debunked the worldly gift, let's take a look at a few spiritual gifts.

John 3:16 'For God so loved the world that He gave His one and only Son, that whoever believes in Him shall not perish but have eternal life.'

Nowhere in this verse does it state you must believe, but rather whomever chooses to believe, free will prevailing, not a demand. While we think of this as a free gift, it comes with a heavy cost; Jesus was nailed to a tree so that we may enjoy the gift of eternal life!

Luke 6:38 'Give, and it will be given to you. A good measure, pressed down, shaken together and running over, will be poured into your lap. For with the measure you use, it will be measured to you.'

You will receive back, what you have freely given. If your gifts were conditional, it is conditional gifts that will come back, measure for measure. In life, we have always learned that we get back what we have put into the act. If we do something halfhearted, then halfhearted is the reward.

Proverbs 18:16 'A gift opens the way for the giver and ushers him into the presence of the great.'

When you give from the heart and for the love of Jesus, greatness becomes a shared event, both the recipient of the gift and the giver of the gift.

I have accomplished exhaustive research and cannot find anywhere, a book or online website that specifically takes the reader point by point, covering all the rules, regulations, and conditions on the art of gift giving. Additionally, the same goes for penalties associated with failure to observe the gifting rules. Wait a moment, now I remember, there are none! That being the case, it must mean that we are the complete package, we decide what the gift will be, we present the gift and ensure the recipient understands the conditions and terms that accompany the gift. It almost sounds as if we are the gift.

I apologize for the sarcasm attached to that last paragraph, but we truly need to understand that what we have gifted away was never ours to begin with; it was a gift from our Lord, freely and unconditionally given. So, in gifting we must give back freely and unconditionally, sharing the blessing as our Lord has requested we do.

One final biblical note:

Deuteronomy 15:14 ' . . . .Give to him as the Lord your God has blessed you.'

Short Arms and Deep Pockets . . .

One of the scariest words in the non-secular world is 'Tithe.' This little five-letter word can wreak havoc on our emotions, ushering in such wondrous feelings of guilt, frugalness, physical and emotional distress and in some lucky cases pure unadulterated joy. A minimum of at least once per year, we will experience the dreaded 'Stewardship Sunday.' You know very well the Sunday I'm referring to; it's the one where little beads of sweat start to form on your forehead; it's the day that your wallet or your purse starts to twitch almost uncontrollably. You're not hungry, yet your stomach starts to churn a bit and it seems like dark clouds start to move across your sunny financial forecast. Loosely translated: 'There goes the swimming pool we promised the kids.'

We have all heard the cute sayings when our financial help is both needed and required. 'The bad news is we're still a bit short on our expansion budget, but the good news is that the needed funds are still in your pocket.' How about 'Don't give what's left, give what's right.'

I have a personal theory on why tithing can be somewhat stressful for some, and I would like to share a few of my thoughts with you. I call my theory the $20.00 Dilemma. You're sitting in church and the basket starts down the aisle. You really want to reach into your pocket and pull out that 'ole twenty,' the one that's been sitting in your pocket so long it now qualifies for residency. Unfortunately, the sacred twenty starts screaming, 'No, don't take me.' They say money talks, and you're a witness, you heard it. One would almost wonder if the twenty was super-glued to the lining of your pocket, it's now become a friend, it's part of who you are. Your empty hand slowly backs out of your pocket and now the dilemma begins. Next enters the 'moment of truth'—how much should I drop in the basket? This then is quickly followed by 'rationalization'—can I really afford to tithe an extra twenty this week? Finally, assertiveness steps into the picture— I give what I can and when I can. And now we have justified to our personal satisfaction why we do not have to spend an extra twenty. How simple was that?

Let's dissect our little dilemma. The truth of the matter is, in all probability, we truly can afford the extra twenty, but we already have plans for this president and perhaps even a few more of his counterparts. After church, we always stop and get bagels and cream cheese on the way home or we always stop at our usual haunt and have brunch; it's like *Cheers*, everyone knows us there. These are certainly both wonderful things to do, especially since I love bagels, but do I really need them every Sunday? My family and my waistline would simultaneously yell 'No.'

If a friend of yours was hospitalized, as all good friends do, you would visit them in the hospital and you might bring a bouquet of flowers, you know the ones we get, a handful of semi-wilted flowers from the hospital lobby gift store. And guess what, they cost $20.00. I'm not casting any negativity on a hospital visit; what I am trying to say is that when we give flowers to a friend, we immediately and physically see the joy that they bring. When we buy the bagels or go to lunch or a movie, we can physically enjoy the experience our twenty provided.

Conversely, could it be that when faced with the dilemma of dropping the extra twenty in the basket, it's like dropping the twenty into a black hole? We know it will be used for good somewhere, but when and where? Will I ever know what good my twenty brought into this world? I think I'm feeling joy, but not sure if it's real or imaginary.

Yes, they tell us in church where our tithing goes and we get a detailed explanation once per year at our annual parish meeting, but maybe that's not enough to pry that $20.00 loose. So, what is the answer?

Perhaps we need to get a little more involved in our church and its direction and then we would certainly experience a more intimate relationship to the many programs and assistance our tithing provides to those less fortunate than ourselves. I'm talking about the folks who consider bagels and cream cheese or a family luncheon on any day, not just Sunday, an extravagance that only happens either on TV or to the very rich.

Every home operates on a budget of one fashion or another; that's the only way we can survive, especially in today's tumultuous financial environment. The church is no different. It relies on tithing to forecast what it can or cannot accomplish in the coming year, just like we do at home. And like our home environments, unplanned events pop up that put a strain on our finances.

Now, let's get back to our $20.00 dilemma. We can easily remove the fear and worry of an extra $20.00 by offering it up to the Lord. Think about it. Do you think it was by sheer luck that we wound up with an extra twenty just floating around in our coffers, or could it be divine intervention? Let's make the first Sunday of every month the 'Extra Twenty Sunday.' We can certainly plan for it, we may have to forego our bagels and cream cheese, but remember, we are offering this first Sundays goodies up to the Lord, and we all know that He would be most appreciative. Now the one hundred-thousand-dollar question: So who wants to get this $20.00 first Sunday event into motion? It begins with you!

And now onto the bigger picture, our annual tithe. We sit down and plan our budget, our rent, car payments, food, entertainment and etc. Some folks ask, 'Is our tithe based on our income before or after taxes? Is our tithe simply a financial commitment or am I supposed to donate a reasonable portion of my time to the church? Where does tithing fall on our budget plan, after entertainment expense allocations, after the new swimming pool or after our much-needed vacation budget?' I could comment on these questions, but I believe they are better discussed between you and the Lord. After all, wasn't our Lord and Savior the one who gave us our finances, a gift from the grace of God, so who better to consult on this dilemma and what your responsibilities are?

Whether it's our annual pledge or the Extra $20.00 Sunday, our Bible is very specific on what our responsibilities are toward tithing both of our time and our money, responsibility being the key word on this matter. When the Lord blessed us with children, it was our responsibility to care for them. When the Lord blesses our congregation with a newly baptized individual, their spiritual growth is part of our responsibly. How seriously are we taking the responsibility set before us?

Want more help in making a tithing decision, try thinking about this. The Lord has graciously loaned you all that you have, finances and otherwise, a loan that can only be made through the absolute grace of God. If you're thinking I earned my money at work and by making sound investments, let me simply say, The Lord giveth and the Lord can taketh away.' Do not allow the Tempter to lead you to believe that it was all you and only you. That kind of thinking not only displays an ungrateful heart, it leads you into all sorts of other slippery slopes, such as greed, theft, illegal or ill-gotten gains, and forsaking those who can truly benefit from the sharing of your financial blessings.

See, you thought you only had to listen to a tithing request only one week per year. Open your heart and your pocketbook, because when the Lord measures your worth, it will not be on what you had, but what you gave. Additionally, when He brings His tape measure out, it's not to measure your head; it will be to measure your heart.

Matthew 10:8 'Freely you have received, freely give.'

Acts 20::35 'In everything I did, I showed you by this kind of hard work, we must help the weak, remembering the words the Lord Jesus Himself said, 'It is more blessed to give than to receive.'

2 Corinthians 9:7 'Each man should give what he has decided in his heart to give, not reluctantly or under compulsion, for God loves a cheerful, giver.'

It Doesn't Pay to be Nice

What a sad state of affairs our world is in when we can state with even mild conviction 'It Doesn't Pay to be Nice.' Okay, so we tried to offer a kind word or a helping hand to one in need and it didn't go as we had hoped or planned. Can the refusal of our offer truly be that brutally obvious, it didn't work and that's the last time I'll ever to offer help anyone? Aren't we lucky that Christ did not take the same misguided approach to our 'Spiritual Slip-Ups'?

Let's dissect what makes us feel the need to remove being helpful to those in need from our repertoire of God given talents. Perhaps it was when I became mad when my offer of help was rejected. Didn't anyone know it was my moment to shine, show off my reconciliatory talents? No, I think it was the embarrassment I was subjected to when I was told to keep my nose out of it and in front of friends and coworkers. Wait just a minute, now I remember, I tried to help and wound up becoming an accessory to the problem, the goat instead of the hero.

One would almost think the offer of help was all about us and not about the person gasping for help. We live in a very complex society; doctors are becoming more and more cautious about offering roadside assistance to an injured driver for fear of being sued. What happens to the poor soul who tries to break up a fight? He always winds up as the casualty, the poor sap who winds up getting the black eye or bloodied nose and more often than not, there is not even a scratch on either of the combatants. I guess when we look at it this way maybe it really does suck to be nice. If you subscribe to this previous sentence, please let someone know so they can pray for you.

Can you think of a time when you were the recipient or benefactor when someone was being nice? Think back, it felt good? If we gave up every time something did not go as planned, we might as well go to the Tattoo Parlor and get 'Quitter' inked across our foreheads. Are we really that naïve that we truly believe everything in life comes up smelling like roses? If you subscribe to this thinking, please immediately GPS your location, you may be unknowingly strolling through Satan's Garden of Bananas and you're about to get peeled.

Okay, this is for the Doubting Thomas's out there. Did you know that the word 'Nice' is not mentioned even once in the Bible? I can hear the 'Ah-has' already. Before you start the victory dance, let's talk about what is mentioned in God's Book.

Genesis 20:13 'This is how you can show your love to me: Everywhere we go, say of me, 'He is my Brother.'

Proverbs 11:23 'The desire of the righteous ends only in good, but the hope of the wicked only in wrath.'

And of course, the greatest commandment of all, 'Love thy Neighbor.'

Ephesians 4:29, 32 ' Do not let any unwholesome talk come out of your mouths, but only what is helpful for building others up.' . . . 'Be kind and compassionate to one another, forgiving each other, just as in Christ God forgave you.'

If one were to peruse the Concordance of the Bible, you would find pages and pages of references to Kindness and Love, so instead of me listing them all, take a scriptural journey through these passages, I'm sure you will 'Love' them.

Sadly, I believe two of the most common impediments to being nice are weakness and what I like to call the transference of kindness. I'll start with the weakness impediment. Some folks honestly believe that being kind can sometimes be interpreted as a sign of weakness, believing that only the strong survive. The Bible has a great deal to say about this but I'll only lift one small quote from the pages: 'The meek shall inherit the earth.' Does this mean we need to roll over and be trampled on? Absolutely not! It does mean, however, that there is significantly more Strength and Power in sharing your spiritual fortitude with one in need. Remember the adage: 'No man stands as tall as when he stoops to help a child.'

The Transference of Kindness is one of the easiest to fall prey to. You're driving along and you see someone on the opposite side of the street that could use an act of kindness, but wait, in order to help you would have to somehow get to the other side of the road. What do we do? We transfer the act of kindness by thinking, surely someone on that side of the road will help rather than me attempting to turn around. Problem solved and life goes on.

I have a thought that probably requires some soul searching. As you were possibly the first one to see help was needed and did not stop, who truly dropped the ball in failing to help one in need? Was it all the 'others' on the other side of the road who should have stopped, or perhaps was it you, the first to witness the need?

A kind act is most probably one of the simplest things we can do, and it can be either a show of support, compassion, an offer of assistance, or simply lending an ear to someone who has no one to turn to. How much gas and time would it have taken to turn the car around and help the person on the other side of the road?

Our final thought must be remembering the greatest act of kindness known to mankind: When a young man who once walked on this earth and through his unselfish act of kindness and caring, allowed himself to be brutalized and hung on a tree so that we may have freedom from death. Good thing He was on the right side of the road when we needed Him!

Nothing Can Match the Power of 'Love'

Recently, during a visit to my home, my mother-in-law, Lady Joy Lockhart and I, her husband was knighted by the Queen of England for his years of philanthropy within the Caribbean, entered into a discussion regarding the power of love. After bestowing accolades on our loved ones and sharing the depth of our love for family, past and present, she shared a story with me which not only touched my heart but a story that clearly demonstrates that love is not limited to that race we commonly refer to as human beings.

One day while sitting on the patio of her home in Antigua in the West Indies and enjoying what my wife and I refer to as a 'million-dollar view' of the Caribbean Sea, she stated that her restful bliss was interrupted by a noise directly behind her. When she turned around, she immediately noticed that a bird apparently flew into the glass sliding doors of her condo and was lying motionless on the floor below. Her first instinct was to go over to the bird and determine if it was still alive but before she could rise from her lounge chair, the mate of the fallen bird immediately appeared on the scene. She tearfully watched as the mate attempted to revive its fallen love to no avail. Seemingly not one to give up, the mate flew a few feet away, pecked at a fallen coconut until it was able to retrieve some of the juice from the fallen fruit. The mate then carried a mouthful of juice to its injured partner and deposited the juice in the little beak of the motionless little bird. This procedure was repeated several times and much to Lady Joy's delight, the fallen mate started to move and show signs of life.

Now the situation was still dangerous, as the fallen bird, while revived, was lying in an area that would most probably be vulnerable to other predators. Most probably sensing these dangers, the mate maneuvered itself underneath its fallen mate and somehow carried the injured bird on its back as it flew them both to a nearby ledge. A short time later, both birds were able to fly away and once again together enjoy the tropical paradise of their island home.

Some skeptics out there might be thinking that my tree hugging heart strings have once again gotten the better of me or perhaps this entire episode was simply a matter of survival instinct and not a love story. Well, to those of you that may subscribe to the aforementioned beliefs, may I offer my heartfelt sympathy to you? I am truly sorry that you apparently have not had the opportunity to stop and smell the roses or you have not had anyone knock on the door within your heart reserved explicitly for love and mistakenly opened the door marked 'deep freeze.' Perhaps you neither have felt the goose bumps of pure emotional joy that raised the hair on your arms and offer up a surge of heart beats when you see the one you truly love and the one who truly loves you.

Okay, so I got a little testy back there about an apparent lack of emotional feelings, but as the author of these little missives, I'm entitled to share my opinions, which then leaves you with the option of accepting them or not.

How many times have we heard stories that can only be explained by the power of love? A husband is working under a car and the car falls off the jack pinning him under the automobile. Seeing what happened, his 120-pound wife comes to the rescue and miraculously is able to lift the car allowing her husband to get out from under the car. Could that incredible moment of strength come from her love for her husband?

One day while waiting on the arrivals level for a ride home at JFK Airport, I witnessed a Port Authority bus run over a woman crossing the street and she was completely pinned under this very large vehicle. Like it was rehearsed, four bystanders and I immediately ran to the bus and lifted it high enough for a policeman to crawl under the bus and pull her out. Since I don't believe I had my Cheerios that morning, I'm giving love for my fellow human being all the credit on this one.

Ask any parent what lengths they would go to in order to save their child? I can answer that; to the ends of the earth and beyond if necessary. One of the biggest mistakes we can ever make in life is to underestimate the undeniable power of love.

It was 'Love' that enabled you and I to be here today and it was an agape love that has gifted each and every one of us with the power over death and has blessed us with the gift of an eternal life with our Lord and Savior. God sent us His One and Only Son to die for our sins so that we may be free from the power of deaths stronghold, now that's love. Jesus, I'm sure in His human state felt great fear as He was nailed to that tree, but He did it in obedience to His Father and in the name of Love.

Ephesians 4:2 'Be completely humble and gentle, be patient, bearing with one another in love.'

Philippians 1:9–11 'And this is my prayer: that your love may abound more and more in knowledge and depth of insight, so that you may be able to discern what is best and may be pure and blameless until the day of Christ, filled with the fruit of righteousness that comes through Jesus Christ, to the glory and praise of God.'

Hebrews 10:24 'And let us consider how we may spur one another on toward love and good deeds.'

I think we can all learn a lesson from the bird in this story. Logistically, there is no way the mate to the fallen bird should have been able to lift a weight equal to its own, no less fly with it on its back. I guess the mate forgot to read the section on weight restrictions for flight or did he know something we don't always remember, love defies all odds.

So, what is the moral of our little story, it's really quite simple but very powerful and poignant, Love transcends everything, every emotion, every feeling, and that's why the greatest commandment our Lord gave us was 'Love Thy Neighbor.'

Love is not the sole property of mankind; love is a gift to be shared. We share a love with:

Our Family and Friends – why is it we look forward with such great anticipation when we're on our way home or when going to visits loved ones? It's more than Grandma's famous apple pie, it's the way she hugs us and how genuinely happy she is to see us. Now that's Love.

Our Pets – every pet owner knows the great joy and love their precious pets give them day in and day out 24/7/365 and never expecting anything in return, their joy comes when they make us happy. Now that's Love.

The Animal Kingdom—we all enjoy a trip to the zoo or to Sea World. Why, because we love to see God's creatures up close and personal. Now that's love whether we realize it or not. Have you ever noticed how closely a mother whale guards her young calf or how monkeys continually groom their off spring? Nothing here has changed; it's still driven by love and affection.

Now I can show you where in your Bible that our Lord has given us dominion over the animals, but I need help finding the biblical passage that states 'love and caring' is specifically limited to mankind. Please let me know when you locate that passage.

And finally, the most important love of our human lives, **the Love for our Lord and Savior.** A God who has told us we will never fall from His grasp no matter what, a God who wants nothing more than to personally welcome each and every one of us into the eternal home He has lovingly prepared for us. This agape love is beyond our earthly comprehension but one that we will experience the moment we walk through those heavenly gates.

Colossians 2:2–3 'My purpose is that they may be encouraged in heart and united in love, so that they may have the full riches of complete understanding, in order that they may know the mystery of God, namely Christ, in whom are hidden all the treasures of wisdom and knowledge.'

I realize that there are many colloquial definitions of the word love and understand many of us have our own twist on what love means to us. One definition I recently came across stated, 'The definition of love is how excited your dog gets when you come home.' LOL.

By now you may have realized that the underlying definition of true and undeniable love in my litany above is 'Jesus Christ.' A love we certainly cannot comprehend in our earthly state, but an agape love that Jesus has reserved especially for you, a love that will transcend anything your brain and heart are capable of imagining.

In closing it is my wish that you catch glimpses of heaven, snippets of abundant joy, that you may grow strong in the reciprocal love between you and your Savior and be thankful for the blessings of this life. Amen!

Spiritual Drift

There are several types or kinds of drifting that each of us will be faced with from time to time and some are carefree and harmless and some may result in unpleasant consequences.

My wife Cathy will tell you her most favorite drifting can best be described as twofold; the first is when she is sitting on a beach listening to the roar of the surf and allowing her thoughts to aimlessly enjoy the splendor of God's creation, the ocean. Her second drift is at our home and on our back deck. She and our puppy, Heidi, sit together in the same chair, enjoying the night air, watching birds frolic in our bird bath and gazing up at the heavens while listening to music selections from the Pandora application on her telephone. Other than prayer, I don't know if there are any other events that bring her closer to God.

As for myself, hiking in many of our national parks provides me with that same degree of drift; I stop constantly to take in all the splendor of a world so magnificent, that only the hand of God could have created the masterpiece before my eyes, one that captures my vision and mind with wonder and awe.

There is another drift out there that is not as pleasant as the two I have just described and it's called spiritual drift. Spiritual drift has but one cause, to keep you distracted and from paying attention to God. If you are feeling this drift, let God be your anchor. When you find yourself being confronted by non-spiritual drifting and you're feeling a distance growing between yourself and the Holy Spirit within you, the very first question you must ask yourself is 'who moved?'

The Holy Spirit will never leave you but the Spirit can become somewhat dormant if it is not fed on a regular basis. Why you ask? The answer is simple, we leak. Band-Aids and patches will not stop this leaking or drifting, but there are many tools at your disposal that will close the distance and halt the drift. I've listed just a few below.

Prayer – Ask God for discernment in your life, for the inner strength needed to keep your focus on Him and to remove those things that are distracting you. I'm sure if you ask, nearby spiritual warriors would love to send up a few arrows to heaven on your behalf. Remember, it's virtually impossible to be distracted when you are on your knees in prayer with the Lord.

The Bible – Open this book to any chapter, any verse, and start reading with an open heart and mind. I promise it will speak to you and anchor that drift. It should be no secret who is behind your drift, the Evil One himself, attempting to distract your focus on God by filling your head and perhaps even your heart with thoughts of work, household issues, financial problems, heavy workloads, and an array of commitments that almost seem impossible to handle.

Church – There is no better place on earth to spend a few precious hours than in the Lord's House. Feel His presence, sing songs of joy and praise, offer supplications, and receive the precious gift of Holy Communion.

Sunday School and/or a sponsored Bible Study – Both of these offerings will not only feed you spiritually but will also give you the opportunity to feed others that may be struggling with any life issue and you're sitting on the resolve they so desperately need. We all have been tasked with feeding one and other.

Community Service – Nothing makes you feel better or puts a spiritual spring in your step than serving others in need. The Lord blessed you with the ability to serve; now it's time to awaken the will to serve. Here are just a few of the areas where blessings can be found: serving at a soup kitchen, home building with Habitat for Humanity, delivering Meals on Wheels, visiting the sick and elderly in either a hospital or nursing home. The choices and opportunities are available and waiting for you. When we come to the end of ourselves is when we come to a new beginning.

Mother Teresa coined this timeless phrase which should help from becoming a Christian couch potato: 'Yesterday is gone. Tomorrow has not yet come. We only have today. Let us begin.'

Proverbs 4:20–22 'My son, pay attention to what I say, listen closely to my words. Do not let them out of your sight, keep them within your heart; for they are the life to those who find them and health to a man's whole body.'

Hebrews 2:1 'We must pay more careful attention, therefore, to what we have heard, so that we do not drift away.'

1 Timothy 6:20 'Timothy, guard what has been entrusted to your care. Turn away from godless chatter and the opposing ideas of what is falsely called knowledge, which some have professed and in so doing have wandered from the faith.'

When you seek and allow the Lord to become your anchor, it does not matter how rough the seas, how deep the waters, how strong the current, once you are in His grasp you will never drift from His loving hands.

Do You Sit in the Spiritual Bleachers?

I remember my first baseball game. My Dad got us seats in left center field, top row at the old New York Yankees stadium. It was indeed a momentous moment for this young man, I brought my baseball glove so I could snag a homerun and I was bursting with excitement at the thought of seeing my favorite Yankee players. Being a rookie attendee, I brought everything except binoculars. The players in the batter's box seemed so far away I couldn't tell who was batting and worse yet, I couldn't see them and they couldn't see me. Their biggest fan was there and not one Yankee player would ever know it.

While being a spectator is an enjoyable outing at any sporting event, when it comes to our individual spirituality, we must be a player, not a fan in the stands. The simple truth is that we should not follow Jesus as a spectator, but as an active believer. It's not the easy way, but it's the only way.

Contained in many of the pages of our Bibles are numerous biblical events that included humanity standing on the sidelines either cheering positively or negatively as spectators or those who were true and active followers. The apostles were not fans but followers; Abraham, Job, Noah, Jeremiah, and Daniel, just to name a few, were active followers of Jesus and his message of salvation.

If I'm at home sitting in my favorite easy chair and watching a Dallas Cowboys game, while the players can assume there is a television audience, they cannot see it nor can they feel it. The television program is essentially for our benefit and not necessarily for theirs. However, if I'm swinging a hammer at a Habitat for Humanity house building or participating in any one of our many church and/or community programs, it is an action that can be seen and felt by others. I'm now an active player and follower; I have surrendered my spectator status for something real and tangible, a true follower of Jesus.

As fans in a stadium, we are there to be entertained, but as active followers of Christ, we have the responsibility of getting folks out of their stadium seats and onto the field as spirit-filled players and bringing the message of God's grace and salvation to others, by what we say and by what we do. A Christian couch potato is nothing more than a spectator; we want the best seats we can get but with none of the responsibility of the game.

If you have Jesus in your heart, then get out there and show it. Be a follower and a role model for others. If you're in a restaurant, say grace before the meal, now that's showing others you are grounded in the word and a true follower of Christ Jesus. Live each day as if you're the star player and all eyes are focused squarely on you and that is the moment that you allow the world to see it's not important as to whom you are, but rather whose you are. And keeping with our baseball game analogy: May all your hits be triples—the Father, Son, and Holy Spirit—and when you hit enough triples, many will cross the plate into their heavenly home.

Matthew 4:19 'Come follow me,' Jesus said, 'and I will make you fishers of men.'

2 Thessalonians 3:9 'We did this, not because we do not have the right to such help, but in order to make ourselves a model for you to follow.'

John 12:26 'Whoever serves me must follow me; and where I am, my servant will also be. My father will honor the one who serves me.'

2 Thessalonians 3:7 'For you yourselves know how you ought to follow our example. We were not idle when we were with you.'

1 Corinthians 11:1 'Follow my example, as I follow the example of Christ.'

Chapter Four:

Faith

Knock, Knock, Who's There?

Let's answer the door, shall we?

When fear knocks on your door, send faith to answer it and you will find there is no one there.

When Jesus knocks on your door, it must be opened from inside the heart.

Matthew 7:7 Ask, Seek, Knock. 'Ask and it will be given to you, seek and you will find it, knock and the door will be opened to you. For everyone who asks receives, he who seeks finds, and to him who knocks, the door will be opened.'

Jeremiah 33:3 (better known as God's Telephone Number) 'Call to me and I will answer you and tell you great and unsearchable things you do not know.'

Why are we backing away from answering the door? Perhaps it's the bill collector, or maybe a problem we just don't want to deal with at this point in time, or a problem we don't feel we're properly equipped to handle. Playing the role of an ostrich, putting our heads in the sand will not make the problem go away. Call upon the Lord. He will not only help with your dilemma, but He will give you great comfort throughout the process. The only way this process can work smoothly is when you lay the problem and your idea of what it will take to fix the issue, at His feet. If you have a pre-conceived fix, you have already removed God from the equation and you will undoubtedly miss His response and the great blessing attached. Don't second guess God, His wisdom will trump your wisdom, time after time after time. Why would we go to Him in prayer if we already know what it will take to fix the problem? I'll tell you why. We want the easy fix, the once in a lifetime miracle, and it's okay if we don't learn a good lesson from the experience, just get us the hell out of the hot water. I purposely chose the use of hell as a potential real estate option for those times when we begin to think we are smarter and wiser than God.

Sometimes fear keeps us from answering the door or the call; it's a natural emotion or reaction, especially when times are tough. It's during times like these that we must pray that the Lord will put a fire in our hearts that will melt the lead in our feet, giving us the desire to face adversity head on—the Lord and us. Just like the air that we breathe, the Lord is with us every single moment of our lives and if you stop and really listen, you just might hear and fell Him saying; 'I love you and I'm here for you.'

But why is it so important to grow through adversity? Perhaps, will I miss the blessing or will someone miss the blessing because I elected to ignore the knock at the door? Or will I turn my back on what surely was a blessing in disguise and subsequently turn away from the spiritual growth the Lord had planned for me? Knowing Jesus is not the way out of trouble, knowing Jesus is the way to triumph through trouble. We learn from our experiences in life, both worldly and spiritually, and they represent the strength and resilience of our growth. If we learn absolutely nothing from an experience, the chances are extremely high that we will continually be repeating and/or making the same mistakes over and over again. Nothing learned, nothing gained; what a miserable credo to have tattooed on your life's résumé.

So, the next time there is a knock on your spiritual door, run, don't walk to answer it, and remember to thank the Lord for the 'gift' that is on the other side.

Matthew 7:8 'For everyone who asks receives; he who seeks finds; and to him who knocks, the door will be opened.'

God can have anything He wants and He wants you and me. Hallelujah!

There's an Old Saying that If You Don't Believe in Something You'll Fall for Anything.

Our faith is the backbone of our beliefs, and so I thought we would spend a few moments dissecting exactly what is faith.

There are acronyms for the word faith . . .

Favorable Action In The Heart

And my favorite:

Forsaking All I Trust Him.

Let's break faith down into what I call the three C's of faith.

Content – Something to believe in, Biblical truth and knowledge.

Consent – A response to the body of knowledge, taking ownership.

Commitment – Giving up control, believing in the truth, confessing the truth, and embracing the truth.

Faith is the eye in which we can see God.

Faith is an empty vessel that wants to be filled.

Faith is the surrender to God

Faith is the way of sacrifice.

Faith lets God have His own way.

Faith asks no questions.

Faith is all of Him and less of me.

Someone once told me that there is no strength for the Christian but to be strong in faith and when you reap from discipline it produces a harvest of faith. So, the question now becomes, how is the harvest going, feeling any stronger yet?

There is an easy way to build on your faith, and simply put it is 'Feed your Faith,' because when you do, your doubts will starve to death. What's the best way to feed your faith? Attend church regularly, join a Sunday school class or Bible Study group, and stay grounded in the Word by reading the Bible daily. Pray to your Lord and Savior for discernment and strength to stay grounded in the light and truth of His Holy Word and that you might enjoy complete peace under His protection and presence.

Romans 1:12 'That is, that you and I may be mutually encouraged by each other's faith.'

Ephesians 3:17 'So that Christ may dwell in your hearts through faith.'

Romans 10:10 'For it is with your heart that you believe and are justified, and it is with your mouth that you confess and are saved.'

Colossians 2:5 'For though I am absent from you in body, I am present with you in spirit and delight to see how orderly you are and how firm your faith in Christ is.'

We are sometimes reluctant to surrender our will to faith because there is 'stuff' out there that our worldly self thinks it needs and wants. It can be hard, it can even be a bit scary, but I think one of the hardest things anyone of us can do is to say with sincerity each and every day, 'Lord, my will for your will.' But fear not, as there is a 'Light' at the end of the tunnel, and the 'Light' is our Lord and Savior. Trust in Him and you will begin to trust in yourself.

If you're still unsure about your faith, let me ask you a few questions. First, we'll begin with worldly faith. When you retire for the night, you do so believing that you will awaken the next morning—that's faith. When you are a passenger on an airplane, you believe that the pilot will get you to your destination safe and sound—that's faith. Even though you cannot see the pilot actually flying the aircraft, you still have faith in the unseen promise of a safe landing.

Now let's look at spiritual faith. When you accept Jesus as your Lord and Savior, you will have secured a place in His eternal kingdom—that's faith. Even though you cannot see Jesus face to face, you still have great faith in His promises to you.

We all need something to cling to; a place to hang our proverbial hats and our beliefs, a vision of the end of the rainbow, and that is all possible through Jesus Christ. Give Him a call; become one of the faithful in heart and spirit, He's been anxiously waiting to hear from you.

Why Does the Grass on the Other Side of the Fence Always Seem Greener?
Maybe it's because the other guy takes better care of his grass or maybe it's because no matter what we have, we're always looking for that one thing to come along that seems to be better than what we already have. Someone shared the following story with me and what struck me about the story was not its probable unauthenticated reliability but how something like this can invade our lives and decision-making process in a very real-world environment.

An elderly couple, each sixty years old, was strolling along a beach one day when a bottle washed up on shore directly in front of them. Being curious types, they picked it up and opened it to see what might be inside. Much to their amazement, a Genie (bear with me on this) popped out and granted then each one wish. The woman did not hesitate; she wanted to take a beautiful cruise around the world with her husband of forty years. Now it came to her husband's turn. After a few minutes of careful thought, his wish was somewhat similar to his wife's. He wanted to take a beautiful cruise around the world, but additionally, he wanted to take it with someone thirty years younger than him. The Genie said no problem, and in the flash of an eye, the man became a ninety-year-old.

Okay, perhaps the story was a bit hokey, but it makes a very good point: we never seem to be satisfied with our blessings. At the first sign of something that we perceive to be bigger and better than what we already have, we want it. Need an example? The majority of us have reasonably good and functional cell phones; they achieve their designed purpose, and we can make and receive telephone calls. The minute the new 'iPhone' came out, perhaps even the first time we saw the commercial, what happened? You know exactly what happened; our old cell phone was no longer good enough. Many of us wanted the new 'iPhone' and the only reason most of us did not run out and buy one was the cost, but we never gave up hope that one day we would own one.

Remember when I said this story gave me real world goose bumps. Think about the following scenarios:

Thank you, Lord for the nice Ford, but I really wanted a Lexus like my neighbor Bill. Thank you, Lord for my fifty-five-inch TV, have you seen my neighbor John's TV, it has a seventy-inch screen.

Thank you, Lord for the one thousand dollars I won in the lottery. If only I had won five thousand, I could be flying first class right now.

Proverbs 11:6 'The righteousness of the upright delivers them, but the unfaithful are trapped by evil desires.'

2 Peter 1:3–4 'His divine power has given us everything we need for life and godliness through our knowledge of him who called us by his own glory and goodness. Through these he has given us his very great and precious promises, so that through them you may participate in the divine nature and escape the corruption in the world caused by evil desires.'

It's okay to desire to become a better person and it's okay to want nice things, but we need to recognize the fine line between our existing blessings and wanting something just because it's bigger and better. There is a huge difference between wanting something and truly needing something. Desire is a slippery slope, and once we taste its forbidden fruits, you need to hang on tight because you'll be going for a fast ride and if I remember my physics properly, gravity pulls you down, not up!

The Cause of Death Was . . .

Imagine the poor soul whose death certificate read as follows: *Cause of Death: Abuse of human 'responsibility,' self-inflicted.* It's the same old story, over and over again; it's not the will of man that will keep him from heaven, it's his won't.

What 'responsibility' is that, you ask? It is your responsibility to share the gospel with others. Oh, I can hear the moans now. I'm not a teacher,

I'm not comfortable in doing this, I'm not a people person, I'm not properly trained, and so forth and so forth. St. Francis said, 'Preach the Gospel. Use words when necessary.'

Why are we so comfortable in being incognito? No one wants to plow the field, although we all want to reap the benefits. Sharing the gospel is both a privilege and the beauty of being believers. Wherever the Bible is preached, Christ speaks.

Romans 10:15 'How beautiful are the feet of those who bring good news.'

We all love to get 'good news' and think how much fun it would be to share 'good news,' especially with those you love. The purpose of the written Word of God is to reveal to man the Living Word of God, the Lord Jesus Christ. It is both life-changing and life-giving. The Gospels are a rich composite picture of Jesus Christ. Now, why would we ever want to keep something that good, that important, that exciting, that life-giving and that precious from those around us?

We must accept the responsibility that was given to us and share the gospel as Christ has requested; our futures depend on it. How long will we ignore the outstretched hands of God? Tomorrow is not guaranteed. There is someone out there with an undetermined lifespan and who is in desperate need of the good news of the gospel. How sad would it be if we filled our heads with excuses and filled the one in need with emptiness and avoidance?

Philemon 6 'I pray that you may be active in sharing your faith, so that you will have a full understanding of every good thing we have in Christ.'

Matthew 10:6–7 'Go rather to the lost sheep of Israel. As you go, preach the message: The kingdom of heaven is near.'

Matthew 10:32–33 'Whoever acknowledges me before men, I will also acknowledge him before my Father in heaven. But whoever disowns me before men, I will disown him before my Father in heaven.'

Remember, the best tact for sharing is 'contact.'

Calling All Holy Rollers

Why are we so worried about what others think of us and why are we not overly concerned about what the Lord thinks of us? It's truly one of life's paradoxes.

> *I don't like to witness because my friends and peers will make fun of me.*
> *I don't like to witness because people will think I'm some kind of religious nut.*
> *I don't like to witness because I never know what to say.*

One of the main reasons we are reluctant to witness is because of what we will call the 'Fear of the Sneer.' We all want to be accepted by our families and by our peer groups, and we are not willing to jeopardize those closely guarded relationships by bringing the Lord into the conversation. So, we rationalize ourselves out of witnessing. So, there we have it, rather than possibly scar our 'worldly popularity,' we have opted to forego the sharing of God's word with one in need. End result: another missed opportunity and another missed blessing for someone out there. What I'm about to say next may seem very bizarre, but when we knowingly fail to share the word with someone in need, are we in some small way contributing to their downfall, their eternal death as opposed to offering them the possibility of an eternal life with Jesus? A soul-searching thought that sometimes plagues my spiritual being when I fail to react to an opportunity the Lord has placed right under my nose.

I once heard someone sarcastically claim that the number of people at your funeral will not be determined by the number of your peers, but by the weather that day. While not an accurate statement by any means, I wonder how many people subscribe to this feeling. Why is this thing we call an ego so fragile that we must protect and guard it at all times and at all cost? Will we be ostracized from society, will be become nothing less than a leper to those we thought would love and support us no matter what the challenges were? Should that be the case, maybe those individuals that now shun us were never the close friends we believed them to be.

Someone figured out that 1 percent of the world reads the Bible and 99 percent of the world reads you, so what better reason to make sure that your popularity is not threatened by people watching? Wrong, if those numbers are correct, you have a captive audience, get out there and spread the Word!

Question: If someone did not take the time and effort to witness to you and me, where would we be today? I don't know about you, but I don't want to go there.

John 1:7 'He came as a witness to testify concerning that light, so that through Him all men might believe.'

Romans 12:13 'Share with God's people who are in need.'

Romans 1:16 'I am not ashamed of the gospel, because it is the power of God, for the salvation of everyone who believes.'

Witnessing is not as complicated as we make it to be. A witness to someone can be as simple as saying 'Didn't the Lord bless us with a beautiful day?' Or instead of taking all the credit for that new car you have, how about saying, 'Look at the beautiful car I have been blessed with.' The next time you sit down to a meal, whether at home or in a restaurant, offer a blessing before eating. Who knows, you might start a trend for not only yourself but for others as well. Now that's witnessing!

Yes, it truly is that easy; try it when the Lord presents you with that next golden opportunity, you'll be glad you did. Break the ice. Be bold for your God because the debt we owe our Lord is payable here on earth. THOSE WHO ARE ON THE ROAD TO HEAVEN SHOULD NEVER BE CONTENT TO GO THERE ALONE!

Us and Them

If you're a Baby Boomer like I am, you might be thinking this is a song title from Pink Floyd's record album *Dark Side of the Moon*. A great album, I might add. Or it might possibly be a struggle between two different factions of people.

I have chosen the latter, a struggle within humanity and spirituality. There are basically two factions of people, those who believe in the word of God and those who do not. I know there are different variations of belief out there, but for the sake of this story, I have chosen those who do and those who don't.

Recently I saw the movie *The Shack*, and afterwards I entered into a discussion with someone regarding what I thought was a great Christian movie with numerous great Christian-centered messages and ideals. The response I received let some air out of my spiritual balloon. I was told that 'Rotten Tomatoes,' a movie-rating system, scored the movie very low. My immediate response was 'That's crazy, the movie was awesome.' I was then informed that apparently people do not like to be preached to when they see a movie, so that was one of the reasons it scored poorly. Well, duh, it's a Christian movie, what did the viewers expect, of course there will be a certain amount of great messaging being delivered, some perhaps even in a 'preaching' style of delivery. It did not take long before I realized I was not going to win this debate and it was rapidly becoming another example of 'us and them.'

I walked away from the conversation with the distinct feeling that I just got my butt whipped by one of 'them.' My pity party did not last long at all; soon the spirit within me brought a sense of spiritual reality back into my wounded soul. Not everyone is going to like what I like and that does not necessarily make them bad people. Perhaps some people don't mind a good sermon in their Sunday pew but do not necessarily like it in their theater seat. Okay, I get it, maybe I got this whole thing wrong and it's not a battle of us and them, it's a battle within me. I was unfairly judging those who did not conform to my way of thinking, my likes, and my dislikes. How does the story go? 'Sometimes we wear our halos so tight we give the other person a headache.' Guilty as charged on this one.

Psalm 7'8 'let the Lord judge the peoples, Judge me O Lord, according to my righteousness, according to my integrity, O Most High.'

Proverbs 3:30 'Do not accuse a man for no reason when he has done you no harm.'

Luke 6:37 'Do not judge, and you will not be judged. Do not condemn and you will not be condemned.'

I would like to believe that I have learned my lesson; however, should I ever falter once again, I know I can quickly turn to the Holy Spirit within me for discernment, strength, and forgiveness.

Oh, one more thing, I also learned that I'm not smarter or more innocent than 'them' and I need to keep my spiritual P's and Q's in line before I let my mouth deceive my beliefs and worse yet, cause someone to stumble because of my indifference to others' opinions.

You're Under Arrest!

Question: If you were arrested as a Christian, would there be enough evidence to convict you?

Before you jump right in with a response, a little soul searching is sometimes needed when attempting to answer this question as we all need to look into the spiritual mirror every now and then. As part of the world, we get caught up in many of the burdens and issues the world seems to cram into our already busy lives. But the world is not always to blame, as sometimes we are more concerned about 'saving face' than about 'saving grace.' Why does this happen? Because at the heart of every problem there is a problem of the heart!

When I first attempted to answer this question for myself, if you were in earshot, you would have thought that I was a highly acclaimed Harvard law professor. I had more excuses and reasons why my shortcomings were really just misdemeanors and not felonies. I was the absolute 'victim' in virtually everything that may have cast a shadow or aspersions on my potential errors in judgment. Even now as I put this to paper, I'm beginning to sound like the lawyer of old. Could our unwillingness to accept ownership of a shortcoming be attributed to our built-in defense mechanisms or perhaps the absurd belief that we have been coated with sin-repellent Teflon? If I can be so bold, it's not the circuit judge that we need to be concerned about, as you will most definitely be answering to a higher power.

And, unlike today's judicial system, a life sentence in this court may be eternal with the very noticeable absence of an appeal process.

Real people, solid spiritual individuals, are not defined by their accomplishments but by their relationship with God. In our humanness, we rank people by their homes, jobs, checkbooks, and toys, but God uses a different ranking system, He measures our spiritual worth and vitality based on what we have done with the gifts and blessings that He so graciously bestowed on us. Did we share or compare?

Remember that time at work when the walls were caving in around you, everyone was running in different directions, confusion was rampant, and out of the corner of your eye, you spot a lone individual? It's the person standing in the midst of all the chaos and she is cool, calm, and very collected. Your first thought is, 'Wow, I don't know what she has but I sure would like some of it right about now.' My guess is that her heart is in the exact place where it needs to be and that individual has turned the entire office debacle over to the Lord, because she knows that it is divinity, not destiny, that will form the outcome of the moment.

One of my favorite retorts when my Christianity is challenged is 'Christians are not perfect, just forgiven.' If you mess up, seek forgiveness, if you cause others to stumble, be humble and ask for their forgiveness as well. Your heavenly Father loves you so very much and given the opportunity, He will always be there with you and for you.

Given the choice in life, if I need to be convicted of something, may I be convicted of unfailing love, abundant humility, unshakable faith, and a forgiving heart? And it is my hope and prayer that you will be convicted of these same charges as well. May the peace of the Lord be always with you!

My closing prayer in every Sunday school class is always, 'Lord, let all that we say and all that we do in this coming week be to the honor and glory of your most holy name and let others see your grace shine through each one of us as we go about the business you have set before us.' Amen!

So, make it your goal to be 'Convicted' as charged.

1 Thessalonians 1:5 'Because our gospel came to you not simply with words, but also with power, with the Holy Spirit and deep conviction.'

I Knew You Could Do It

Encouraging words can be wings to the sprinter or endurance to the long-distance runner. They lift up would-be and professional athletes and amateurs alike. It's that all-important shot of Gatorade that brings you to and across the finish line.

I was watching a morning television show where the commentators were suggesting that the best way to offer encouragement to an athlete, especially the younger ones, was to simply say, 'I really enjoy watching you play,' as opposed to the good old 'We'll get them next time, when things don't go our way.'

Encouragement is not solely limited to sporting events. You can encourage academic achievement: I love to read your works, musical abilities; I love to listen to you play the violin, creativity within the arts or the landscape novice who just tackled that mess in your backyard. Encouragement is that magic potion that stimulates us to go beyond the norm and reach new and lofty goals that previously may have seemed out of reach.

Some of the best descriptions of encouragement can be found in that wonderful book we call the Bible.

> *In the Book of Ruth*, God encourages a very caring and loving Ruth to forsake the comfort and safety of her home and remain in a foreign land to care for Naomi, her ailing mother in-law.
>
> *In the Book of John*, Jesus encourages a somewhat skeptical Nicodemus to be born of water and the spirit and shares with him the power of light over darkness, a message that must be spread to the world.
>
> *In the Book of Acts*, Jesus encourages Saul, a feared executioner with the blood of many Israelites on his hands,

to repent from his evil ways and become a disciple of Jesus.

In the Book of Genesis, God encourages Noah to build an Ark of an enormous size so that it can accommodate the animals of the earth by pairs.

It would have been very easy for God to flip a switch and the folks above would automatically have answered the call. God chose loving and comforting words to strengthen the resolve in each person, affording each the opportunity to learn and grow from their newfound confidence.

Job 16:5 'But my mouth would encourage you; comfort from my lips would bring you relief.'

Acts 15:32 'Judas and Silas, who themselves were prophets, said much to encourage and strengthen the brothers.'

2 Thessalonians 2:16–17 'May our Lord Jesus Christ himself and God our Father, who loved us and by his grace gave us eternal encouragement and good hope, encourage your hearts and strengthen you in every good deed and work.'

Hebrews 3:13 'But encourage one another daily, as long as it is called today, so that none of you may be hardened by sins deceitfulness.'

Colossians 2:2–3 'My purpose is that they may be encouraged in heart and united in love, so that they may have the full riches of complete understanding, in order that they may know all the treasures of wisdom and knowledge.'

My written missives, which I hope you are both enjoying and finding solace in, were a direct result of the encouraging words of several of my church family members. After several years of leading Sunday school, some of the class attendees suggested that it would be very helpful to them if I would put pen to paper and capture many of the analogies that I used during our sessions. I never thought of myself as a writer and internally questioned if my skills were sufficient enough to even attempt such a task. After some wonderful words of encouragement, supported by many prayers, our Heavenly Father blessed and encouraged me with the confidence and the ability to deliver these messages to you. A gift of encouragement I will forever be thankful for.

All's WELL that Ends WELL

I have many favorite Bible stories, but one that really strikes home with me is the story about Jesus and the Samaritan woman at the well: **John 4.**

Jesus and the disciples arrive in Samaria, a place that is not known for rolling out the welcome mat to Jewish visitors. Jesus sends the disciples into town and while they are gone he enters into dialogue with an apparent outcast Samaritan woman. Knowing her heart, Jesus shares the gospel of living and eternal water with her. After their discussion, the woman also leaves for town. Now comes my favorite part. The disciples come back from town and all they bring back with them is lunch. The woman comes back from town and she brings with her the entire town, so they may also hear the gospel message! Wow!

I must truly ask myself, had I been in that same situation, would I have brought back the mayo or the mayor. It's easy on the conscience to opt for the town, but when was the last time I brought a single newcomer to our church, no less multiple individuals? I guess I need to spend a little more time at the well.

How many trips have you made to the well? How many opportunities have you had in your lifetime to share the gospel with someone, or did they unfortunately slip right through your fingers without even a sip of living water? Tough questions we must ask ourselves each and every day. Perhaps our morning prayers should include 'Father, when the opportunity to share the gospel with one in need does arise, bless me with the will and the words to comfort that person and share your story with them.' All too often I seem to lack the courage or confidence to step forward and profess the word, so help me Lord be a bold witness to your mighty name. Trust me on this, you don't have to quote scripture or frantically wave a Bible; you simply need to let the other person know what your Heavenly Father has done for you. The Holy Spirit will take care of the rest.

A good friend of mine shared a story about a flight he had between Dallas and San Antonio. He said that when he sat down, it was easy to see that his seat mate seemed down in the dumps. He introduced himself and before the flight left the ground, the seat mate said to him, 'I wish I had some of that joyfulness you seem to have.' The spiritual door just swung open, and over the course of the one-hour flight, my friend shared how Jesus had turned his own less-than-stellar life around. Upon landing in San Antonio, the seat mate had accepted Jesus as his Lord and Savior; the two had a quick but low-key prayer together. If my friend had not shared his story with his seat mate, this poor soul could have been stumbling and fumbling through life, a missed opportunity on saving someone in need.

Now, I'm not suggesting you start preaching to your seat mate on your next flight, but what I am suggesting is to keep an open heart and mind to those around you, and if you come across someone that would benefit from having Jesus in their life, do the right thing. Remember, someone shared the word with you.

So, on your next visit to the well, aside from quenching your own spiritual thirst, please remember to share a cup with one in need. Somewhere along our journey through life, someone took the time to share a cup with you and me. Thanks be to God on that faithful gesture!

John 4:13 'Jesus answered, "Everyone who drinks this water will be thirsty again, but whoever drinks the water I give him will never thirst. Indeed, the water I give him will become in him a spring of water, welling up to eternal life."'

Romans 1:16 'I am not ashamed of the gospel, because it is the power of God for the salvation of everyone who believes.'

1 Corinthians 9:16 'Yet when I preach the gospel, I cannot boast, for I am compelled to preach. Woe to me if I do not preach the gospel.'

Romans 15:16 'to be a minister of Christ Jesus to the Gentiles with the priestly duty of proclaiming the gospel of God, so that the Gentile might become an offering acceptable to God, sanctified by the Holy Spirit.'

See you at the well.

The Hardest Questions in the World to Answer

No, I'm not talking about quantum theories or matters of relativity, I'm talking about some of the most simple and basic functions on earth. These questions will plague mankind from now until the end of time. For example;

Why is it so hard to drop a twenty in the collection basket, yet we will drop several twenties at our favorite restaurant or movie theater?

Why is a little white lie okay, but a big white lie is not okay?

Why do our minds wander in church but in front of a television or movie screen we don't miss a single word or action?

Why is it sometimes so hard to get up in the morning for church, yet even after a full night of partying we would be up at the crack of dawn to catch our vacation flights?

Why do we tithe what's left and not what's right?

Why do we keep repeating the same sins over and over again?

Why is it so hard for us to say 'grace' before a meal in a public restaurant?

Why is it okay to take the pencil from work but don't let anyone take any of your stuff?

Why does misery like company?

And my non-spiritual favorite, **why** do they leave the door to the bank vault open and chain the $.25 stick pen to the desk in the bank lobby?

Tired of all the same old whys? Then I have one final why question for you.

Why not consider a change? Instead of a litany of 'why' issues, try the one 'who' wants to help you avoid that repetitious repartee; His name is Jesus.

So, if you're ever looking for answers to tough questions, you're wondering how you will ever get out of your current predicament, might I suggest your Bible! It is the Living Word of God and can guide you through anything you will ever have to face and answer, in great peace and comfort.

Jeremiah 33:3 'Call to me and I will answer you and tell you great and unsearchable things you do not know.'

You're either a Saint or an Ain't

In order that we may better live with ourselves, we put varying degrees of value on our sins or wrong doings such as 'That was just a little white lie.' 'That was only a small sin, nothing major, or my personal favorite, 'Good grief, it's not like I killed someone.' The fact of the matter is that sin, no matter what value we place on it, sin is still sin in the eyes of the Lord. The Lord does not have our human sliding scale of justice. Now, the danger we are facing is the fact that when we employ the use of a sliding scale of right and wrong, it is you and I, not God, who are setting the parameters of good and evil. We have taken it upon ourselves to decide how far we can push the spiritual envelop and still feel good about ourselves.

Another of my favorite pitfalls is when we are forced to choose the lesser of the two evils. Have you ever given any thought to choosing neither one? Seriously, if they're both evil, doesn't this become a no brainer?

When it comes to Christianity, it is a far better thing to wear out than to rust out.

Don't be a Christian Couch Potato, as that surely will get you into trouble one day. We have this thought process in our heads and it goes something like this: I go to church, I tithe, and therefore I am. Well, while that is all well and good, when the Lord asked us to tithe, He meant more than just our money; He meant our time as well. Lead a Sunday school class, get involved in an outreach program or get involved in a youth or music programs. The key here, which I hope is becoming abundantly clear, is that you need to get involved. Don't rely on the other person to complete the job the Lord has given all of us to do.

Getting involved is a personal choice and must come from the heart. Be very careful when it comes to the spiritual choices that you make in life, they can have eternal consequences. Not sure how to get started? The shortest distance to the resolution of a problem is the distance between your knees and the floor.

Our task on earth is singular, to choose our eternal home. You can afford many wrong choices in life. You can choose the wrong career and survive or the wrong city and survive. You can even choose the wrong mate and survive. But there is one choice that must be made correctly, and that is your eternal destiny.

Psalm 30: 'Sing to the Lord, you saints of his, praise his holy name.'

Luke 9:25 'What good is it for man to gain the whole world and yet lose or forfeit his very self?'

John 15:16 'You did not choose me, but I chose you and appointed you to go and bear fruit, fruit that will last. Then the Father will give you whatever you ask in my name.'

2 Thessalonians 2:13 'But we ought always to thank God for you, brothers loved by the Lord, because from the beginning God chose you to be saved through the sanctifying work of the Spirit and through belief in the truth.'

Remember, God chooses us and then looks at us through the heart.

So, are you going to be a Saint or an Ain't?

Selecting the Right Course

We live in busy times. Our jobs can be very demanding and stressful. Our equally demanding family matters consume much of our time and energy, and we seem to constantly face those financial issues that hang around every corner. It's understandable that we are always on the lookout for an easier path to travel. While an easier path may be okay for some worldly issues we encounter, be careful on the spiritual course you choose, as our selections can have eternal effects.

The Dilemma: We want the short course in spiritual intellect.

We do not want the intensive course in spiritual intellect.

The Truth: We are choosing the course of our eternal lives.

I don't believe God owes us an easy curriculum.

The Fix: When we come to the end of ourselves is when we come to a new beginning with Jesus.

Proverbs 15:21 'Folly delights a man who lacks judgment, but a man of understanding keeps a straight course.'

Proverbs 16:9 'In his heart a man plans his course, but the Lord determines his steps.'

Proverbs 2:8 'for he guards the course of the just and protects the way of the faithful ones.'

We need to remember that skillful sailors were not made on smooth seas. When the Lord brings us into deep waters, it is not to drown us, but to cleanse us and allow us to spiritually mature. So how do we go about selecting which course is best for us?

The very first step is by accepting Jesus Christ as your Lord and Savior. Congratulations, you have just completed all the steps necessary in the pursuit of selecting the right course. Yes, it really is that easy, and as your relationship with Jesus develops and as your spiritual maturity grows through the study of the living word, before you know it, you will become a master navigator of life. When the people and things around you begin to crumble out of control, you will be the one who possesses the peace and understanding of God.

I think it was Mother Theresa who said, 'Worry does not empty tomorrow of its difficulty, worry empties today of its strength and its peace.' All too often we seek the peace of God, without seeking God.

So, try a new approach to life, instead of continually occupying your mind with your problems, try occupying your mind with God's promises.

A Stumble through Faith

Faith is one of my favorite beliefs to write about because it congers up such a wide variety of thoughts and ideas, but truth be told it can be truly uncomplicated and rewarding if we allow it to be. Faith is the cornerstone of our beliefs and spirituality, it is also the tenacity of our tenets, that gut check that says I believe. However, Faith can sometimes be our willingness to put more trust in what we can see and do as opposed to what we cannot.

Okay, a very strange opening line perhaps but let's dissect faith and start with some every day garden variety faith dilemmas.

One of the most precious gifts our Lord has given many of us is our children. Yet, we take these precious children and leave them with a perfect stranger at day care because it's 'supposed to be safe.' Do you personally know the individual who will be taking care of your child? Can this be considered blind faith?

You get on an airplane, you have full faith that the guys flying the aircraft will get you there safely. How do you know this? Is the captain your neighbor, a relative, or a close friend? Or is it a numbers game, the majority of time they land safely, or is it true and undeniable faith?

Okay, we may have to do these things like fly and use day care facilities, but is it an act of faith or a matter of necessity that helps to make us believe all will be well.

My personal belief is that Spiritual faith comes from the deepest recess of our hearts and not our brains. Our brains will argue with our heart all day long if we allow it, trying to scientifically prove or disprove something. We're human, and that's just one of the flaws in our human nature, but it's not a flaw that cannot be overcome and controlled.

My two favorite acronyms for Faith are: 'Forsaking all I trust Him' and 'Favorable action in the Heart.' True faith, as I see it, must be a combination of trust and a sound spiritual heart. Does faith know that God can, or that God will?

Faith is the eye in which we can see God.
Faith is an empty vessel that wants to be filled.
Faith is the surrender to God.
Faith is the way of sacrifice.

115

Faith lets God have His own way.

Faith asks no questions.

Knowing the above, why do we sometimes 'stumble' around a bit when it comes to spiritual faith?

We go to our Lord in prayer and offer up our petitions but only on those that we feel very strongly about, we also offer Him solutions that we feel would work. Where is our faith, do we truly think He needs our help in providing answers and solutions? Do we believe he cannot handle these problems without our input?

Going back to the Day Care and Airline Pilot scenarios, is it that we can see the pilot, even though we weren't there to witness it, we know he has been thoroughly trained by the airline. As for the Day Care providers, we know they must be licensed and certified by the state and that certification must be posted at the facility. So why then when it comes to God, do we sometimes experience moments of doubt in our faith? Is it because we cannot physically see God but can see the pilot and the Day Care Workers' certifications?

We see and experience God every day of our lives through the birth of a child, a sunrise and sunset, the majesty of the earth and sky, the simple beauty of a flower in bloom. We see God when people come together in prayer when tragedy strikes and we see humble servants of the Lord tirelessly working in soup kitchens, hospitals, and food banks to name just a few. Hey, want to see the Lord? Look into a mirror; we were made in His image. If you don't like what you see, do something about it, become involved in a service program, pray for spiritual direction, and He will answer you.

We have great trust in our parents, our clergy, our families and friends. This trust did not materialize overnight or with the wave of a magic wand; it was developed by a longstanding, continuous, and very loving relationship. Yes, it that's simple, it all starts with a relationship between you and the Lord. He loves you so very much, and nothing would make him happier than to hear from you on a regular basis. So, start a good spiritually-rooted relationship today, and if you already have one that's so-so, dust it off and awaken your inner spirit. And if your relationship is already awesome, please send up a resounding hallelujah.

Some churches experience very high attendance during Easter and Christmas, and while this is a wonderful thing, was the rise in attendance based on Calendar Holidays? Can the increase in attendance be a faithful belief in our Lord's Birth and Resurrection, or is the rise solely predicated on the fact you're supposed to go to church on these dates, it's tradition?

A faith that cannot be tested is a faith that cannot be trusted, so accept trials and tribulations as part of your spiritual growth and above all, open the doors of your heart and invite the Holy Spirit in. He wants to be with you always.

And remember we must always feed our faith through righteous acts, loving our neighbors, prayer, reading the Bible and having a humble servant's heart. Do all of this and no one will ever have to say to you; 'Hey Brother, Keep the Faith.'

What Am I Worth?

I ask that you look into your heart before you answer this question, I did. I'm not referring to your financial status but rather your spiritual status. If I cannot be used for the Lord's word, if indeed I am not 'usable,' then am I just taking up space on this big blue marble?

In order for me to self-evaluate my worth; I'm going to use the word usable in an acronym form.

Usable—am I 'Unstained 'by the culture I was brought up in or the culture that I now reside in? They say people are a product of their environment, if that's the case was I a follower or a dissenter in my culture. Were the beliefs of my culture spiritually strong or as diverse and unstructured as shifting sand on a wave beaten beach? No one wants to be an outcast, especially in their own culture, so did I acquiesce on moral issues or did I hold my spiritual ground. If I did become stained by my culture, did I seek forgiveness and direction from my Lord to avoid future stains? Did

I offer a thank you for His spot cleaning of my soul? Surface stains are usually easily washed away but beware of the stains of Satan as he has been known to use a permanent marker.

Have I **'Stretched'** myself to the absolute limits of my ability, my being and beyond or have I just done enough to get by? Have you ever heard someone say, if he only applied himself he would have been great? I know some folks seem to have the Midas touch, everything they touch turns to gold, and then there are those of us who have to claw our way to the top through a quagmire of sweat and tears. While gold may be a precious metal, it can melt away to nothing, but the satisfaction of achievement can never melt away. When I was a small child, my mother would bake the most delicious cookies the universe has ever known. She would place the plate of warm treasures on top of the counter, just beyond my flatfooted reach. It did not take long before I realized that if I stretched myself as far as could, on tippy toes, the reward would be as close to heavenly as a cookie thief could get.

Do I **'Adhere'**; to all that I have learned, all that my Savior has taught me? Do I walk the walk or just talk the talk? I can profess all I want but if I can't back it up, I'm just full of 'hot air' and we all know where hot air comes from, an attack by the Evil One, Satan. Do I cause others to stumble because of my inconsistent faith? If I am not spiritually grounded in the word, then the only person I'm fooling is myself. The Lord reads my heart not my empty head. One of the most common dangers in adhering to scripture is that it doesn't always fit into what we desire and so we make what we believe to be small compromises in our faith. There are only so many cornerstones that can be pulled out of the base of a building before it crashes and crumbles to the ground. You cannot compromise the structure of a building and you cannot compromise the structure if your faith.

Am I **'Bold'** in my witness for the Lord? Do I wear my faith on my sleeve or on my lips and my actions? Am I concerned about what others think so I do not witness when indeed I should have? Do I let peer pressure keep me from professing my love for Jesus or am I afraid of being labeled as some kind of religious nut or holy roller gone wild? Will I feel better if I declare myself to be semi-bold? When it comes to spirituality and boldness, you are either all in or all out, because working for the Lord has never and will never be a part time position as the goal should always be full time spiritual growth.

Have I been '*liberal*' in my tithing and the giving of my talents and my time to serve the Lord or have I become a part-time warrior, sometimes I am in the game and sometimes I'm content just sitting on the bench. If I find a twenty-dollar bill, do I put half in the collection plate or does the whole twenty stay tucked safely away in my pocket? When my church or community is seeking volunteers for a cause, do I rattle off a litany of untruthful excuses or do I boldly state, where can I sign up?

Finally, have I taken the necessary steps to be **'Equipped'**; in scripture? Do I start or end each day reading a few verses or a chapter of my Bible? Do I even own a Bible and have I ever read the entire book? My church offers many Christian education classes throughout the week, have I attempted to sign up for a class or do all of these offerings interfere with my busy social life? Most sane people would never think of going out into subzero weather in just a tee shirt, we would want layers of clothing to protect us from the bitter cold and ultimately pneumonia. It's no different spiritually; we should always make sure we are equipped in the full armor of God. Should we fail in this endeavor, it's not going to be the bitter cold we need to be concerned about.

So now that I have taken this personal evaluation of my spiritual walk, the next questions I need to address are; Is my Christian walk worth following and is there anyone following me? To those that may have difficulty in answering these last questions, help is closer than you think. Dust off the Bible and start reading again, go to the Lord in prayer, let Him know your heart's desire and ask for His loving hand to not only lift you up but strengthen you to the point whereby in the glorious name of Jesus Christ, you may lead a parade of believers to their heavenly home.

What are you worth? Everything to the God that created you and the God that loves you more than mere words can describe.

1 Peter 1:7 'These have come so that your faith, of greater worth than gold, which perishes even though refined by fire, may be proved genuine and may result in praise, glory and honor when Jesus Christ is revealed'

Temptation

Temptation has to be one of Satan's most effective ploys in his evil bags of tricks, all of which are designed to cast doubt on our spirituality. He works on the premise of not what is good for you, but what feels good to you, and unfortunately, he gets many of us to slip, trip and fall from grace when we get lured into this web of deceit. It is important to remember that temptation comes from our own desire, God does not tempt us; God strengthens us.

When we look into what causes you and I to submit to temptation, I'm willing to bet that nine out of ten times, we succumb to temptation when we are at either at our weakest moments or we are in need of some type of quick fix to what we believe is a developing disaster. It is at these very moments, when we drop our spiritual guard, even ever so slightly, the Evil One is ready to pounce on our beliefs.

You're out shopping and your spending budget is very tight. The cashier rings up your purchases, but you notice they did not catch a major purchase item on the bottom of the cart and could you ever use that savings for other much-needed items. Next, enter the Great Tempter and the temptation. He whispers into your soul, 'What's the big deal, the store can afford it and can you ever use the extra savings. Besides, it's their fault they did not look underneath the cart.' Are you tempted to walk away with the item not paid for or will you advise the cashier they missed an item?

You're driving to a party and you are running late. Construction has closed your normal route with a Do Not Enter sign, but it's pretty obvious to you that you can easily maneuver around the sign and get to your destination. Enter the Tempter and the temptation. He whispers into your soul, 'What's the big deal; other cars have probably driven around the barrier already, so go ahead and do it.' Do you find a legal route to your destination, or since you're running late, you make this one-time exception and pay no heed to the do not enter sign?

We are tempted more times each day than we probably care to think about, even down to the smallest of decisions. If you're on a diet, you're tempted by the dessert cart; if you're running late to work, you're tempted to drive over the posted speed limit; and the list goes on and on. The majority of the time, we do a great job in avoiding temptation and not falling into well-laid traps. Where we do get into trouble is when we make those 'little exceptions' to help ease us through the difficult choices. While exceptions may seem like a minor blip on our spiritual radar screen, compounded over time they can turn into very slippery slopes and lead to a fall from grace. Once we realize how easy it was to make the exception and it really did not cause any recognizable harm, what's the problem with a little shortcut here and there? It's not like we killed someone for goodness sake.

Each time we attempt to justify an exception, regardless of how small or finite it may be, we are essentially chipping away at our Christian armor and it's only a matter of time before the small exceptions grow to such a dimension that we are no longer capable of discerning right from wrong.

In Luke 4, Satan tempts Jesus on three separate fronts, from performing magic to obtaining power and authority over the land and finally to jumping off a mountain to prove He can save himself. Jesus replied, 'Do not put the Lord your God to the test.'

A good rule of thumb in avoiding the temptation trap quite simply: If you need to think about whether or not an action is okay, it probably is not.

1 Corinthians 10:12–13 'So, if you think you are standing firm, be careful that you do not fall! No temptation has seized you except what is common to man. And God is faithful; he will not let you be tempted beyond what you can bear. But when you are tempted, he will also provide a way out so that you can stand up under it.'

Mark 14:38 'Watch and pray so that you will not fall into temptation. The spirit is willing, but the body is weak.'

Luke 11:2–4 'He said to them, 'when you pray say: Father, hallowed be your name, your kingdom come. Give us each day our daily bread. Forgive us our sins, for we also forgive everyone who sins against us. And lead us not into temptation.'

Two Serious and Important Questions

Question 1 – Is your Christian walk worth following?

Question 2 – Is there anyone following you?

If you have answered either no or I'm not sure to the questions above, may I suggest you start with a prayer and then open your Bible and let the Lord turn your life around.

Why are the simplest of questions, sometimes the hardest to answer? I sometimes wonder if the difficulty is either a direct result of our not wanting to know the answers or if it is the age-old adage 'What I don't know can't hurt me.' Let me offer a resounding 'Wrong' to that misnomer as it will not only hurt you, it may have eternal consequences.

Let's look at question one. It's a well-known fact that most people will take your example far more serious than your advice. Are you a 'do as I say and not as I do' type of individual? Once you profess to be a Christian, there is an obligation tied to that declaration. People who are struggling with their own Christian walk will look to your inspiration and guidance, and this happens whether or not you are aware that someone is closely watching your Christian walk. The 'watchers' have put their trust and their spiritual wellbeing that you are on the right path and would never lead them astray. Yes, it is a mighty responsibility but one well worth the effort.

Let's take an imaginary walk together. When something does not go our way, do we get upset and mumble an unsavory expletive or two, or do we allow the Spirit within us to help us stay the course and find wholesome solutions to the dilemma at hand? Next, we come across someone struggling with packages and children while attempting to cross a busy intersection. Since you and I are already on the other side, do we continue on our way or double back to help one in need? We're now in our car driving to work and we come upon a young woman stranded on the side of the road with a flat tire. Unfortunately, we're already going to be late for work, so should we take the position that surely someone will come along to help her or do pull over and make an offer of assistance? And finally, we're at a neighbor's party and it's a hot day and there is a tub of your favorite beer and it's ice cold. Everyone seems to be knocking back the suds one after another and the air is festive and fun. Do we over-indulge and keep pace with the party revelers because we certainly do not want to be the wet blanket, or do we maintain a safe intake according to what would be socially acceptable? It truly is easy to claim to be a good person and that we are on a good Christian walk, but when the defining moments arise, how well do we respond? If only one person is influenced by a good Christian decision in the events described above, get ready for a spiritual high five from Jesus himself, compliments of the Holy Spirit.

Question two, is anyone following our walk? The very first thing that would set off my spiritual alarm would be the realization that no one was following my walk. My next and immediate thought would be; why? What am I doing or not doing that is making others leery of my walk? As a Christian, the last thing I would ever want to do is to knowingly cause another Christian to stumble. Worse yet, I never want to turn around and realize the only one following me is the Evil One himself.

Our Christian responsibility is a simple one, to make sure that as we travel the path to heaven, we bring others along with us. So that means the bigger the crowd behind you, the more followers that join your walk all equates to a job well done Christian solider. Never be content to take a Christian walk by yourself; always bring a friend, loved one or one in need.

One final thought, please do not get discouraged or be dismayed from your appointed course by a slip or trip here and there. None of us are perfect and things will inevitably happen; however, these can be easily overcome by seeking forgiveness from our Lord and help to get back on the righteousness path. You can minimize potholes on your walk by offering a prayer to the Lord before your take the first step of your journey, seeking strength and wisdom to stay the course.

Psalm 27:11 'Teach me your way, O Lord; lead me in a straight path because of my oppressors.'

Psalm 23:3 '... He guides me in paths of righteousness for his names sake.'

Proverbs 15:10 'Stern discipline awaits him who leaves the path; he who hates correction will die.'

Proverbs 4:26–27 'Make level paths for your feet and take only ways that are firm. Do not swerve to the right or the left; keep your foot from evil.'

1 John 3:7 'Dear children, do not let anyone lead you astray.'

The School of Life

If there is one constant about life, it's that we will never graduate as life is an ongoing and constant learning process. Life lessons can be both helpful and hurtful, but lessons just the same. The key to learning and understanding these lessons is how we emerge from them and did we recognize the value of the experience?

Life is like a school; the Lord knows when to give us a lesson and when to give us a test. God will test us not for His benefit but for our benefit.

No one enjoys a harsh lesson, especially the Apostle Peter.

Matthew 14:27–30 'But Jesus immediately said to them: "Take courage! It is I. Don't be afraid." "Lord, if it's you," Peter replied, "tell me to come to you on the water." "Come," he said. Then Peter got down out of the boat, walked on the water, and came toward Jesus. But when he saw the wind, he was afraid, and, beginning to sink, cried out, "Lord save me!" Immediately Jesus reached out his hand and caught him. "You of little faith," he said, "Why did you doubt?"

Peter's lesson was fearful, harsh, and wet. He became fearful once he saw the wind and the waves swirling around him and I'm pretty sure he got a little wet on the waves. His biggest lesson was getting a harsh reprimand from Jesus, chastising him for being of little faith. We all know what went down beside Peter. He was doing just fine until he became distracted by the wind and waves which caused him to take his eyes off the Jesus. A lesson learned; keep your eyes and your attention on Jesus.

One of the best known life lessons was that of Adam and Eve. God gave them one very specific command; they were not to eat from the tree of knowledge. Well we all know how that went, a serpent, an apple, a woman and a man changed the course of life events and in the process unknowingly cast a death sentence on Gods Son.

Genesis 3:23 'So the Lord God banished him from the Garden of Eden to work the ground from which he had been taken"

Not all life lessons are harsh; many are helpful and fulfilling and serve to make our lives that much better. Remember a time when your parents told you not to hang with a certain crowd, they were looking for trouble. Well, you heeded their advice and later learned that many members of the 'crowd' you wanted to be a part of are now all serving time in a criminal institution. Thanks, Mom and Dad!

Both Peter and Adam thoroughly understood their life lessons and they took great value from the experience and neither one is known to have committed a repeat offense. I'm sure both were disappointed in their actions yet both also knew that a loving and forgiving God would never abandon them. They paid a price for their actions and accepted the consequences, a life learning experience. Had neither one given any credence to their actions and continued along the same path, I wonder if heaven would be minus two great men of God.

The Lord does not bring us into deep waters to drown us, but rather to cleanse us through the experience. A faith that cannot be tested is a faith that cannot be trusted!

Chapter Five:

Salvation

✝ A Faithful Salvation

A smart man once told me that salvation is not achieved but received. The more I thought about it, he was right; faith opens the door of salvation to all. As a matter of fact, one might even say, what other offer can make such a claim?

I should point out that there is a difference between religion and salvation. Religion is man trying to do something for God; salvation is God doing something for man, so it is my opinion that salvation is totally dependent upon God.

Salvation is certainly free, but it is by no means cheap. It is free to you and me, but it cost Jesus His life, as He shed His blood for each of us.

Now, that we have all that cleared up, let's pose the million-dollar question, 'What right do we have to enter into heaven?' How should we answer that question? One thought I had about an answer goes something like this. I have no right other than the right Jesus gave me, because He has become my righteousness. Jesus took our place that we might have His peace, He took our sin that we might have His salvation. Another way to explain that last paragraph would be to simply say, The Son of

God became the Son of man that He might change the sons of men to be the Sons of God.

A final thought on salvation. While it is true, salvation may come to us quietly, we must not remain quiet about it. Sharing the gospel message about salvation is without a doubt the most important thing happening in the world today! Is salvation just a word and a blessing we simply and casually accept? Do we ever stop and think that Jesus allowed himself the pain and agony of being nailed to a cross for me, so that I will receive the gift of salvation? While it is certainly easy for us to accept this free gift, we need to remember that our part of the bargain is to become faithful stewards of His word. When someone hands you a birthday gift, most people would respond by saying thank you. Regardless of the cost of the gift, we always say it's not the gift but the thoughtfulness behind it. When was the last time we looked up toward heaven and said, 'Thank you Jesus for that very thoughtful and free gift of salvation'?

Romans 1:16 'I am not ashamed of the gospel, because it is the power of God, for the salvation of everyone who believes.'

Psalm 62:1–2 'My soul finds rest in God alone, my salvation comes from Him. He alone is my rock and my salvation, He is my fortress, I will never be shaken.'

And if you're still not sure about what to do about salvation and sharing the gospel, let me leave you with this thought.

'Our obedience to God is Critical; our relationship with God is Vital.'

Do You Know that You Have More than One Address?

Yes, you have two addresses, and no matter where you live or where you move to, these are the two most vital and important addresses you should ever be concerned with.

In God the Father . . . this is your **Home Address**

Why we are here . . . this is your **Work Address**

Let's look at the 'Home Address' **John 14:2–3**

'In my Father's House are many rooms; if it were not so I would have told you. I am going there to prepare a place for you. And if I go and prepare a place for you. I will come back and take you, to be with me that you also may be where I am.'

The price of this heavenly real estate was extremely high; the blood of Jesus Christ was required as payment in full to secure a place for both you and I in heaven. Did we deserve to be in this neighborhood? Not really, it was not until Christ was sacrificed for our sins were we upgraded from a hellish environment to a heavenly environment.

John 3:16 'For God so love the world that He gave His One and Only Son that whoever believes in Him shall not perish but have eternal life.'

Let's look at the 'Work Address' **Colossians 3:23–24**

'Whatever you do, work at it with all your heart, as working for the Lord, not for men, since you know that you will receive an inheritance from the Lord as a reward. It is the Lord Christ you are serving.'

There is a large mission statement banner than hangs in the front of the sanctuary of my church and it states simply and profoundly that as a church family, as Christians, we are responsible 'To Raise up the Children of God.'

During each Baptism, our Pastors ask if we, the Church Family, will accept the responsibility of ensuring the newly baptized become strong Christian individuals and we all reply in unison: 'We will with God's help.'

1 Peter 4:10 'Each one should use whatever gift he has received to serve others, faithfully administering God's Grace in its various forms.'

So, my advice is to maintain a very close eye on these addresses, live up to the covenants of the neighborhood (The Ten Commandments), and most importantly live up to the expectations of the one whom gifted us with these two fine addresses.

How do you start? Read the Bible, it will scare the Hell out of you, and trust me, I'm thinking that is one address that you definitely do not want listed on your life's résumé! Go to church regularly and get involved with your church community. Attend Sunday school or join a Bible study.

We should never be content by traveling alone on the road to heaven. Bring others with you, leave no soul behind. Nothing would please our Lord more than to see you show up at the gates of heaven with a huge crowd behind you and hearing them say, 'We're with him.'

The Great Inheritance

When we think of the term 'inheritance,' typically our first thoughts begin tabulating and fantasy spending an impending windfall. Our prayers have been answered, we can now afford the around-the-world cruise, a new home, several new cars, and who knows what else. If we stop for just a moment and look back at our spending list, every item on there is of a physical nature and I'm sorry to say that donations to a church or charity were not at the top of our list or in some cases such as ours above, not even on the list.

Yes, we all would enjoy being the recipient of an incredible inheritance; it would certainly take care of those nagging bills, tuitions, and credit card bills for sure. Can your financial windfall guarantee you an equitable happiness, eternal life, and a life free from pain and suffering? I don't believe this question requires an answer, but I'll say it anyway—a resounding No! As good as our 'wishful windfall' might be, there is another inheritance that far exceeds any worldly spending spree we can ever imagine; it is the inheritance of eternal life with our Lord and Savior. This inheritance is free to anyone who wishes to possess it and all that is required on your part is a heart filled acceptance of Jesus Christ as your Lord and Savior. Congratulations, you are now on the inheritance list, and whether you choose to believe it or not, you are now rich beyond your dreams.

No amount of money can buy the eternal happiness you will enjoy from this inheritance. No amount of money can provide the heavenly garments that will adorn your new body, one that is free from pain and pestilence. No amount of money can provide a home that can even begin to compete with the home your Heavenly Father has prepared for your arrival; also part of your magnificent inheritance.

130

Every once in a while, we may daydream of being as wealthy as a Bill Gates, but even with all of his money and resources, spiritually, you are much wealthier than he is. Your thoughts might be, 'if I had that much money I would help as many people as I can.' Well, you can share your inheritance right now, right here on earth, by bringing others to Jesus Christ. Spend that spiritual inheritance as liberally and as often as you can. I'm pretty sure there are people you may even know who would benefit greatly from your inheritance. Think of yourself as a great philanthropist with unlimited checks to distribute as often and as freely as you would like, knowing your account balance is as eternal as your salvation. Don't leave would-be recipients of your generosity out there as easy pickings for the Evil One. I'm sure he also believes he has an inheritance waiting for them, and it is most assuredly not a pretty one. Honestly, how many times in your life can you be told? Go out there and spend, spend, and spend.

Mark 10:17 'As Jesus started on his way, a man ran up to him and fell on his knees before him. "Good teacher," he asked "what must I do to inherit eternal life?"'

Hebrews 9:15 'For this reason Christ is the mediator of a new covenant, that those who are called may receive the promised eternal inheritance now that he has died as a ransom to set them free from the sins committed under the first covenant.'

1 Peter 1:4 'And into an inheritance that can never perish, spoil or fade, kept in heaven for you.'

Ephesians 1:13–14 'And you were also included in Christ when you heard the word of truth, the gospel of your salvation. Having believed, you were marked in him with a seal, the promised Holy Spirit, who is a deposit guaranteeing your inheritance until the redemption of those who are God's possession, to the praise of his glory?'

One last thought on inheritance. Our children inherit more than the resources we leave behind, they also inherit our spirituality. Think carefully before you answer this last question; what is the balance in the spiritual checkbook you have left as an inheritance for them?

So I'm a Little Bit Out of Shape . . .

Okay, so I should go to the gym more than I do and I should watch what I eat, but wait, this is not about my physical self, it's about my spiritual self. God did not write the Burger King slogan, 'Have it your way.' So how does one get out of spiritual shape anyway? By having it your way!

Christian Life today is not going out to the playground; it's going out to the battlefield. Satan is out there leaving a path of banana peels for us to slip, stumble and fumble in faith. Make no mistake about it, Satan knows your weaknesses and he is waiting for the opportunity to capitalize of them and sadly, at your expense.

Satan's plan to keep us out of shape:

1. Distract them from gaining hold of their Savior and maintaining that vital daily relationship.
2. Keep them busy with the business of the world, tempt them to spend, spend, spend and borrow, borrow, borrow.
3. Keep them from spending time with their children, fragment their family life.
4. Give them idols such as Santa to distract them from teaching the real meaning of Christmas.
5. Keep them excessive in their recreation and make sure they return very tired.
6. Flood their minds and their mailboxes and their media with junk, junk, and more junk, especially the sweepstakes mailers that always give them false hope.

It's not the will of man that will keep him out of heaven, it's his won't. Any of these sound familiar? I'm just too tired to go to church today. I don't have time for the Bible this morning, I'm going golfing, and I just love to golf. I can't help out with Sunday school, I'm just too busy to bring others to the Lord at this time in my life. Do we ever stop and wonder about the fact that from time to time, we are simply too busy for the Lord's work, yet when we need Him, we want an instant response, no excuses, I need you right now please. I don't believe we do this intentionally, but it still happens, and ergo, we just let Satan back into the house and back into our lives. What really irritates me is when I make it too easy for Satan to distract me; feeling that he probably didn't even have to break a sweat on my stumble. Was I that vulnerable, that easily distracted that perhaps he didn't even have to show up; he simply phoned my stumble in?

The best plan for spiritual fitness is your Bible. It's low in calories and high in spirit. Faith is like a muscle, it needs to be exercised regularly. Feeling a bit tired? Offer it up to the Lord by saying, 'Lord, please expand my time and my energy so that I may do the things you have set before me.'

Challenge yourself and try this for just one week and see if it doesn't improve your spiritual fitness. Each morning, set aside ten minutes, ten measly little minutes, and read a Psalm or a Proverb. I guarantee that by the end of the week you'll be wondering how you made it through all those prior weeks before you started this daily ritual.

And now the best part of this whole spiritual exercise plan. The Lord wants to shape us down here so we fit perfectly up there. Can I get a hallelujah!

Luke 10:38–42 'As Jesus and his disciples were on their way, he came to a village where a woman named Martha opened her home to him. She had a sister called Mary, who sat at the Lord's feet, listening to what he said. But Martha was distracted by all the preparations that had to be made. She came to him and asked, "Lord, don't you care that my sister has left me to do the work by myself? Tell her to help me." "Martha, Martha," the Lord answered, "you are worried and upset about many things, but only one thing is needed. Mary has chosen what is better, and it will not be taken away from her."'

What Will Your Tombstone Read?

Slightly morbid perhaps, but I have two tombstone stories I would like to share with you.

The first is about the simple wording on some poor soul's tombstone, it read: 'I expected this but just not yet.' The sad but simple fact of the matter was he was not ready yet; which then begs the question; are you ready?

Luke 12:40 'You also must be ready, because the Son of Man will come at an hour when you do not expect him.'

We are all suffering from a terminal disease: it's called life, because life in and of itself is terminal. So, like the poor soul above, don't get caught running out of time. Do not let doubt make you feel that your disease is incurable, because if you feed you faith, your doubts will starve to death. Additionally, another self-inflicted and life-altering disease is procrastination. How many times have we thought to ourselves, 'I could have, I should have, I would have, and yet I did nothing'? Contrary to what you may believe, time is not on our side. Time is relentless, it never stops, even long after we are gone.

The second story is about that little dash (-) on your tombstone, you know the one I mean, it's in between the years of your life span. Although it's such a small and insignificant little mark, it represents something huge; it is who you were and what you accomplished, all that you did or did not do in your time here on earth. Did you spend it wisely, did you apologize to that person whom you hurt a very long time ago, did you build a close relationship with your Lord, did you always repent for your sins, and did you go on that world cruise you longed for all your days? Yes, that little dash can say a lot about who you were. So as you think about this reading, think about your dash, what will it say about you?

People complain about old age. I say if you're old, don't complain about it, thank God for getting you this far, because you certainly had nothing to do about it, it was through His grace and only His grace.

So, in closing I'll simply ask you, did you ask God about His plan and purpose for your life, your dash, and if not, why not? God's will has found you but did it find you willing?

Separation is the way of things on earth,

Reunion is the way of things in heaven.

Tick, tock, tick, tock, tick, tock . . .

1 Peter 4:17 'For it is time for the judgment to begin with the family of God, and if it begins with us, what will the outcome be for those who do not obey the gospel of God?'

Repentance

Is the word 'repentance' just a byline or is it an act of contrition?

We know that the cross of Jesus Christ guaranteed man the ability to seek forgiveness and repent for his sins. The death of Christ saved man from deaths mighty grip and afforded him the blessing of repentance, the ability to seek forgiveness from our Heavenly Father for our transgressions. The Bible has numerous passages whereby we are commanded to repent for our sins and seek His forgiveness.

Job 36:10 'He commands them to listen to correction and commands them to repent of their evil.'

Acts 20:21 'I have declared to both Jews and Greeks that they must turn to God in repentance and have faith in our Lord Jesus.'

There are two very succinct thoughts that come to my mind when I think of repentance and I hope you will find these helpful in your walk.

• Repentance is an inward conviction that expresses itself in outward action.

When we seek forgiveness, it must be more than a fashioned statement; it must come from the heart. When the Lord measures our sincerity, I'd like to think that he puts His spiritual tape measure around our hearts and not our heads. May I suggest you find a quiet spot and while on your knees in prayer and with heartfelt conviction, not only seek His forgiveness but feel the peace within your spirit that comes as you lay your burdens at His feet. It is not until you have accepted inwardly a wrong doing that you can outwardly profess His grace. Empty words and empty promises offered in prayer may temporarily take you away from His will, but fortunately for all of us, never out of His grasp. Even when we falter, He is standing right next to us and like the 'footsteps in the sand'; He wants to carry you through your anguish.

When you have come to terms with the Spirit within you, people will most certainly notice a newfound peace about you and your attitude toward achieving a oneness with God will hopefully become a beacon of hope for others. A Christian must keep the faith but not just to himself. And through this oneness with God, you are now equipped to help others by sharing a wonderful truth; knowing Jesus is not the way out of trouble, knowing Jesus is the way to triumph through trouble. What is the old saying? 'If Jesus brings you to it, He will bring you through it.'

- Repentance is not just saying I'm sorry, it's saying *I'm through*.

I worked with a man who would openly repeat the same transgressions time after time, day after day. After a short time, my spirit nudged me into a conversation with him, questioning why he seems to be comfortable in dancing on the edge of evil. He quickly replied that when the end times were near, he would seek forgiveness but right now he was going to enjoy all the fruits of life, no matter what tree they may have come from. My quick and astounded retort was, 'But what if you don't get the chance to earnestly seek forgiveness?' and I was sure that God was not an advocate of do 'whatever you want as long as you quickly add an I'm sorry.' Well, it doesn't work that way ,and I'm sorry to say he was not interested in what I had to say. He seemed to be very content frolicking in his own little world for as long as it may or may not last.

When I reflect back on the scenario above, I'm hurt that he would think one could use or take advantage of God's grace in such a careless and carefree manner. Then my very next thought is that I probably did not pray enough for him to see the light. Shame on me, I know better.

As we seek repentance, are we saying; Lord, I can't believe I keep doing the same bone head thing over and over again, which when loosely translated might mean 'We're not ready to give the deed up yet because it brings some type of worldly satisfaction.' This type of thinking is probably not the best approach to repentance. Perhaps we should be saying; Lord, please help me avoid this unsavory deed that seems to have a hold on me,

I truly want to release it from my life and cannot do so without your help. I'm thinking this is a much better approach.

It's hard to let go of things that we believe are minor transgressions and besides, they really do not harm anyone. The rest of the previous sentence should have said, and really do not harm anyone that I'm aware of. Aside from the Lord, you never know who else may be watching and without realizing it, we may cause them a stumble in faith. So knowingly or unknowingly, we just pulled someone under the transgression bus with us. This attitude certainly doesn't shed very much Son Light on the 'I'm not ready to give this up' mentality.

When you see a sign that says 'wet paint,' you instinctively touch it (don't really know why we do this) and then you get paint on your finger, you will only do this once. If you burn your hand on a hot pot, you do not repeat the same careless action. The question then becomes, why it is so difficult for us to add to our repentance prayer 'Lord, I'm through'?

We are all familiar with the axiom; the definition of stupidity is doing the same thing over and over and expecting a different result. There is a very serious difference between external feel good and internal feel good, one is physical and temporary and the other is spiritual and eternal. Which one is right for you?

The Dreaded Conscience

A Conscience—everyone has one, and everyone at one time or another has wrestled with this self-acclaimed sense of right and wrong. Some folks compare a conscience to those little imps perched on our shoulders pleading their justifications in our ears and tugging at our beliefs.

I sometimes wonder what the value of a conscience is, as it seems to me it's not an iron-clad guarantee of making the right decision. I mean, at best you only have a fifty-fifty shot that your choice was a correct one, or was it?

Well, let me try and clear this anomaly up right now. A conscience is only valuable when illuminated by the word of God. Consider a conscience to be like a sun dial; when God's truth shines on it, it will always point you in the right direction. I guess that eliminates the Vegas 50/50 odds dilemma on decision making. Another way of explaining conscience is knowing and believing that the word of God is like a spotlight, it reveals our sins, and with the possible exception of a few, I'm sure most folks do not like getting caught in the spotlight.

Personally, I have always been somewhat of a skeptic when it comes down to literally chalking things up to the result of a decision of conscience. My beliefs are more spiritual than worldly, I firmly believe that it's not a matter of conscience but rather an active Holy Spirit within me that dictates my choices between what's right and what's wrong.

Now for a disclaimer I find no joy in making. If one is not solidly grounded in the word of God, then the only choice typically made is based on the worldly 50/50 conscience decision, the flip of the coin and maybe you will make a wise decision and perhaps you may not. When the proverbial rubber of life meets the road and the decision your about to make is critical, you want and need the odds in your favor and that my friend is the word of God and the indwelling of the Holy Spirit.

I once knew a young man whose life credo was all about fate; if you come to a fork in the road, take the first one that pops in your mind, fly by the seat of your pants, and enjoy the ride. While I sometimes accept that impromptu decision making can have an air of fun and excitement attached to it, I also believe there is a time and place for this type of frivolity and should never be a substitute for sound spiritual thinking.

We have all heard the phrase 'let your conscience be your guide.' Well, consider the fact that if your conscience does not have a solid foundation, if it is not rooted in faith and backed by the word of God, your life may turn into a board game and every decision is based on a roll of the dice. I hope you will agree this is not a very sound or comforting hook to openly hang one's credo or beliefs on.

Hebrews 9:14 'How much more, then, will the blood of Christ, who through the eternal Spirit offered himself unblemished to God, cleanse our consciences from acts that lead to death, so that we may serve the living God.'

Job 27:6 'I will maintain my righteousness and never let it go; my conscience will not reproach me as long as I live.'

Acts 24:16 'So I strive always to keep my conscience clear before God and man'

2 Corinthians 4:2 'Rather, we have renounced secret and shameful ways; we do not use deception, nor do we distort the word of God. On the contrary, by setting forth the truth plainly, we commend ourselves to every man's conscience in the sight of God.'

Someone once told me the easiest way to ensure a clear conscience was to make every decision as if you were standing in front of your mother or the *20/20* camera crew. While humorous no doubt, I prefer another approach: What would Jesus say and do?

If you opt to let your conscience be your guide, please make sure it is hard wired into the Holy Spirit within you and then stand back and feel the presence of the Lord at work.

Amen my Brothers and Sisters.

Mr. Lu Cifer, the Infamous Button Pusher

If you're an animal lover, may I suggest you please skip this narrative?

Last year, an old friend, whom I have not seen or heard from in many years, tracked me down through one of the social media sites. After the obligatory 'how has life been treating you, how is the family and a number of remember when's,' the tapestry of events he called life, just handed him one final challenge under the title of life expectancy. My old friend informed my wife and I that he was dying from cancer.

I won't dwell on a lot of background information but what I will share is that Cathy and I both decided rather quickly that since he is alone in life, no nearby family members, very few friends, it was our Christian duty to make numerous trips to his bedside as his surrogate family. No one should have to die alone. Over the next year, we would fly to and from Texas to the East Coast to spend some quality time with an old friend. Now, we're not related to Bill Gates, so airfares, car rentals, and hotel bookings were taking its toll on our savings and our budget, but you simply make adjustments and start crossing off a few things from the monthly wish list (the household budget) that you can do without or items that no longer seem important.

Many hours were spent closing up his old apartment; he would never go back to the little piece of real-estate he called home. Life going forward for our dear friend was going to be a series of chemo treatments and being shuttled between hospitals and nursing homes in a bumpy van that caused great pain on every trip as his backbone was deteriorating from the cancer and every bump that transport van hit seemed like someone was thrusting a hot knife into his back and twisting it. That painful description was shared with us from tear-filled eyes upon his last return to the nursing home.

Undaunted by his oncologist's dismal prognosis, we sat with him days on end, ran errands, and attempted to fulfill many of his wishes and needs. I'd like to think we brought not only a ray of sunshine into his overcast life but also a ray of hope. Deep in our hearts we tried not to rain on his determination to win this battle over life and death; however, we were acutely aware of how much of his body was wracked and filled with this ugly and terrible disease.

After numerous trips to his bedside, before we knew it, it was almost as if we had never lived apart, we were becoming neighbors again. After all, isn't that the second greatest commandment from our Lord, 'Love Thy Neighbor as you love Thy Self'?

On our last visit, our friend, feeling time slip away, asked if we would accept the ownership of his few remaining possessions in life. We acknowledged the beautiful gesture and his generosity, but advised him the gift we prayerfully wanted to see was him walking out of the nursing home under his own power.

Now, enter the button pusher. One day during one of our many daily telephone calls, my friend elected to share a story with my wife, a story from his past, and one that we have never heard before. He spoke about a lady friend he was visiting and how her cat never seemed to like him, it was always hissing whenever he came near. He continued to almost brag that he had enough of that damn cat and one day he simply picked it up and flung it against the wall. When his lady friend came back to the room, she questioned how odd it was that the cat was sleeping so early in the day. No, he didn't kill the cat, but I'm sure it was severely dazed for quite some time. To make matters even worse, he bragged how after that episode, he and the cat got along just fine.

Needless to say, my wife was devastated and fashioned a quick and flimsy excuse to get off the telephone. She came to me almost in tears and painfully related the gruesome story and shared its effect on her. After learning what my friend did, I became incensed with anger.

That evening I tried to go to sleep but could not get the image of the cat and that vile and cruel act out of my mind. As I lay in bed that night, a knot began to form in the pit of my stomach and the more I thought about the cat, the angrier I became and the more the knot hurt. How could he do such an evil thing? I am ashamed to say I began to seethe with anger and thought, 'That's it, I won't do another damn thing for that miserable little ass.' The offer of our accepting his possessions flashed before me, and it was just as quickly dismissed with not only a 'No' but with a resounding 'Hell No, I don't want anything from this evil fool.'

I was getting myself worked up into a full-blown frenzy and realizing the direction I was heading was not spiritually healthy, so I asked the Lord for guidance. 'Dear Lord, I cannot get these feelings of hatred under control and I need your help and guidance to understand what I am dealing with and how I should act. Now, a key element here is if you are going to the Lord in prayer for guidance, keep your heart and mind open, clear, and attentive to the spirit within you. Do not presuppose what you think His answer will be; if that happens, you will definitely miss the message.

My prayer of help turned into a prayer of my seeking forgiveness, not for my friend, but for me. I took my eyes and concentration off my Lord and paid a horrible price; hatred. Satan knew how I felt about animals, so he pushed the cruelty to animals button of my soul and good old me jumped right in, hook, line, and sinker. I allowed my faith to be tested and I failed.

Remember when I mentioned the Love thy Neighbor passage earlier? Well, my answered prayer went something like this. Gary, you have been a good steward in caring for your friend in action and in prayer and Satan must be getting very annoyed at your success, so he diverted the love and faith in your heart to one of hatred, now Satan is happy again. Yes, the Evil One, knowing my love for animals, knew exactly how to unravel a year's worth of compassion with one little story, a simple push of the button.

How could I have been so gullible to allow Satan to do that to me? This feeling only lasted for a brief moment because I knew the greater glory here was that my Lord and Savior once again blessed me with answered prayer, he once again pulled me from the clutches of the Evil Ones grip. Yes, it hit me right between the eyes, the Lord allows and wants me to come to Him whenever I am seeking forgiveness yet I was unwilling to extend the same courtesies provided to me through grace, to one in need.

I still occasionally think about the cat and pray that nothing like that will ever happen again. I pray my friend will gain control of his anger if not by himself than through my constant prayers on his behalf.

If you're still not convinced about who's behind all the nonsense and button pushing, go back and look at my opening title. Take the first and last name of the person mentioned, put them together to form one word and you will have your answer.

P.S. Unfortunately, my old friend finally succumbed to his disease, but not until I had repeatedly asked the Lord to have mercy on his soul.

Light versus Dark

Do you ever think about how in the course of a day we go from the beautiful light of day and then before we are ready for it, we plunge into the depths of nightfall? We enter into an eerie darkness that seems to pull down the shade on the wonders on the day, obscuring the magnificent visions that were commonplace in the sunlight. And yes, Virginia, there are beautiful starry nights as well, the awesome wonder of the galaxies, but to my way of thinking, albeit right or wrong, one cannot appreciate the full intensity of beauty unless their heart can translate what the eyes can see.

I know I have not given this daily occurrence much thought, at least until recently that is. While preparing a Sunday school lesson, I became very intrigued with this concept and the more I thought about it, the more questions began to plague my thoughts. The movie *Star Wars* took our imaginations to a place called the Dark Side, a fictional world developed by the skill and imagination of a team of talented writers, yet how often has the world shared stories from the dark side of life with us? Can you think of a time when you were watching the evening news and there were no reports of dark deeds; no stories of murder, kidnapping, arson, genocide and etcetera?

Can someone who is totally bathed in sunlight be living in darkness? Let's see if we can shed some 'Light' on that.

I am an acronym nut, but they help me to provide clarity to many of life's anomalies.

Light: Living In God's Heavenly Tapestry

Dark: Demons Are Rarely Kind or Demons Are Roaming Kingdoms

Let's start with the Light side of this equation. The Lord did in fact tell us He is the 'Light 'and He will take us out of Darkness into the Light. That's a wonderful truth and certainly one that should warm our Christian Cloaks, but what exactly does this mean?

To me, the light that shines eternally in each of us is without a doubt the gift of the Holy Spirit, lovingly offered to each one of us by our Lord and Savior. This internal and eternal light helps us to see clearly, no matter what the conditions may be and like the light in the night sky for the Israelites during the Exodus, it is the guiding light that keeps us on the path to our spiritual home.

If you're wondering about the actual brightness of your own light, I believe we were all given a 300-Watt Spiritual Bulb (Father, Son, and Holy

Spirit) of intensity and we have been given the ability to keep our spiritual lights glowing at full strength. Occasionally, we may stumble on the edge of darkness but the secret to our Soul-ar power is our ability to get on our knees and pray; the ability to exercise the God given grace to seek forgiveness which will certainly keep each of us spiritually illuminated. The technical term for this is 'Son Light,' and continued exposure may prevent burning.

Now, let's take a look at the Dark Side of life.

During the brightest times of the day, we can sometimes come upon a poor soul who seems to be shielded from the light and either knowingly or unknowingly seems to be lurking in the dark shadows of life. Can this individual be self-absorbed to the point that all honor and glory is theirs? Could it be something much more personal, life dealt them a bad hand and now life owes them? In either case, the darkness represents a more personal need and also comes in three distinct levels of power as well; it's called the other trinity, Me, Myself, and I.

I often wonder if those moving in darkness despise light, as they view light as a spotlight designed for the sole purpose of revealing sin, weakness, and despair. Have you ever heard or, for that matter, used the expression, 'Oh, his bulb does not burn brightly'? When we entertain comments such as this, are we helping or hindering the power level of this bulb? I have always found that when dealing with someone who feels down and out, salvos of criticism, whether satirical or serious, seem to confirm the need for darkness. Many of us Baby Boomers will remember a light that was very prevalent during our teen years; it was called a Black Light, and it was almost always used in conjunction with a strobe light. Looking back now, I can hardly remember a dance that did not offer this Dynamic Duo of technology, and to non-dancers like me, it was great. The light was obviously dark, as its name suggests, and the strobe cleverly distorted all images within its spell, so it afforded me the ability to get on the dance floor and no matter how awful my dancing may have been, in the cover of dark distortion, no one could tell if I had two or three left feet.

As with my pathetic attempts at dancing, could this be exactly what darkness attempts to convey in a worldly fashion, specifically, little if any light (No Spirituality) and a bunch of distortion (No Truth) all cleverly designed by the Evil One to keep us wandering hopelessly in the dark?

Those of you that are outdoorsmen know that whether on land or in the sea, the majority of predatory hunting happens under the cover of darkness. While I am not suggesting we are animals, I am suggesting that when we travel in worldly darkness, we truly become the hunted—we are the prey of Satan, who would love nothing more than to bag another lost soul.

At the beginning of my thoughts on the Dark Side, I listed two acronyms for the word dark, the first being 'Demons Are Rarely Kind.' I don't believe demons are remotely kind, but how many times have we said or heard, 'Better the devil you know than the devil you don't'? Why do we feel the need to have a relationship with a devil or demon on any level? To me, this is right up there with the choice of the lesser of two evils. Why do we have to choose either one?

My second acronym was 'Demons are Roaming Kingdoms,' which for me ties beautifully into a passage from the Book of Job. When asked where he has been, Satan responds to Christ by stating that he has been here and there roaming the earth. Now, with this thought in mind, choosing the Son Light over Darkness should be a no brainier, but don't be discouraged if you feel your light has dimmed; get on your knees and from your heart let your Lord know you need a slight power surge, I'm sure he would be most happy to give you a spiritual jolt.

In closing, let me simply state that the very next time you read or hear our Lord's statement; 'I am the Light,' your next thought should always be 'The light that shines gloriously within me.' And should a little darkness be in the forecast, immediately get onto your knees and use the POP defense, the 'Power of Prayer,' and turn those dark clouds into a ray of Son Shine, compliments of our Lord and the Holy Spirit.

Home

The word 'home' conjures so many meanings for each of us. The first one that I'm sure comes to most everyone's mind is that place we go to after a hard day's work, that place of solitude, that safe harbor with all of its creature comforts. In the techie realm, home takes you back to the beginning of the program you were in. In baseball, home is the plate that each player wants to cross. Even in the movies, remember Dorothy's line in the *Wizard of Oz*, 'There's no place like home.'

While all these images of home are wonderful, there is one home that each and every one of us should be clearly focused on, our eternal home in heaven. Our Lord has told us that He's so excited about our coming home that He has already created a spot for us.

John 14:1–3 'Do not let your hearts be troubled, Trust in God, trust also in me. In my father's house are many rooms; if it were not so, I would have told you. I am going there to prepare a place for you. And if I go and prepare a place for you, I will come back and take you to be with me, that you also may be where I am.'

Wow, Jesus wants you and me for eternity! Brothers and Sisters, it just doesn't get any better than that.

The journey to our earthly home is an easy one; we've made the trip so many times we could almost accomplish it blindfolded, but how do we get to our eternal home? Sorry, a Garmin, Google Maps, and a Road Map will be of no use on this trip. But please do not despair, I know of a book that has all that you will need to get you there. It has step by step directions and for those that follow and believe, it comes with a guarantee. You already know the spiritual atlas I'm referring to, it's the Bible. I know you've heard this acronym before, but it's appropriate here:

Basic Instructions Before Leaving Earth.

Now, just owning the book and not reading it will not get the job done. To become a book club member, you will need the following; a healthy measure of Faith, a huge dose of Humility, a Forgiving heart, and an abundance of Love. Next is the hardest step because many cannot believe it's that easy; accept Jesus as your Lord and Savior.

Okay, we're almost ready, but we still have a little more work to be done. To begin with, we must never be content to take this journey alone, always plan on bringing others with you. In my church, we refer to this as 'Raise up the Children of God.'

We're getting closer. Next, be thankful for all the gifts that you have been blessed with by our Lord, ensuring that you share the blessings, making sure those less fortunate than you receive alms from your heart. Start each day with an exchange of wills, His will for your will and don't forget to thank him for the fabulous sunset you enjoyed last night and the phenomenal sunrise this morning that gave you goose bumps because it was so magnificent.

You're doing great. Now, Love your Lord with all your heart, Love your neighbor as you Love yourself, and seek forgiveness whenever you falter.

Okay, my Brothers and Sisters, that wasn't so bad was it. In the vernacular of today, let me be the first to say 'Congratulations,' you just had your ticket punched for your heavenly home. May the peace of the Lord be always with you.

You've heard me say I'm a bit of an acronym nut, so here goes my spin on the word home. Home is . . . **H**eavens **O**wn **M**ajestic **E**den.

What makes all of the above happen . . . it's also simple, Prayer. Talk to your Father in Heaven who loves you more than you could ever imagine and who is always thrilled to hear from you. Ask for guidance, help, direction or whatever it is you need, and then listen carefully as He shares His love right back to you.

Now, if all of this did not get you fired up about your eternal address, may I offer a word of caution? Satan also has a place that he would very much like to have you come down for an extended stay, but don't be fooled, he bills it as the hottest place in town.

Some folks say 'home is where the heart is,' and while that's an amazing phrase, I believe home is 'where the Lord is,' and that just may build you a better castle in the sky.

The final question is what makes a home, that place that seems so wonderfully hidden from the trials and tribulations of the day, that place that boasts an air of safety and contentment? Now, close your eyes and imagine, if you will, you're now in your heavenly home and Jesus has wrapped his arms lovingly around you and states, 'This one is with me'! If that's not worth the price of admission, there is absolutely nothing in this universe that will ring your chimes.

Psalm 23:6 'Surely goodness and love shall follow me all the days of my life, and I will dwell in the house of the Lord forever.'

Psalm 122:1 'I rejoiced with those who said to me, 'Let us go to the house of the Lord.'

The Infamous 'Do Over'

I was taking our dog, Heidi, for a walk the other day, or maybe it was the other way around, perhaps she was taking me for a walk, but the end result was the same. We came upon a group of young children playing what looked like a redefined version of an old American standard, the great game of street baseball.

I took a few moments to take in the action and found myself reliving some of my own memories, standing in the sidewalk chalk batter's box, looking down at an old flattened hub cap which was given the great distinction of home plate, when I heard that long forgotten cry 'Do Over.' I laughed to myself recounting the numerous 'Do Over's I must have demanded during my illustrious career as cleanup hitter.

The more I thought about the 'Do Over,' the more it became obvious to me that not much has changed since those glorious youthful summer days. While I have indeed made the transition to a responsible adult, pure conjecture on my part, what did this mature adult yell from the links when he hit an errant shot? You guessed it, 'I'm going to take a Mulligan,' the adult version of the 'Do Over.'

Don't laugh, we are all guilty of some version of this inalienable right we so truly believe to be an inherent gift, even though we really do not know where it came from, yet it's out there for our exclusive use when needed. How many times have we uttered in a low and painful sigh; 'Oh would I love to do that over again.'

So, where do you think this phenomenon originated? The truth of the matter is that we have all been given the greatest 'Do Over' or 'Mulligan' that one can imagine and certainly one that we did not earn or deserve. We have been graciously taken from the Old Testament to the New Testament, free from the bonds of sin and each one of us have either knowingly or unknowingly, benefited greatly from the day a young man named Jesus was nailed to a tree. He could have asked for a 'Do Over' and some biblical scholars firmly believe He would have been granted that request by His Father, but He knew the score and it was the bottom of the ninth inning in the Old Testament.

John19:30 'Jesus said, It is finished.' With that, he lowered his head and gave up his spirit.'

In my heart of hearts, I truly believe it was that very moment, that unselfish sacrifice, that we became benefactors of the most incredible 'Do Over' in the history of creation. So, I must ask everyone who has just read this, have you thanked Him for your 'Do Over'?

In order to appreciate how truly fortunate we are, we must take a brief walk back to the Old Testament, a time and place where 'Do Overs' were not the golden parachutes of the general public.

In the Book of 2 Samuel, David lost his first born son with Bathsheba. Could it have been a result of David's devious act of sending Bathsheba's husband to the front lines of battle where he would most certainly be killed, thus leaving Bathsheba exclusively available to David? I'm pretty sure David would have loved to use a 'Do Over.'

Also in the Book of Genesis, as God prepares to destroy Sodom and Gomorrah, He warns Lot and his wife not to turn around and watch the destruction of the cities. Lots wife, most probably unable to resist the temptation to take a quick peek at what was happening behind her, turns around and is immediately turned into a pillar of salt. I'm real sure she would have liked a Do Over.

Need more proof? When the high priests would enter the tent of The Most Holy, they had a rope tied around their waist and bells affixed to the hems of their garments. The only person authorized by God to enter this tent was the High Priest; however, these Priests had a very specific routine to follow as dictated by God. If the Priest did not follow God's instructions to the letter, he was struck down within the tent. When the priests outside of the tent did not hear the jingle of the bells, they instinctively knew something was wrong and summarily extracted the High Priest from the tent by the sash tied around his waist. Perhaps another good time for the all-encompassing 'Do Over'?

There is an old saying that 'Christians are not perfect, just forgiven.' In addition to the gift of life over death, we have also been given the gift of 'Free Will' the right to make life choices that hopefully have been thought out and are spiritually centered. We are not perfect and by virtue of our human or worldly nature, we will sometimes make inappropriate choices. When this happens, we can go to our Lord and Savior and request a 'Do Over' and if our request is sincere, He will never let us slip from his grasp, He loves each and every one of His children too much to ever let that happen.

Keep the following thought in the forefront of your mind: 'You are not holding onto Him, He is holding onto you.'

You will never fall from my grasp . . . Amen!

Prey or Pray?

Every now and again, we get this strange feeling that something or someone has this weird hold on us, making us say and/or do things that are not typical of who we really are. I have a thought on who is always getting us in his grasp and I think you have already surmised who I am referring too; that's right, the Evil One himself, Satan.

While none of us are comfortable even thinking about the possibility that Satan plays an active role in our lives, let's see if we can see how slick he really is.

One phrase I'm sure many of us may have used on one occasion or another is 'I had to pick the lesser of the two evils.' My question is really quite simple, 'Why?' Why do we feel the need to make a choice between two evils, why not simply say, 'If both are evil, I choice neither!' No one was holding a gun to our heads when we were confronted with that choice, so why then does it seem normal or correct to opt for the lesser evil?

Enter Satan. Remember, I said he was slick. Who else but Satan would have us justify why choosing one evil over another is a good thing and make us believe we have no other solutions? We have all seen the cartoon where some poor soul in a dilemma has a good angel whispering in one ear and a bad one whispering in the other, the classic good versus evil campaign. Now the question arises, if I have a good angel on one shoulder, why should I even entertain any whispers from the evil-sided shoulder? The reason is simple; unconsciously or perhaps even consciously, you made what you think are the right choice already, now all you need is a little justification to make you feel it was the right choice. What follows next are the mind games; 'it's really okay, I didn't have much of a choice anyway' or 'Oh go on, it's going to be just fine.' The danger that lies within becomes our ability to rationalize and justify why an evil choice needed to be made at all. Another part of this inherent danger occurs when we become somewhat comfortable with the choice. Does this sound familiar: 'I really did not want to lie, but it seemed like the best option at the time'? What just happened? A bad decision was made followed immediately by a positive justification on why a bad decision was okay. When we do this, does it signify in any way, shape, or form that we are supporting evil? Think about it, when we analyze what just happened, it does have a sinister overtone.

I have a theory on how the above scenario can manifest itself. Whenever we step out of our spirituality and dabble in the world, we will get just what we are asking for, a worldly response. If we do not seek the guidance of our Lord, either through the Bible or prayer, how can we possibly expect the Lord's blessing on something we did not consult Him on? Satan knows all too well our weaknesses and he knows which buttons to push and when, he truly is the master of disaster. There is a very significant difference between what we think we need or want and the blessings already bestowed upon us by our Lord. Knowing this, Satan loves to prey on our choices and whenever possible, he's out there dangling the proverbial carrot in front of us, hoping that we will succumb and choose one of the two evils, hoping for a spiritual stumble and worse yet, enjoying the fact that we may have been feeling good about an ill guided choice.

What's the simplest answer to the above? 'You will never become Prey if you Pray.'

Another favorite little ploy of the Evil One is what I like to call 'False but Comfortable Values.' Okay, I know that statement may sound strange, so let's take a closer look at its meaning.

Have you ever heard of or used the following statement? 'It's only a little white lie.' I always seem to ask myself, what exactly is a little white lie? Is it bigger than a small black lie? No matter how we attempt to justify a lie, regardless of the myriad of colors we prefix the lie with, most of which I believe is intended to soften its effect, it is still a lie. Now to some, a little white lie does not register high on their personal sin scale, so to those individuals that ascribe to this thought process, I have just two questions. Exactly how many white lies does it take to make a bad lie and where might I find the scale that measures this process. I'll give you a hint, the reference material was a gift from God.

All right, a bit sarcastic perhaps, but the point remains the same, why do we allow ourselves to participate in assessing levels of sin. Yes, it certainly makes us feel better about ourselves but truly, in the eyes of the Lord, sin is sin, plain and simple as that may sound. There are no sliding scales, no bell curves, no levels of mild, bad, or terrible, just one accountable action; sin. The slippery slope that Satan is trying to get us on is accepting and associating our own grading system of sin. Most unfortunately, it's usually too late before we realize that the co-author of our system is Satan.

If I keep repeating a little white lie, either to myself or others, does it always remain little or does it take on a sinister life of its own and become a bigger issue? Once again, the trap we fall into here is; what are a few little lies among friends. The value that we have given to the white lie (sin) is so small that it becomes easier and easier to repeat making white lies and sadly, most probably without even giving it a second thought. Now it's time for the big question. Where does it all end? Does it end once we hit twelve little white lies in a calendar year or when we have unknowingly accepted sin as no big deal? Remember, I warned you that the Evil One is slick, and it seems that many of the times that he gets us to stumble, it's usually a subtle but most effective fall. Chalk one up for the evil side!

Okay, how do we avoid keeping a foot off his banana peel? Always be truthful in all that you say, there is no need to embellish the story, let it stand on its own merits. Pray for strength in avoiding these pitfalls and thank your Heavenly Father daily for allowing you to be a bold witness to the truth. A very wise man once said that if you always told the truth, you will never have to remember what you said. Think about that, it makes perfect sense both as character strength and as spiritual strength.

Job 1:6–7 'One day the angels came to present themselves before the Lord, and Satan also came with them. The Lord said to Satan, 'Where have you come from'? Satan answered the Lord, 'From roaming through the earth and going back and forth in it.'

A Ram in the Bush

Our Heavenly Father has put a very special woman on this planet and filled her heart and soul with the Wisdom of Solomon, and her name is Mrs. Nichols. I have dipped into her 'purse of pearls' before and now I'm about to do so once again.

On numerous occasions when her young son Willie was experiencing one of those moments in life when he felt the glimmer of hope was slowly fading around him, she lovingly would look him square in the eyes and state, 'Baby, God always has a ram in the bush for you.' Another Hallelujah moment compliments of Mrs. Nichols.

Let's revisit the origin of that very wise advice. In the Book of Genesis, Abraham was asked by God to offer his son, Isaac, up as a burnt offering, the son who was a gift from God as Abraham's wife, Sarah, was barren, yet God allowed her to conceive the child. Isaac's parents loved him beyond any words one could pen to paper and raised their son to love God with the same passion they exhibited throughout his young life. Faithful Abraham explained to his equally faithful son what God had asked and Isaac's love for God was so strong that he accepted his fate. Moments before his father was about to take his son's life, the Lord commanded Abraham to stop, acknowledged his faithfulness and directed Abraham to a ram stuck in a nearby bush and said to use the ram for the offering and release Isaac.

Taking Mrs. Nichols' analogy to heart, I went back over the years of my life to try and recall the number of 'rams' the Lord has provided for me. Here are two incidents that immediately came to mind.

- I was boarding a flight in JFK when I was paged back to my office and subsequently missed the flight. Three hours later the flight crashed in St. Thomas. I was assigned a first-class seat and later learned that the entire first-class cabin was burned beyond recognition. Fate or a Ram?
- I was on an operating table in a hospital in Buffalo, New York, for a simple operation which, unfortunately, went horribly wrong. The operating room nurse said a voice in her head kept telling her to get a tracheotomy kit, even though she was chastised by the physician for bringing unnecessary equipment into the OR. Thirty minutes later when I went into respiratory arrest and was clinically dead, had it not been for the tracheotomy kit, I would not be here today. Fate or a Ram?

I personally believe that our Lord has an unlimited number of rams that He has strategically placed throughout each and every one of His faithful servants lives as a measure of love. Does this mean if you're not faithful you don't get a ram in the bush? Absolutely not, God loves and provides for all of His children, the only difference is the faithful know it was a ram provided by God and not a quirk of fate or a stroke of luck.

Let's look at another event in which there was not a ram in the bush to save a young man and we should all be on our knees always in praise and thanksgiving.

John 3:16 'For God so loved the world, that He gave His one and only Son, that whoever believes in Him shall not perish but have eternal life.'

Like Abraham, God provided the ultimate sacrifice, His one and only Son, to suffer an excruciating death, only this time He could not put a ram in the bushes as the ram was already on the cross. The same love was there, like Abraham, a father's love for his son, but God possesses an agape love, a love for you and for me and all those yet to come, that in order to free us from the chains of death, there would be no ram for His Son. While many of us may believe we have a good handle on 'love,' we may never fully understand the magnitude of this sacrifice until such time that we are sitting next to our Father in the heavenly home he has prepared for us.

I can't help but wonder if there really was a ram in the bush, but it was a ram for all mankind.

John 14:2–3 'In my Father's house are many rooms; if it were not so I would not have told you. I am going there to prepare a place for you. And if I go and prepare a place for you, I will come back and take you to be with me, that you also may be where I am.'

So once again, thank you Mrs. Nichols for the love and wisdom you bring to life, your spirit-filled convictions that seem to transcend time and for sharing some of that Son Light that burns deeply in your soul, you have been truly blessed.

Pardon or Punishment

In our lives, we have only two options, pardon or punishment. So what choice have you made? It's also important to note that even in inaction, you have made a choice.

We certainly do not need to make this a difficult choice, we are not kids in a candy store with hundreds of choices that overwhelm and confuse the issue at hand; we simply have two, a 50/50 chance of whether we plan on riding the elevator to the top floor (heaven) or the bottom floor (hell). Two choices!

I think this should be a relatively easy choice; we all want to be pardoned, or do we? Some folks would say that only a sadist would want punishment, and while that may be true, I wonder if some of us have ever flirted with a wisp of sadism.

Hold on, I'm not saying you're a sadist and I'm not a heretic. My point is that when we fall into the trap such as 'oh well, I'll do better next time,' 'I really didn't mean to hurt you,' or 'I really hope he gets what's coming to him,' and we have not sought forgiveness for these seemingly harmless transgressions, have we inadvertently crossed over to the punishment side of the scale? Have we knowingly or unknowingly simply accepted the end result as finality to the event at hand? Does 'I'll do better next time' wipe the slate clean in the eyes of the Lord?

We have all been blessed with the option of choosing to be pardoned and the best part of this gift is that it's free to each and every one of us; it was paid in full by the blood of Christ. Just think, we don't have to apply for this blessing nor do we have to fill out an application or write an essay, we simply need to drop to our knees and seek to be pardoned for the inevitable miscues of life. Honestly, could it be any easier?

Another salient point to pay keen attention to is timing, don't wait until the last minute to seek the pardon, life's clock does not always run in concert to the exact beat of our hearts. It's quite possible that procrastination may lead to damnation, and that's not our goal or desire nor is it God's desire for you or me.

We must, unfortunately, spend a few lines on the flip side of this coin, punishment. No one likes to be punished, but what may provide some hope to this action is that not all punishment is designed to be hurtful or eternal. When we receive punishment from God, it is not designed to cast us away from Him but for us to grow from the experience and thereby grow closer to Him. This is not an easy concept for some to accept as its' right up there with that famous parental saying 'This is going to hurt me more than it's going to hurt you.' Well, guess what? That's God. He wants to shape you down here so that you will fit perfectly up there. I think a hallelujah is in order on that note!

When you were punished as a child, even though at the time it seemed like your world was coming to an end, how many of us remember thinking years later, when watching a friend or classmate struggle through difficult times, thought, 'Wow, I'm so glad my parents were as strict as they were, that could have been me.' Don't deny it, you've had that same thought process that we all experienced, and I'm sure other generations will also be thinking along these same lines.

Your Heavenly Father wants the same happiness and joy for your life that your earthly family wants for you, an abundance of love, peace and a life filled with the grace and glory of the Holy Spirit.

Isaiah 54:7 'Let the wicked forsake his way and the evil man his thoughts. Let him turn to the Lord, and he will have mercy on him, and to our God, for he will freely pardon.'

2 Chronicles 30:18 ' . . . May the Lord, who is good, pardon everyone, who sets his heart on seeking God.'

Proverbs 23:13–14 'Do not withhold discipline from a child; if you punish him with the rod, he will not die. Punish him with the rod and save his soul from death.'

Hebrews 12:5–7 'My son, do not make light of the Lord's discipline, and do not lose heart when he rebukes you, because the Lord disciplines those he loves, and he punishes every one he accepts as a son. Endure hardship as discipline; God is treating you as sons. For what son is not disciplined by his father.'

So, when choosing pardon or punishment, exercise your God given gift of repentance, seek to be pardoned, but when discipline is the order of the day, gratefully accept His caring intent, as it is being administered with the unceasing love of a Father for the unceasing love of His Child.

Easter Blood or Easter Bunny

Let me start with a disclaimer: The story is not as bizarre as the title.

We have all heard the saying 'we never cry over spilled milk,' but maybe we should give a little more attention to blood that was spilled on our behalf. Christ spilled His own blood so that we would not have to spill ours. We all know the story; Christ had to die and He was brutally beaten and tortured which culminated in being painfully nailed to a tree for our sins, so that you and I may receive the gift of salvation.

That was one of the most epic and pivotal events in biblical history and yet how often do we reflect on the crucifixion and the gift? Could it be that the Easter liturgical season of the church is one of the few times we actually remember to offer a heartfelt thank you to Jesus? Or, not be crass, do our reflections during this period become blurred by chocolate bunnies, marshmallow peeps, and colorful eggs?

While nowhere in the Bible will we find any mention of our candy-dispersing bunny, however, somewhere along the way the Easter bunny has become a very prominent part of the culture of Christianity, especially so during this most important religious holiday. Some theorists believe that Easter eggs represent a new life being brought into the world, and when the bunny brings the eggs to children, it symbolizes bringing new life to man, just as Christ did after the crucifixion. In some cultures, it is claimed that the Easter Bunny would don clothing and bring toys and gifts to those in need. Since there is nothing very definitive on the Easter Bunny's role during this period, we are left with several plausible theories to choose from. Regardless of the theory we choose to believe, the Easter Bunny will continue to remain as a spiritual icon of the Easter season.

If your church is like mine, we celebrate the Eucharist every Sunday offering the bread and cup of Christ to all congregants but when we get to the communion rail, are we offering a silent message of gratitude from the heart or are we just going through the motions of the ritual?

My aim is not to cast aspersions on your relationship with Christ or our lovable Easter Bunny; it is to help keep this momentous event in the forefront of our minds. Had the crucifixion never taken place, the burden of sin and of an unknown destiny would surely have taken its toll on our hearts and minds as well as our ability to function with any degree of confidence or assuredness in the fate we would eventually face.

One of the most important and fundamental aspects of the sacrifice of Christ is captured in **John 3:16**, 'For God so loved the world that He gave His ONE and ONLY SON that whoever believes in Him shall not perish but have eternal life.'

There are many gifts we will be blessed with throughout our lives, but nothing that will ever match the magnitude of the agape love in the John passage.

In a fairly recent television news story, a woman was reliving the story of how a Good Samaritan came to her rescue and saved her life. What struck me in her story were her comments about repeatedly thanking the gentleman who came to her aid. She related that she was so thankful; she must have thanked him at least ten times for saving her life. If a perfect stranger can be a recipient of our gratitude, shouldn't our Lord and Savior also be the recipient of our gratitude?

Let's make a pact right on this page. Going forward, we will all do our level best to remember to offer a sincere thank you to the Lord for the gift of eternal salvation in both our daily prayers and more specifically, right before we receive the cup of salvation. I'm pretty sure both the Lord and you will appreciate the effort.

Matthew 26:28 'This is my blood of the new covenant, which is poured out for many for the forgiveness of sins.'

Romans 3:25 'God presented him as a sacrifice of atonement, through faith in his blood.'

Ephesians 1:7–8 'In him we have redemption through his blood, the forgiveness of sins, in accordance with the riches of God's grace that he lavished upon us with all wisdom and understanding.'

Hebrews 9:12 'He did not enter by the means of the blood of goats and calves; but he entered the Most Holy Place once for all, by his own blood, having obtained eternal redemption.'

No Passport or Visa Required

There is absolutely no place outside of the United States that one can travel without having in their possession a valid Passport or Visa. These items are mandatory requirements for access and egress to and from your country of origin, and without them you are going absolutely nowhere.

Well, lucky for us (the entire world) that when it becomes time to enter our heavenly home, the kingdom of God, no travel documents are necessary or required. The terms to enter His kingdom are clear and concise, simply be clothed in the righteousness of God. Okay, so that sounds simple enough, but what exactly does that mean?

Righteousness is defined by possessing the attributes of virtue, morality, decency, uprightness, and honesty. These traits are certainly an integral part of your spiritual wardrobe, but the main premise that ties all this together is one must wholeheartedly accept Jesus Christ as their Lord and Savior. I used the term wholeheartedly as professing this acceptance as a 'get out of jail free card,' or a golden parachute when needed, does not qualify you for the trip home. One must be sincere of heart and mind and be willing to be a witness to their faith in the message of Salvation.

It's not as complicated as it may seem, and actually, it's probably significantly more difficult to get a Travel Visa too many countries around the world, than it is to be clothed in the righteousness of God. Now, that should make you feel warm and fuzzy.

The harsh reality of most travel is that the destination you have chosen is mostly interested in how much money you will spend at their resort or in their country and unfortunately not in your clothing, albeit righteous or not. In Christianity, money and possessions play a zero role in your qualifications to enter the Kingdom. I'm sure you have heard the saying; 'it's not what you know but who you know' that gains entrance into those highly sought-after locales. In the Christian world, I believe it's a good combination of both. Your knowledge of the Word provides the wisdom and strength to walk in the ways of the Lord, but equally as important is the fact that you know Jesus as referenced in the John passage below.

John 14:6 'Jesus answered, I am the way and the truth and the life. No one comes to the Father except through me.'

Righteous clothing can sometimes get a little soiled by sin, so whenever this happens, go to the Lord in prayer, seeking forgiveness, protection, and direction and before you know it, your righteous clothing is dazzling bright again.

Chapter Six:
Spiritual Food

The Vending Machine

You're hungry for something to eat so you wander over to the vending machine make your selection, insert your coins, press the appropriate button and the machine dispenses the food. What could be easier than that?

So, when we need spiritual food, do we apply the same vending machine logic? Dear Lord, I need a new car; I've made my selection, so now I'll press A6 and my new vehicle pops out. Ladies and Gentlemen, *God is not a vending machine!* He does not exist to ensure that we possess every worldly toy we want nor does He exist to ensure we have an overabundance of stuff. I wonder if there is anyone out there who feels providing an overabundance of stuff is the job of an earthly parent? Of course, we all want to provide for our children but somewhere along the way, controls have to be established. When is enough, enough?

Unfortunately, we sometimes become very callous in our relationship with the Lord; we really are looking for the vending machine God. It's so easy, make your selection, and press the button for the item you think you need and then sit back and wait for the Lord to deliver it. Machines take all the labor and guesswork out of what we need, simply make a selection.

I wonder if prayers should be like that. Press 101 for purchases, press 102 for money; press 103 spiritual direction, and so forth. Wouldn't that be just so easy? Well, as we know, you cannot develop a relationship with a machine, no matter how hard we try, and machines are emotionless, they have no feelings and only do what they have been programmed to do. God on the other hand cares deeply for us, He wants to hear from us, He wants to help us and love us always, and unlike the machine, He never leaves your side. Also, His only requirement is that you talk with Him; He does not require money to be inserted, electrical outlets, fuel, or any other type of propellant. Think about it, just you and God in prayerful discussion, now that's easy.

What are vending machines anyway? Aren't they just impulse units? You don't really want the item, you don't really need the item, but it's there and it's convenient; it's the easy way. So, the question becomes, 'Do you desire to be a vending machine junkie?' Seriously, when you take your family out to dinner, do you look for a vending machine mart or do you prefer a good quality restaurant, one where you can trust the food being served to your family? God does not make junk food nor does He serve junk food; He feeds you with hope, love, discernment, and guidance. Oh, by the way, if you really need to use the machine, save your quarters; He has already prepaid for everything you could ever want or desire.

The next time you're standing in front of that spiritual vending machine, think about passing on the junk food and then find a quiet spot, get on your knees, and talk to the one who really loves you, who really knows what you need and while you're down there, remember to thank him for all that He has already blessed you with. You might find after all is said and done, that you truly have more than you need or deserve. So, choose God over everything else, I promise you will be eternally satisfied and so very glad you did.

Genesis 22:8 'God himself will provide the lamb for the burnt offering, my son.'

Psalm 111:9 'He provided redemption for His people.'

1 Corinthians 10:13 'No temptation has seized you except what is common to man. And God is faithful; He will not let you be tempted beyond what you can bear. But when you are tempted, He will also provide a way out so that you can stand up under it.'

The Infamous Pecking Order

When I worked in the airline industry, seniority ruled above all else, even unfortunately, over talent. There was a pecking order that simply had to be observed, no exceptions. Some of that twisted methodology must have rubbed off on me because I remember a time when my youngest daughter, Breanna, wanted to know why Genese, her older sister, got first crack at something. I found myself saying, 'Because she's older.' What an idiotic answer to give a teenager. Some people might argue that seniority is the most popular answer. To that I can only say, the person who exchanges their principles for popularity always gets badly cheated.

So, let's clarify where the world should now stand on pecking orders, from a spiritual standpoint. Once Jesus was born, the only family line (pecking order) that God recognizes henceforth is that which has its direct source in Christ. Every individual who becomes a child of God through faith in Christ is thus a member of the new humanity, the church; this is all the genealogy or pecking order one needs. Amen! (This paragraph is a personal opinion, and not meant to offend non-Christian denominations or beliefs).

I know that birthrights played a significant role in the Old Testament lives, but we are now living in New Testament times, for which by the way, we should all be eternally grateful. The scarlet thread of redemption, that runs through the entire Bible has emerged in New Testament times, dictating that faith in Christ, not years of service, will be the order on how we enter into heaven.

Colossians 4:23–25 'Whatever you do, work at it with all your heart, as working for the Lord, not for men, since you know that you will receive an inheritance from the Lord as a reward. It is the Lord Christ you are serving. Anyone who does wrong will be repaid for his wrong, and there is no favoritism.'

Birthrights also come with a promise of being the 'first' to inherit power and riches, another enticement for those of us who want the rights of first birth. The Bible offers a warning about that kind of thinking.

2 Peter 2:19 'They promise them freedom while they themselves are slaves of depravity; for a man is a slave to whatever has mastered him.'

In an attempt make the pecking order easy for us all, I have reduced it down to three simple letters . . . **J O Y** (Jesus, Others, and Yourself). Maintain this pecking order in your life and you will always remain on the spiritual straight and narrow.

The plain and simple truth is that the Lord owes us absolutely nothing; furthermore, we deserve absolutely nothing, even if you are the most senior soul in town, yet we have been given so very much. So, remember to thank God that His gifts have been given freely, not by seniority, but through grace, His loving grace.

You Are What You Eat

Spiritually we are what we eat: We are to read, mark, learn, and inwardly digest the Word of God and 'take and eat.' 'This is my body given for you.' Now, think about that for a moment. Where are your thoughts, are they always yearning for something more than what you have already been blessed with? Are you always envious of others and their stuff?

Let's take at a look at the word envy.

E very

N erve

V iciously

Y earning

It doesn't sound very nice, wholesome, or Christian-like, once we dissect what the true meaning of envy is. When we want something that bad, we always seem to find a way to get it, right? Well, why not apply that same energy and talent into a loving and thankful relationship with the

Lord? Be thankful for all your blessings and the blessings of others as well, you'll be much happier. So, turn those yearnings for worldly items into a yearning for your Lord. Truth be known; envy is a poor marksman, it shoots at everyone but invariably, it shoots itself.

When I think of the word envy, I sometimes think of it as a disease. It's like some type of entity, like a cancer, that has taken ownership of your physical and emotional being and it can seem as if we have no control or will to overcome this perilous anomaly. Envy has been deemed to be so consuming of one's thoughts and actions that it has driven some people to do the unthinkable; lives may be lost in the pursuit of this horrible addiction.

To me, envy is like an escalator that only goes down, and I don't think you have to be a Rhodes Scholar to figure out where that is leading to. Have you ever stopped to think about the fact that while you may envy something of a friend or neighbor, someone less fortunate than you envies your gifts? Without the help of professionals and the Lord, envy could become an all-consuming plague and you and I would then be destined to face a life of unhappiness and emptiness, as each and every day will bring more dissatisfaction and hopelessness.

Something that helps keep me grounded and far from envy is the thought that one day I will have to explain this nasty emotion that has reshaped my Christian soul to the Lord. Aside from an envious nature, I will also have to address why I felt the gifts the Lord blessed me with were insufficient pawns in my happiness. I really do not want to go there, so I pray and accept my blessing from the Lord with happiness and thankfulness.

However, if you really need to feel envy, may I suggest you direct the envy at yourself and accept the fact that you have more than you need in life and donate to those who truly will be thankful for the blessings? Not only will you make others happy, you may have taken the first step in curing your own internal strife, letting go of envy and getting back on the path to the Lord.

A true believer cannot do what he pleases but what pleases God because when you enter into Christianity. It is not a religion; it is entering into a relationship, a relationship with God.

Romans 8:14 'Those who are led by the Spirit of God are sons of God.'

Proverbs 24:19 'Do not fret because of evil men or be envious of the wicked.'

Proverbs 14:30 'A heart at peace gives life to the body; but envy rots the bones.'

Now, I ask you, what better relationship can there be other than one between a parent and his child?

Some relationships take time to cultivate, and sometimes they don't always work out the way you had hoped, but a relationship with your Heavenly Father will stand the test of time, trial and tribulation—it's eternal.

There is an old saying I stumbled across and it fits perfectly here: He who has a 'why' to live for can bear almost any 'how.' So, make the Lord your 'why' and I'm sure He will be most pleased to show you 'how.'

Which Dictionary Do You Own?

Do you ever think about how the world has changed some of the ways we think about things and what is the 'new' or 'accepted' definition of some of the most basic words that once held a strong spiritual meaning for us?

Listed below are what I call the 'Spiritual' definition and the 'Worldly' definition of just a few of those words we once knew. Which ones do you use most often?

Spiritual Meaning	*Worldly Meaning*
Hell – the domain of Satan, a place Christians want to avoid.	**Hell** – getting your license renewed at Motor Vehicles.
Heaven – Our Father's Home, a place of eternity with The Lord.	**Heaven** – Being the proud owner of a brewery.
Grace – a gift from our Lord.	**Grace** – the girl next door.
Pride – living and effectively applying your spiritual gifts.	**Pride** – I am the gift!
Sin – a direct violation of God's laws.	**Sin** – A possible violation, to be determined by the violator.

Churches – the houses of God, a place of worship.	**Churches** – a place we go to for fried chicken.
Love – Jesus Christ.	**Love** – all my stuff.
Sermon – your Pastor's message during church.	**Sermon** – what you get when you do something wrong.
Peace – living in harmony, a wish for fellow Christians.	**Peace** – when the children go to bed.
Savior – The Lord Jesus Christ	**Savior** – the person who saved you from BIG trouble at work

So, I'll repeat the opening question: Which dictionary is on your shelf, which dictionary fits most closely to how you live and how you worship?

Lord I Need Patience and I Want It Now

If you don't think I'm busy, just ask me. Our lives are so busy that it even creeps into the church pews on Sunday. Instead of listening to a great sermon and praising and thanking the Lord for allowing us to come into His House, yet one more time, we're sitting there thinking: 'When I get home, I have to clean the house, wash the car, cut the grass,' . . . should I go on? Need I mention who is enjoying those distractions you are experiencing? He loves it when he can score a victory in the house of the Lord.

We are living in the 'instant' generation; we want everything now, not in a few minutes, now! How did we get this way? Do you think Fast Food, Microwaves, Fast Cars, Fast Jets, anything that will speed up the result and make our lives Faster had anything to do with it?

Recently, I overheard a friend of mine turn down tickets to a very critical sporting event because he was sure there would be long lines waiting to park the car, get into the venue, and when it was time to get something to eat and drink. There is an old saying that patience is a virtue, so I need to ask, are we becoming a virtue less society? What is so pressing and so critical in our lives that we cannot tolerate waiting an extra twenty to thirty minutes in a line? Are we making ourselves and our time out to be significantly more important than it really is?

I was recently at a stoplight when the car next to me blasted of the line the split second the light turned green. I guess he was in a hurry. The funny thing was; after he consumed all the gas charging up the road, here we sat once again, side by side at the next light. The only visible gain I could see from this whole episode was all the smoke in the air from the burning of tires and running a wide-open carburetor.

When we go to the Lord with a prayer request, does it go something like this; 'Dear Lord, please grant me patience and I want it right now.' Hello, our heavenly Father has blessed us with so many wonders of beauty, take time to; stop and smell the roses, enjoy the magical sunrise or sunset, the night sky that glistens like a tiara right out of Tiffany's. I'm pretty sure that if God wanted us to move fast he would have motorized our legs and would not have spent time creating the majestic beauty of nature since we were going to be far too busy to take it all in. I'd like to believe that God placed all this beauty around us so that we would indeed slow down and take in His magnificent creation.

How about a few spiritual speed bumps to help slow you down?

'Heavenly Father, help us to remember that the jerk who cut us off in traffic last night while I was already late for an appointment is a single mother who worked nine hours that day and is rushing home to cook dinner, help with homework, do the laundry and spend a few precious moments with her children.'

'Help us to remember that the pierced, tattooed, disinterested young man who can't make change correctly or fast enough is a worried nineteen-year-old college student, balancing his apprehension over final exams with his fear of not getting his student loans for next semester.'

'Help us to remember that the old couple walking annoyingly slowly through the store aisles and blocking our shopping progress are savoring this moment, knowing that based on the biopsy report she got last week, this will be the last year they go shopping together.'

Still feel the need for speed? Then how about this little gem:

'Let us be *slow* to judge and *quick* to forgive, show patience and empathy and love, after all, isn't that what our Lord shows us day after day, after day, after day, after day . . . .'

Proverbs 19:11 'A man's wisdom gives him patience.'

Isaiah 7:13 'Is it not enough to try the patience of men? Will you try the patience of my God also?'

Hebrews 6:15 'And so after waiting patiently, Abraham received what was promised.'

I'll close by letting you answer this question: Who is the one person who is always patient with us, no matter how many times we mess up?

The Four 'R's in Journey

We take journeys all the time; we visit friends, family, take vacations and go to work, each being its own little journey through life. Life can sometimes be painful—we could lose a loved one. Life can sometimes be stressful—bills piling up faster than the money rolls in, the car breaks down again, the air conditioning system is making a very funny noise, and so forth and so on. We've all been on many similar journeys. If you're still having trouble putting your finger on issues facing life's journeys, let me ask you a few simple biblical questions.

Would you take a sea cruise with the Apostle Paul?

Would you like to spend your summer vacation on a missionary journey with Paul?

Would you be willing to journey anywhere with Paul?

Would you be a survivor if you had lived in Old Testament times?

So, what's up with the four 'R's in journey? *The Life Application Bible Commentary* really puts this together nicely for us.

Recognize the presence of God – understand that God is with you, even in darkest times.

Rely on the people of God – lean on the people whom God has so graciously put in your life.

Rest on the promise of God – know that what God has said, God will do.

Remember the purpose of God – keep your eyes on the destination and the ultimate goal.

I wonder how close Moses would have got to the Promised Land if he did not:

Recognize the presence of the Lord **(Exodus 3:12)**, 'And God said, I will be with you.'

Rely on those God gave him **(Exodus 7:1)** 'See I have made you like God to Pharaoh, and your brother Aaron will be your prophet'

Rest on the promise of God **(Exodus 6:6–7)** 'I am the Lord and I will bring you out from under the yoke of the Egyptians . . . 'I will take you as my own people and I will be your God.'

Remember the purpose **(Exodus 3:17)** 'And I have promised to bring you up out of your misery in Egypt, into the land of the Canaanites, Hittites . . . .a land flowing with milk and honey.'

So, take heed. No matter how short or trivial you may think the journey, always invite the Lord to join you on your adventure. You'll be glad you did.

P.S. Driving Tip – never drive faster than your Guardian Angel can fly.

Pants on Fire

Remember as kids when we caught someone in an outright lie, we immediately broke into song: 'Liar, Liar, pants on fire' and the world was good again.

We can call them fibs, falsehoods, half-truths, or the imitation pearls of a prevaricator; it doesn't matter how we choose to color or camouflage it, a lie is a lie, a misleading untruth. Aside from lies being offensive to God, our earthly friends do not take kindly to our suspicious rhetoric either. Once we're tagged as a 'provider of untruths,' people will take everything we say with that proverbial grain of salt because of the inconsistencies that spew from our lips. Unfortunately, we only need to get caught in one lie, that's all it takes to shift your integrity from the trustworthy to the suspicious side of the coin. What a terrible cancer to keep in your soul, or worse yet, as a sorrowful testament to leave behind as your life's legacy: He was a nice guy but he was also a terrible liar.

A popular and favorite excuse we like to unleash when necessary is 'It was only a little white lie.' So I must ask a question on that philosophy. If I shoot someone and they die, can my defense be that it was only a little bullet, not a big one? One tiny lie, placed at the right time and in the right place, can literally devastate and ruin someone's reputation and life. In today's society, we call that kind of negligence and injustice 'slander.'

Another dangerous trap we seem to find ourselves in happens when we justify and rationalize why it's okay to lie. Have you ever participated in the following? I did not want to hurt his/her feelings so I told a little lie. Yes, we never want to intentionally hurt someone's feelings, but I still wonder what Jesus would say about this practice. I'm certainly not presumptuous enough to answer on His behalf, but I'm wondering if it may be similar to: sin is sin in the eyes of the Lord, albeit a big sin or little sin. If you don't want to lie, then keep your sentiments to yourself, mind your own ministry.

Today's children are significantly more savvy and intelligent that our generation, so as parents we need to be especially mindful about keeping our responses to them truthful and honest. When we have been untruthful to someone, and then later at the postmortem reconciliation meeting, you hear the dreaded phrase; 'I wish you would have been honest with me and told me the truth.' The damage is done and unfortunately it may become a living nightmare; how can I ever trust you again. Trust in this, while you may be extended the olive branch of forgiveness, the internalized hurt of the one you have deceived can turn out to be one long hard road to hoe. Casually offering a lackluster apology such as 'pay no attention to the man behind the curtain' only works in the movies and will not get you back home or back into the heart that you have deceived.

Some people, and you may know of one, have lied so much and so often, they have great difficulty in distinguishing what is truth and what is not. I know of a woman who lied so much about her age, she truly did not know how old she actually was.

Think of lying as planting a bad seed. Once the lie is out there, it takes on a life of its own and continues to grow and grow. If you happen to be the originator of the lie, now you must always remember the story your perpetrated as at some point in time you will be required to re-confirm its authenticity.

Proverbs 19:22 'What a man desires is unfailing love; better to be poor than a liar.'

Psalm 63:11 'But the king will rejoice in God; all who swear by God's name will praise him, while the mouths of liars will be silenced.'

Isaiah 57:4 'Whom are you mocking? At whom do you sneer and stick out your tongues? Are you not a brood of rebels, the offspring of liars?'

Deuteronomy 19:18–19 'The judges must make a thorough investigation, and if the witness proves to be a liar, giving false testimony against his brother, then do to him as he intended to do to his brother.'

1 Kings 22:16 'The king said to him, 'How many times must I make you swear to tell me nothing but the truth in the name of the Lord?'

1John 8:32 'Then you will know the truth and the truth will set you free.'

Someone once told me that there was a fine line between what is true and what is not. I don't subscribe to that philosophy at all. This slippery logic leads me to believe that the person, who coined that phrase was building in an escape clause for his lies. A fine line means there's room for negotiation on whether something is true or not. I'm from the old school; it's either a bold truth or a bold lie!

Hope

For some people, the word 'hope' means the ability to chase life's rainbows, hoping for that pot of gold that is just waiting to be claimed. You know the worldly examples I'm referring to; I hope I win the lottery, I hope the Spurs win the championship, I hope it won't rain today as I'm going to the beach, and hope endures and endures.

There is absolutely nothing wrong with having aspirations of hope; it shows your inner fortitude, your great resolve, and we can also enjoy a modicum of fun through hope, as long as we keep it in perspective and do not become obsessive in our hopes and dreams.

Another great hope in our lives is God; He is the only true and everlasting hope. In addressing spiritual hope, I personally feel it's a good mixture of faith and with generous sprinklings of love. Our life's hope must be the knowledge and belief that God has a plan for us; it must be our spiritual goal, it must be the light at the end of life's tunnel, the undeniable and comforting feeling that God is saying; 'Don't worry my child, I've got you covered.'

Biblical or spiritual hope is comprised of three distinct actions of faith, the first being believing in the promises of God, accepting in your heart that God does not make empty promises. The promises of God are the foundations of what we believe and profess deep within our hearts; they are the golden rays of hope. The second action is to believe in the one who made the promise; believing in God himself with our entire heart and soul, that He truly is the hope that lights the path home for each and every one of us. Finally, living and acting on the hope of God in our daily walk through life. Our actions and words need to reflect our hope and belief in all that we say and do. We must share the hope so that others will see and feel God's presence in their lives and that each may enjoy a renewed sense of hope.

We can also think of hope as an insurance policy. Regardless of how many premiums we may have or have not made, God has stamped each policy at the time of its inception with 'paid in full' and is redeemable upon arrival in your heavenly home. I wonder, can anyone possibly hope for something more than this?

Back in my college days, there was a young man we all called 'Hopeful Harry.' He had more hope stored in that scarecrow frame of his than most of our entire dorm put together. At the time, I thought it was humorous how Harry was hopeful for good grades, a girlfriend, a new motorcycle, and the same hope as the rest of us, I hope I get to go home soon as see my friends and family. He was never without hope. Looking back now, I wish I would have let more of Harry rub off on me.

Psalm 42:5 'Why are you downcast, O my soul? Why so disturbed within me? Put your hope in God, for I will yet praise him my Savior and my God.'

Psalm 62:5–6 'Find rest, O my soul, in God alone; my hope comes from him. He is my rock and my salvation; he is my fortress, I will not be shaken.'

Romans 12:12 'Be joyful in hope, patient in affliction, faithful in prayer.'

Hebrews 11:1 'Now faith is being sure of what we hope for and certain of what we do not see.'

I Don't Need Help; I Can Do It Myself

Does the title sound familiar? Do you know anyone that fits that description? What makes us think we are smart enough to do anything by ourselves? What continually amazes me is the number of times I found myself, the great and wonderful problem solver, either in way over my head or in hot water, and one would think I would have learned my lesson by now.

Two of my favorite oxymorons are 'Jumbo Shrimp' and 'Self Help,' the latter of which I'll focus on for this discussion. In our complex lives today, we have become so accustomed to and so successful at putting out 'fires' that we truly begin to believe we are exceptionally talented, we can accomplish practically anything on our own. WRONG! Do not think for one moment that is was your individual driving skills that got you to work safe and sound today? Or was it that invisible co-pilot who was in the seat next to you? Feelings of grandeur are further endorsed by the financial bonuses we receive for a job well done. Additionally, let us not forget all those well-deserved 'pats on the back' and all those gushing 'atta boys.' I think part of the problem is that somewhere along the line we go from playing Superman to actually believing we are indeed Superman. It's the same old story that has plagued so many for so long; we go from being somewhat 'competent' to 'completely convinced' we are the ultimate answer to all the maladies of life. You don't have to go looking for this person, as they will tell you of their prowess at every available opportunity.

We cannot save ourselves, we must have Jesus.

John 14:6 'Jesus answered, I am the way and the truth and the life. No one comes to the Father except through me.'

Three very simple truths are: Christ died to save us, Christ lives to keep us, and Christ will come back for us. Knowing there is absolutely no humanly possible way we can get to heaven on our own, the Lord sent us help, The Holy Spirit.

John 14:16–17 'And I will ask the Father, and He will give you another Counselor, to be with you forever, the Spirit of truth.'

So, knowing we have been blessed with help, why do we sometimes choose not to accept the help? When we choose not to believe in the gifts we have been given and that Christ is our Savior, we become a walking, talking definition of hopelessness; more specifically put, we are tied to a dead person. Should we expect God to save us from that which we refuse to repent and that which we refuse to believe? I don't think an answer is required here.

The next time you feel that it was all you and only you and you accept all the accolades on behalf of yourself, remember this, 'The man who exchanges his principles and his spirituality for popularity, always gets badly cheated.'

I Never Graduated

Question: What's the only school one never graduates from?

Answer: Sunday school.

Justification: In order to fit perfectly up in heaven, we must be continually spiritually shaped down here.

I have personally been either attending or leading Sunday school classes for the past twenty years, and I know in my heart that my spiritual graduation day will be when I take my last breath on earth. If I'm still of a sound mind when this happens, I hope I can remember to once again thank my Savior for all the Sundays that He has fed me with both spiritual food and spiritual knowledge.

I have a thought about Sunday school. I wonder if our Lord was thinking since He only get most folks on a Sunday, why not create a Sunday school class and really pack in as much spiritual richness as possible?

Life on this big blue marble is full if not overfull with family and work obligations, distractions and moments that can keep us from spending time during the week studying our Bibles, God's word. Is it any wonder then that Sunday school came into being, a spiritual learning event, intended to provide the direction and spiritual knowledge that God has so graciously and lovingly offered to all His children? In doing so, clearing the way and guaranteeing our journey to the heavenly home he has prepared for us?

I was reading an article from a website that claimed Sunday school was originally formed as a place where less fortunate or poor children could learn to read and write. During the Industrial Revolution, the majority of children apparently were needed to work very long hours, six days per week to help support their home life and Sunday was the only day they had to expand their education.

It wasn't until the 1870s that Sunday schools became a little more evangelically organized, and by the 1960s, Sunday schools became the place to deposit the children of parents who did not attend church, yet wanted their children to receive a Christian education.

If we think about these last paragraphs, they indeed show to my way of thinking how our Lord is most definitely in control and does work in mysterious ways. In the early formation of Sunday school, it was a venue to learn how to read and write, as one surely cannot learn anything from a Bible if they are illiterate. Now we have generations of knowledgeable children, many may be potential teachers, now being groomed for years of spiritual richness ahead of them, and while some parents did not fully buy into the concept of Sunday school for themselves, they saw the benefit of this institution for their children. Finally, parents soon began to recognize the fruits of spiritual enrichment developing within their children and wanting to become supportive in this movement, paved the way for adult Christian education.

Now, while I may have taken some literary license in describing my thoughts on how we may have evolved into today's formation of Sunday school, it does not deter from the fact that Sunday school was indeed a gift from God, no matter how it is presented or explained.

Now let's look at the benefits of a Sunday school education. To begin with, you are enrolled in an ongoing Christian educational program, one which provides a lifetime of spiritual enrichment. Akin to the Greek symbols of Alpha and Omega, this education is eternal; the more you know, the more you grow.

Next, your life takes on a new direction; it becomes less stressful because you now know and understand that our Lord wants each of us to place our trials and tribulations at His feet so that He may take our worry from us. Your new mantra becomes 'If the Lord brought me to it, He will bring me through it.'

Additionally, you now become the benefactor of hearing friends and colleagues comment, 'You look so relaxed lately, what's changed in your life?' or 'There is a great peacefulness and calmness about you.' These are just a sampling of the many changes and blessings people will immediately recognize in you.

Another great benefit is that you will master the 'Doctrine of Christianity.' What an awesome achievement to list on your life's résumé. People will begin to take direction from your actions and your wisdom and in turn will receive great blessings and comfort because of who you have become. You now fully understand that the road to eternity is not to be traveled alone; you are encouraged to bring others along with you.

I mentioned at the very beginning that one never truly graduates form Sunday school as it is an ongoing process. Well, for those that have the need for that Christian sheepskin, I believe they will be handed out by our Lord on the day we enter the gates of heaven. Your diploma will be the loving hand that reaches out for you and with an agape love like no other, tells you how He has longed for the day you would come home to Him.

So, don't blow off Sunday school; no one has reached the epitome of spiritual oneness on this side of the grass, so join, participate, and become the person your loving Father in Heaven wants you to be. See you in Sunday school.

But . . . It was Such a Good Plan, What Happened?

There's a tough problem looming on the horizon, so without having to give it a second thought, I put on my shirt with the big letter 'S' on the front and dive right in. I'm the man of the hour, a superhero to the rescue, and all that is left to do is stop and pose for the cameras.

It's day two, and I'm being summoned to yet another rescue. I whip off my glasses and run into a bathroom to change—there are no phonebooths any more—and off for another brilliant and spectacular save of the day. Oops, nothing seems to be going right, so I quickly looked over the plan I made. Nope, it looks good. I double checked the numbers, and they were also as I had planned. So, I asked myself, what in the world went wrong?

After a few moments of utter exasperation, that small voice in my head said, 'Excuse me, but I think I know what went wrong.' 'Tell me,' I begged, 'I'm going crazy here.' The voice said, 'Don't expect God's approval on plans for which He has not been consulted.'

That message struck a chord within me, but yet I kept thinking, 'Hold on, Gary, this is your thing, this is what you do best, you're so good at this, why would you need help?' The mysterious voice returned stating, 'Yes, you are good, but sometimes being good is not enough, sometimes greatness is required.' Ouch! It appears that it's time to put my shirt with the big 'S' on Craig's List.

Perhaps it's true what they say, you cannot counterfeit spiritual fruit. I foolishly believed that I had all the juice needed to handle any problem big or small. Once I came to my senses, I quickly offered an apologetic arrow in the direction of heaven, seeking forgiveness for being so obnoxious in believing I was running things and I was in complete control. What's crazy about this is that I do know better, but somehow I allowed Satan to tap into my ego. Good old 20/20 hindsight uncovered a brief lapse of faith, those chinks in my armor that set me up for failure. Had my faith been operating at full capacity I would have known that faith looks beyond all obstacles and faith does not operate well in a rebellious heart.

When 'man' makes a plan or states that he will do something, he might do it, but when God says He will do something, it is done. And correctly I might add.

Psalm 20:4 'May He give you the desire of your heart and make all your plans succeed.'

Proverbs 15:22 'Plans fail for lack of counsel, but with many advisors they succeed.'

Isaiah 29:15 'Woe to those who go to great depths to hide their plans from the Lord, who do their work in darkness and think, Who sees us? Who will know?'

2 Corinthians 1:17 'When I planned this, did I do it lightly? Or do I make my plans in a worldly manner so that in the same breath I say, Yes, yes and No, no.'

Got a job to do, a decision looming on the horizon, take it from me, shake off the cobwebs, clear the worldly clutter (your ego), and seek the advice of your Heavenly Father. He keeps an open line for consultation, no waiting and I know He would be thrilled to get you started in the right direction. Some of you millennial folk out there may remember a television show back in the day called *Father Knows Best*. Who knew the producers were that spiritually savvy? LOL!

Say What . . . !

We have a favorite colloquium, and it goes like this: 'Don't throw me under the bus.' Unfortunately, equally as popular are the theories 'no one likes to go under the bus alone' and 'there's plenty of room under there for others.'

Unknowingly or sadly knowingly, we have the propensity to say things that will make others stumble in their personal walk of faith. How, you ask? It's those little gems that pop out of our mouths before we engage both our brain and our spiritual upbringing.

You're with a group of friends and the name of Hopeful Hank comes up in conversation, he wants desperately to join your clique. A well-meaning group member blurts out, 'Oh no, not Hank, he's a cross between an idiot and a jerk, or at least so I've heard.' As the accuser is a respected member of your peer group, the group immediately forms a negative opinion of Hank. Yes, your group does consist of solid Christians, but as small and as subtle the remark may have been, it has disparaged and tarnished the fine name of Hank. Sadly, since you truly value your group standing so dearly and rather than form your own opinion, you allow the sentiments of one lone voice to penetrate your mind and heart and with absolutely no provocation, sadly you mentally and emotionally convict a fellow human being, Guilty as Charged! So much for love thy neighbor.

You've heard that Alan Alcohol may have the beginnings of a drinking problem and while you're not 100 percent sure, you have heard the rumors. You like Alan so you invite him to your home for a BBQ. The food is good, the conversation is good, and the drinks are good, but it's time to bring the festivities to an end. Being the gracious host you say, 'Let's have another drink, we're both off tomorrow,' or the infamous, 'Let's have one for the road.' Sadly, the road wins far too many of these challenges. How does that saying go? 'The road to hell is paved with good intentions and well-meaning folks.' I added the last part.

And last but not least, one incredulous incident. My daughters Genese, Breanna and I were watching the Olympics one year and the event was gymnastics, the woman's balance beam. The gymnast on the beam was favored to win a gold medal but faltered slightly and subsequently won a Bronze Medal. When the scores were posted, the commentator announced, 'And she tragically wound up with a bronze medal.' Say what? Can you even use the words tragic and Olympic Bronze Medal in the same sentence?

While I understand there were expectations for this gymnast, here is a young woman who has been blessed with exceptional talents by the Lord and we unknowingly diminished those blessings down to a rating of 'tragic.' Had this gymnast not been secure in her talents, performance, and faith, she could have been led to think that the Lord 'tragically' short-changed her on her abilities and blessings!

Ladies and Gentlemen, our Lord does not make junk. Win, lose, or draw, life is a blessing, a gift to be cherished and nurtured, giving all honor and praise and glory to the Lord your God.

1 Corinthians 10:32 'Do not cause anyone to stumble.'

If I may, I would like to put a spiritual spin on the 'penny wise, dollar foolish' axiom. I wonder if we are becoming a nation of being worldly wise but spiritually foolish.

We go to church, we tithe, and we are basically very nice people. On Sundays, our spirituality captivates our very soul, gushing out from every part of our being, we share the peace and we pray for peace, we are all about loving one and other. Then we hit the wall, the clock strikes midnight and Sunday is over and the world takes control of us again until next Sunday. All right, I hear resounding choruses of 'You're full of baloney, Gary, you're way off base on this.' Well, actually I hope so, but I can't help but think of how easily we fall into the Monday to Saturday traps listed above. If our cir-cles of friends or co-workers are not spiritually sound, we make allowances for certain behaviors; we try and fit into our surroundings as opposed to in-troducing change. We easily transition into the accepted norm, the proverbial 'comfort zone' where perhaps saying grace before a meal or having spiritual discussions is reserved for Sundays and not acceptable behavior in the work-place. So, I have to ask myself, am I becoming a part-time Christian, am I causing others to stumble because I only show my Christian colors and ideals one or two days per week? Am I giving others the impression that Christianity is applied as needed or a last-resort religion?

I know the above was harsh, and I did not mean to cast aspersions on the many good people whose faith shines brightly each and every day. My point was to demonstrate whether we choose to accept it or not, we can easily become a product of our environment, and the best way to avoid this pitfall is to pray for those in the 'world zone' of your life.

2 Corinthians 13:14 'May the grace of the Lord Jesus Christ, and the love of God, and the fellowship of the Holy Spirit, be with you all.'

And one final pearl or wisdom; 'Most people are far more willing to follow your example rather than follow your advice.' Amen!

Who Does Your Thinking for You?

Back in the early frontier days, there was something called a 'Buffalo Jump.' This jump was a cliff formation in which Native American Indians and early settlers historically used in order to hunt and kill plains bison in mass quantities. A follow-the-leader, so to speak, the buffalo stayed as a herd and followed the leader one by one over the edge of the cliff to certain death.

Does the above scenario ring any bells with you? Have you ever let others do your thinking for you because it was easier? Have you ever allowed someone else do the thinking for you because you didn't want to be the 'wet blanket'? May I drop a pearl of wisdom here? Sometimes a wet blanket is the best device at hand to smother the beginnings of a five-alarm blaze. Your wet blanket might have saved another who also did not want to be there.

When we allow others do our thinking for us, to my mind, several things can happen as evidenced hypothetically in this all too familiar stumble in faith. Your group wants to go to this new bar, but you've heard it's not the most savory of places to spend an evening. You go along with the crowd and less than five minutes under the roof of this unsavory dive, you're thinking 'What am I doing here?' You suggest 'we' should all leave, but the group retorts, 'Oh, we're here now, let's make the best of it and have a few drinks.' You concede to the group. Whether you choose to accept it or not, you have just let others do your thinking for you. You just compromised your ethics and values and most probably put a small dent in the armor of God you're so proud to wear.

When we get those feelings or voices in our heads that say, 'Hey, bud, you may want to re-think what you're planning on doing here,' that's not intuition, it's your internal GPS—God's Perfect Spirit. Is it possible that we may be ignoring the Spirit within us for the sake of the crowd? Or is it just easier than having to make an unpopular and perhaps even embarrassing declaration; that you're leaving; this place is not for you.

Okay, back to the dive. So here you sit, most probably very uncomfortable, wondering why you're in this place and, better yet, when are we going to leave? Then one of your worst fears materializes right before your eyes. OMG, my daughter's boyfriend just walked in. What will he think if he sees me here, will he tell his parents he saw me here, worse yet, will he tell my daughter?! Wait a minute, what the heck is he doing here? Yep, the brain cells switch into overload, conjuring up all sorts of horrible Monday morning explanations that may have to be made. I know, if I turn my back to the door he won't see me, but that means my back is also to the group. All of this embarrassment and trauma because it was easier to let someone else do my thinking for me. I swear I'll never let this happen to me again.

Next comes my favorite lamentation: I can't believe I let them take me here; I really did not want to go. 'Hello' . . . if you did not want to be there, then why in the world are you there? That's a rhetorical question. We all know the answer to that question; we allowed someone else to do our thinking for us.

Our Heavenly Father gave us a wonderful discerning mind, He gave us free will to make the choices we believe are right, and if that was not enough, he also blessed us with the most precious gift one could ever wish for, the indwelling of the Holy Spirit. A Spirit filled with an agape love, who wants nothing more than to keep us safe, provide spiritual growth and direction, our internal compass where the directional arrow always points up.

In our worldly existence, we all seem to find ourselves at one time or another in compromising positions either self-imposed or truly by accident, but how we react to the dilemma at hand not only determines who we are, but most importantly, whose we are.

Proverbs 14:15 'A simple man believes anything, but a prudent man gives thought to his steps.'

1 John 3:7 'Dear children, do not let anyone lead you astray. He who does what is right is righteous, just as he is righteous.'

By now I hope you're saying to yourself, 'I'm not falling for that follow the leader baloney anymore, from now on I'm going to do my own thinking.' Excellent, and the best way to get started on this quest is to go to the Lord in prayer and He will be with you every step of the way. Even if there is a little wobble in your step, His loving steady hand will always be holding on to you.

Take on the role of leadership and don't be afraid to say, 'I don't believe that's a good plan and I seriously doubt our Lord would approve of this nonsense.' If your group doesn't turn a quick 180 and offer a wholesome option, then it's time for you to start thinking about who exactly are your following? I'm guessing it may not be the path you were hoping to be on, but fear not, if you have a 'burning' desire to get off the ill-chosen path, be bold in your faith and trust in your Lord, He will lead you back to green pastures.

So, my fellow believers, keep your GPS running always, don't forget to keep it fueled; Prayer, Church, Reading your Bible, Sunday school, and you too will find that while there are many directions we can take, the best direction is and will always be—UP!

Everyone Has a Price!

I would imagine that as you begin reading this narrative, you're already becoming upset because I brazenly declared that you have a sellout price; you can be bought, purchased, or bribed.

Please allow me to categorically state that it is not my intention to attack your character. What I do want to bring to your attention is a cleverly designed satanic pitfall that goes by the name of the Great Tempter. He knows which of our desire buttons to push, and he can be quite masterful in helping you justify the choices you make.

Personally, I can see myself as being one of the first defenders against bribery by donning my Robe of Christianity and openly declaring that I would never sell out, no matter the price. Well, sitting here typing away and not being faced with such an offensive choice, it's very easy to boast, 'No way, man, not me'; however, in my heart of hearts, I guess I need to do a little soul searching first before I make a prevaricator out of myself.

First, let's take a look at a few Biblical negotiations that while they may have seemed like a good sale at the time, they ultimately became a burden of shame and agony. The first one that comes to mind is our dear friend Judas, who sold Christ out to the Romans for thirty pieces of silver. At that time, silver was going for approximately $5.00 dollars an ounce and was primarily used for the purchase of slaves. The long and short of this story becomes one wrought with deception, and those thirty pieces of silver did not bring Judas the happiness he so desired and out of extreme guilt for his actions, he later hung himself.

Next, let's look at Joseph and his beautiful coat of many colors. Recognizing that Joseph was the apple of his father's eye, the favorite son, his envious brothers conspired to eliminate him and accomplished what they set out to do; selling their flesh and blood to a traveling caravan. Nice family values in that household.

Finally let's look at a 'price' that paid for generations of people who have done very little to deserve its epic price tag; one that each and every one of us, should be eternally thankful for: the crucifixion of our Lord and Savior Jesus Christ. It is without a doubt the greatest price ever to be rendered, it was the ultimate sacrifice, it paid for our salvation, it removed the shadow of death from our lives, and it secured our eternity with God. While Jesus had the power and countless opportunities to avoid being hung on that tree, He knew the 'Price' had to be paid.

Now that we have established there are prices out there to be paid and deals to be made, let's get back to the twentieth century where our daily personal struggles in meeting the demands and sometimes the desires of life reside and seemly are always demanding our undivided attention. Deep in every one of our vulnerable hearts we want to believe that selling out would never be an option, but what if the price and the circumstances demanded a sale, a compromise of our values or even worse, a sale driven by envy with little or no regard to what it may cost others.

As human beings, it is in our very nature, a force ingrained within our very being to want a deal, to score big, to purchase something at half its value and our only thought is not that we may have just ripped off an unsuspecting seller, all we know is we just got the deal of the century. To make matters worse, we can't wait to share this conquest with anyone who is willing to listen. I mean it's not like we just killed someone, right?

Let's look at a few scenarios that could tip the scales of our inherent values.

- You're desperately in need of cash and find a wallet stuffed with over $1000.00 in cash, no ID or credit cards, just filled with cold hard cash.
- You are due for that long-awaited promotion at work but it appears your old nemesis Gary may get it. If only the boss knew that Gary has been goofing off for months.
- You're out in the parking lot of a big box store; you just purchased the long-awaited big screen TV that was listed at $999.00. While checking your sales slip, you see that the cashier mistakenly rang the sale up as $399.00.

Can we be tempted into selling out? Below is what the 'Great Tempter' might be whispering in our ears.

The wallet full of cash: 'Hey, there's no ID, it would be impossible to locate the owner and besides, a wallet with nothing but cash, it's probably drug money, just keep it.'

Total Sale: $1000.00

The Promotion: 'Hey, you worked your butt off for that promotion, you worked weekends, worked days off without being compensated, and now this clown Gary, the firm's biggest goof-off, may get the job. You would be doing the firm a huge favor by somehow letting the big bosses know that Gary is not a company man, he's actually costing the company money by being non-productive.'

Total Sale: The tragic cost and loss of someone's career.

The Big Screen TV: 'Hey, it's not your fault the clerk messed up, besides, if you go back in to rectify the error, management may fire him for making the mistake and what good would that be. Furthermore, the poor clerk probably has a family to support and you caused him to lose his job.'

Total Sale: $600.00

Please do not be offended by my examples. I am in no way suggesting the majority of people are dishonest. I'm simply attempting to dramatize Satan's ability to make us rationalize a wrong deed. It's comforting to know there are countless numbers of folks out there that always do the right thing, turn the wallet in, don't let themselves by guided by envy and would go back into the store to correct a sales slip whether its $600.00 or 60 cents.

What then is the moral to this story? Actually, it is simply this: We must constantly be on our guard as Satan knows when we are at our weakest moments. He is without a doubt the master of justification; he purposely fills our minds with unsavory thoughts, even if only for a moment in an attempt to capitalize on a brief moment of distraction to chalk up another victory against Christianity. We must take life's 'price advantages' very seriously as even the casual consideration of an improper act can turn into another notch of victory on Satan's belt. Sadly, even when we do the right thing, if we entertain a non-spiritual resolution, we have allowed Satan to plant a seed in our thoughts to be harvested on another day at another time, at another price.

In closing, pray that you are always cloaked in the full armor of God, do not let life's mishaps allow you to sell out for the 'Worldly Deals,' be a vigilant prayer warrior, and allow our Lord to fight the good fight on your behalf.

And a final tidbit or food for thought. 'Today's Bargains are Tomorrow's Garage Sale Items'

Matthew 27:3–4 'When Judas, who had betrayed him, saw that Jesus was condemned, he was seized with remorse and returned the thirty silver coins to the chief priests and the elders. "I have sinned," he said, "for I have betrayed innocent blood."'

Genesis 37: 26–28 'Judah said to his brothers, "What will we gain if we kill our brother and cover up his blood? Come, let's sell him to the Ishmaelite and not lay our hands on him; after all he is our brother, our own flesh and blood." His brothers agreed. So when the travelling Merchants came by, his brothers pulled Joseph up out of the cistern and sold him for twenty shekels of silver to the Ishmaelite, who took him to Egypt.'

Fleas

There is a very wise woman whom I will refer to as Mrs. Nichols. She is a lady who has been blessed with wisdom well beyond her years. One day, concerned that her young son Willie might stumble down a wrong path, she sat him down, looked him straight in the eyes and with steadfast assuredness said, 'Son, you know that when you hang around with a dog that has fleas, it's only a matter of time before you get fleas.' Amen, Mrs. Nichols.

Well, I'm happy to report that Mrs. Nichols' young son took this bit of advice as well as many other precious offerings to heart, fed on them, believed in them, and grew up to be a strong and loving Christian man. I wonder if Mrs. Nichols knew how profound her examples to her son were and how perceptive of life's many unsavory infestations were avoided due to her loving wisdom.

With respect and reverence for Mrs. Nichols, I would like to expand on her flea concept. Do we realize or understand how susceptible we are to life's many infestations that surround us, each and every day? Having said that, let's look at a few of life's more common ailments.

There's the 'person' at your office, always unsettled about something and always using unsavory or foul language when it suits them. It's only a matter of time, either knowingly or unknowingly, before expletives begin to flow and finally spew from your lips as well. Whether you care to accept it or not, when surrounded by fleas, it is fleas that you will get, but most unfortunately, it's fleas that you will pass on to unsuspecting others. What is the old saying? 'Garbage in, Garbage out.' I guess the big questions here are 'Does the Lord feel welcome in this person's heart?' or do you think the Holy Spirit who dwells in this person, is now thinking 'What happened to the neighborhood'?

Ephesians 5:4 'Nor should there be obscenity, foolish talk or coarse joking, which are out of place, but rather Thanksgiving.'

It's late in the evening, you've decided you're not tired so why not stay up and watch a little television and tomorrow is your day off. You begin to channel surf up and down the hundreds of mindless avenues of 'entertainment' and land on a show rated 'MA' for mature audiences. You might be thinking, it's late, there's no harm in checking what this show is all about. Baloney, we know exactly what to expect from this secular choice: sex, nudity, violence, and foul language. Now your Christian mind is no longer in a calm and spiritual state; it's now being infested by depravity at its best. How about a few more curious and soul-searching questions on this poorly chosen adventure? Who do you think it was whispering in your ear about watching this show, the Spirit or Satan? What kinds of thoughts and images are now occupying your Christian Walk? Are you thinking about the beautiful sunset our Lord has blessed us with or the newly baptized child, or are your thoughts now centered on the obscenities which Satan beckoned into your heart and mind? Another fine example of Garbage in or Garbage out!

Ephesians 5:3 'But among you there must not be even a hint of sexual immorality or of any kind of impurity, or of greed, because these are improper for God's holy people.'

Ephesians 5:5 'For of this you can be sure: No immoral, impure or greedy person—such as a man is an idolater—has any inheritance in the kingdom of Christ and of God.'

I would like to offer a quick and easy solution for those moments when we are challenged by these satanic invites; drop to your knees in prayer. It is very difficult if not impossible to think evil thoughts when on your knees in prayer with your Heavenly Father. In the event you cannot readily get to your knees, no problem. Shoot a quick arrow up toward God; He will hear you and He will help you.

Imagine, if you will, that you have been working at the city's dump site for the past five years as a bulldozer operator. Most folks are somewhat repelled on their first visit there because of the smell, but you have been there so long you don't even recognize the odor any longer. It's no different with sin or idolatry; if you ramble around in the muck and mire long enough, you too will no longer be mindful of the stench or recognize the lack of spirituality in your existence.

Whether or not the things we invite into our lives are good or not so good, after a while the environment becomes the accepted norm and we fail to see that we have settled for secular soup as opposed to seeking spiritual greatness. How then do we avoid this unpleasantness?

Matthew 7:7–8 Ask. Seek. Knock. 'Ask and it will be given to you, seek and you will find; knock and the door will be opened for you. For everyone who asks receives; he who seeks finds, and to him who knocks, the door will be opened.'

Still need help, use the Lord's direct line, **Jeremiah 33:3** 'Call to me and I will answer you and tell you great and unsearchable things you do not know.'

Please make no mistake about this fact. Satan is a relentless taskmaster, he does not take days off, and he likes to go to church as sometimes this can be where he does some of his best work. He's out there 365/24/7 dropping banana peels for you to slip on, filling your head with nonsense, enticing you into believing it's only a small lie or a small sin. Need more proof? Let's look at what the Bible has to say about it.

Job 1:6–7 'One day the angels came to present themselves before the Lord, and Satan also came with them. The Lord said to Satan, "Where have you come from?" Satan answered the Lord, "From roaming through the earth and going back and forth in it."'

I don't know about you, but the fact that Satan is out there every moment of every day roaming all over the earth looking for his next victims, using all his cunning ploys and all the sly tricks of his trade, all in an effort to keep your spirituality path sliding rapidly downward as opposed to soaring upward, is very scary indeed.

So, make it your passion to avoid catching the Evil Ones fleas by a daily dose of God's Perfect Pest Control, the Bible, it will scare the hell out of those pesky fleas.

One more thing, the next time you're talking with our Heavenly Father, send an arrow up for all of the Mrs. Nichols of this world, who have dedicated their entire lives to serving and praising God, a life committed to raising up the children of God.

Complaining

While we have all complained about one thing or another from time to time, we also know of someone who makes an art form out of complaining. Complaining has become a way of life and we have immortalized complaints with select phrases. How about 'the squeaky wheel gets the oil' or 'if you don't complain, it will never get fixed.' We even complain about the weather; 'Oh, it's so hot out today' or 'when is it going to stop raining?' Wait, almost forgot my favorite, 'Ugh, I have to go to work today!' Sadly, when we complain, I'm willing to bet the majority of the folks we complain too are thinking 'Give it a rest already,' or 'I have enough of my own problems, I don't need to hear all about yours as well.' To that I say, 'Touché.'

The fact of the matter is that when we complain, are we being ungrateful for the blessings the Lord has bestowed upon us? Or worse yet, are we in some small way saying that we know better than God what is best for us?

Complaints are our way of saying, 'Lord, I know exactly what I need to be happy and I really wish you would have paid more attention when I sent you my request list.' Or better yet, 'Lord, I asked for a brother not a sister.'

Instead of complaining, I wonder if we should try embracing the issue at hand. Like so many folks out there today, going to work may not be the most exciting event of our day, but at least we have a job to go to. Guess what, there are countless thousands of folks out there that would love to go to work but unfortunately cannot. Could it be yet another blessing in disguise?

I once worked with someone who could have won an Olympic Complaining event. Nothing made this poor soul happy, or at least it always appeared that way. Now, the craziness of this story is that complaining must in some way be contagious, because when I saw our perennial complainer coming toward me, I found myself complaining, 'Good grief, he's going to start complaining again.' So maybe I wasn't as smart as I thought I was, as I plugged into the complaining instead of the person who may have needed my help or a prayer. Shame on both of us, but in truth, shame on me, I supposedly knew better. Another example of how sin begets sin.

Complaining has become such a staple in our lives that most companies now have a complaint department. I recently read an article on MSN which spoke of an airline that hired a company to take complaints on their behalf, and further, they were going to charge a fee of $20.00 to lodge a complaint. Are complaints so rampant that now we are going to make a business out of complaints? After reading this absurdity, I did something equally as absurd, I wondered if I could make a complaint about having to pay to make a complaint. Good Lord, I took this one hook, line and sinker, no bait required.

Philippians 2:14 'Do everything without complaining or arguing.'

The above passage is a perfect segue into part two of complaining. Evidently, when we become so passionate about our complaint, we will argue and defend our position until the proverbial cows come home. Through constant complaining, we have developed an impenetrable layer of thick skin, protecting what was once a simple issue and now has now morphed its way to becoming a mantra, a credo to hang our hats on. Passion trumps brilliance almost every time so chalk another one up for a 'let the arguments begin.'

I sometimes wonder why complainers are so dissatisfied with life. Is it because they simply want more and more? Do they feel they were short changed at the festival of blessings? Could it be a very blatant lack of spirituality? Could we have been influenced by The Rolling Stones' 'I Can't Get No Satisfaction'? We are only as close to God as we choose to be. If we ever were able to completely dissect dissatisfaction in our lives or every complaint we have made in our lives, I believe we would be shocked right down to our argumentative ankles to learn that most of everything that upsets us has no eternal significance.

Proverbs 13:4 'The sluggard craves and gets nothing, but the desires of the diligent are fully satisfied.'

Satisfaction is a funny duck; we can be standing at the counter of a Marble Slab with an awesome ice cream flavor adorning the top of our waffle cone, and while we're standing there waiting for our change, we are still looking into the case to see what other flavor we could have selected. How many times have we been offered a choice between A or B and we're thinking; why can't I have both?

In my younger days, I was a cartoon groupie. Saturday morning would find me pajama clad and camped out in front of the idiot box being thoroughly entertained by Bugs, Elmer, Daffy, and Wile E. I remember watching Aladdin and the Genie in the bottle. You know how the story goes; whoever opens the bottle will be granted one wish. I would sit there thinking, 'Boy, if that were me, my wish would be for a hundred more wishes.' Some people are just never satisfied.

Well, it took more years than I care to disclose, but in time I finally learned a most valuable lesson, in that I would be far more satisfied in serving God than serving myself. How come it took so long to figure out something so simple yet so profound? The answer was too simple to see at the time, back then it was always all about me until I learned what true JOY meant: Jesus, Others, Yourself!

It took a while but I eventually got the order right.

I'm Perfect, Therefore I Judge

Whether we choose to accept it or not, we have become a world of judges. Furthermore, why, oh, why can't the world be as perfect as I am?

My wife participates in a community blog and related the following story to me by one of the blog participants.

'A young couple moved into the neighborhood and while looking out her window one day, she stated to her husband, look how dirty our neighbor's sheets are, I cannot believe she would put them on her clothes line in that condition. The conversation on the deplorable condition of her neighbor's dirty sheets repeated itself for several weeks until she announced to her husband, 'I think tomorrow I'm going to visit our neighbor and see if she needs help in proper washing techniques.' The following day, she looked out her window and saw sparkling white sheets on the woman's clothesline. She immediately called her husband, stating, 'Well, it looks like someone finally straightened her out, the sheets are bright white,' to which her husband replied, 'I got up at five o'clock this morning and cleaned our windows.'

How many times have we been forced to swallow our pride and judgmental nature and yank at a foot that was buried knee deep into our mouths? If you're thinking 'That's not me,' how about a stroll down memory lane?

'Oh my, have you seen her hair, it looks like it was cut with a lawn mower.'

Can't you hear someone whispering in the judger's ear, 'Didn't you hear? Her hair is finally coming back after her Chemo treatments.' (Extract Foot)

'Look at the shoes that he is wearing with that suit, no fashion statement there.'

Can't you just hear someone whispering in the judger's ear, 'Didn't you know that he's color blind? Poor thing must have mislabeled his shoe color.' (Extract Foot)

'I can't believe a mother would send her child out in this weather without a proper coat.'

Once again, can't you just hear someone whispering in the judger's ear, 'Didn't you hear? Both parents have been laid off and they can barely afford to put food on the table.' (Extract Foot)

Thankfully, the majority of us are not mean people by nature, but we struggle so when there is an open opportunity for us to let the world know just how smart and savvy we think we are. And worse yet, we simply cannot resist the opportunity to offer our unsolicited judgmental opinion. Have you ever wondered what shape the world would be in without our expertise?

Let's see what our Bibles have to say about 'judging' others!

Leviticus 18:16 'Do not go about spreading slander among your people.'

2 Chronicles 19:6 'He told them, consider carefully what you do, because you are not judging for man but for the Lord, who is with you whenever you give a verdict.'

Matthew 7: 1–2 'Do not judge or you too will be judged. For in the same way that you judge others, you will be judged and with the measure you use, it will be measured to you.'

Please pay particular attention to the Matthew verse, as you will be judged with the very same measure that you judged others says our Lord. So, my friends, this should capture your immediate and undivided attention.

Recently my daughters Genese and Breanna and I were watching the Olympics, when a friend sent her a humorous email on how we (the world) elevate ourselves to Olympic experts in almost every sport, when in truth and in fact, we have never seen or heard of half the events we are watching. Below is just a small sampling of our bravado, and we must surely wonder how it was that the major television networks didn't ask us to be Olympic Commentators.

- 'He's not going to medal unless he does a better job on his turns in the pool.'
- 'She needs to be a lot crisper on the beam or she's out.'
- 'The next event is "Dressage," is this one with horses?'
- 'She's never going to win a swimming medal unless she develops a better kick.'

Here we sit, in our favorite easy chair with potato chip crumbs on our stomachs and chest, queso drippings on our shirts, a large cold beverage at our sides, and possessing not one iota of technical expertise. We sit poised to judge any athlete we are watching. So, what do we do? After a loud resonating belch, we begin to judge men and woman who have given up years of their lives, are most probably deep in debt, who have endured numerous hardships, and what drives them to this point, they simply want to honor their country.

Shame on us would-be armchair experts.

There's an old saying that's goes like this: 'People who live in glass houses should never throw stones.' While this old adage does indeed bring great insight into how we should conduct our lives, to me it goes much deeper than a few glass walls.

While I do enjoy living in a respectable, spiritually-based glass home, I'm not so concerned about a pillow out of place or a chair not tucked back under the table. What I truly wish is that people would look beyond my glass walls and look directly into my glass heart and hopefully they see Jesus, an abundance of Love, Compassion, and Humility. If indeed this is the case, I hereby promise I will be out there daily with Windex in one hand and my Bible in the other.

Idols

What is the definition of an idol? An idol is anything that becomes a substitute for God in your life.

As we amass 'stuff' which supports our lifestyles and discerns who we are, we must be very cautious about the amount of importance we bestow upon our treasures.

I love my car; it has all the bells and whistles one could wish for, it literally does just about everything I need in a car with the exception of self-navigating. I wash my car weekly if not more depending on the weather. I offer a ride to anyone who needs one, though not so much that I'm trying to be a good servant; I just love getting behind the wheel of this beauty. I constantly brag about my car to anyone who will listen. Is my car becoming an idol?

I adore my wife and children. When I'm showing a picture of my wife, I always preface the showing with the statement 'I guess I'm an over-achiever.' I usually show their pictures to anyone who is standing still and not moving. I always can tell the ones who have already seen my pictures; they run when they see me coming. There is absolutely not a thing wrong with my love for my family as long as everyone knows my love for the Lord is much greater. If the answer is 'not really,' then I need to ask myself, 'Is my family becoming an idol?'

How many of us rent storage lockers because we can't part with our seriously overabundance of stuff? Any idols hiding amongst the cache you have in your secret silo of treasures? How many of us have garages that will never see tire marks on the floor because the garage is bursting at the seams with stuff that could no longer fit into the storage locker? Any idols hiding in there and can you even see in there?

The million-dollar question is, why do we need all that stuff? I'm pretty sure there are idols hiding in these strongholds of stuff; otherwise, we would have parted ways a long time ago. Is there anything within your treasure trove that you have not even used or have actually laid eyes on in the past two years, five years, ten years? So, the question then becomes, why do you even have it?

The inherent danger of collecting stuff can sometimes result in a very subtle transition from 'One day I may have a need for this' to 'Wow, is thing awesome, how lucky I am.' Once we begin to convince ourselves of the magnitude and incredible importance of our treasures, typically the following may happen: the treasures begin to take on a whole new role; they seem to beg for idol status.

Throughout the Bible we have seen over and over multitudes of poor souls who dabbled in idol worship, and then we have seen the disastrous effects of idolizing false gods. Idol worship was rampant in Old Testament times. So much so, certain cultures were like the Hallmark of Idols, they had an idol for every occasion. And if that wasn't enough coverage for these idol fanciers, they even had unnamed idols to be announced at a later time, when the already abundance of idols did not cover a specific need. Now, if you have ever read any Bible stories regarding idolatry, then you are very familiar with the complete absence of tolerance our Lord has for this nonsense. Most of these folks either wound up as burn marks on the ground or they met violent deaths in battle. Where were their idol protectors when this happened?

Habakkuk 2:18–20 'Of what value is an idol, since a man has carved it? Or an image that teaches lies? For he who makes it, trusts in his own creation; he makes idols that cannot speak. Woe to him that says to wood, 'Come to life!' Or to lifeless stone; 'Wake up.' Can it give guidance? Is it covered with gold and silver; there is no breath in it. But the Lord is in his holy temple; let all the earth be silent before him.'

1 Corinthians 8:4 'So then about eating food sacrificed to idols: We know that an idol is nothing at all in the world and that there is no God but one.'

1 Corinthians 10:14 'Therefore, my dear friends, flee from idolatry.'

Psalm 78: 56–58 'But they put God to the test and rebelled against the Most High; they did not keep his statutes. Like their fathers, they were disloyal and faithless, as unreliable as a faulty bow. They angered him with their high places; they aroused his jealousy with their idols.'

I think it's pretty clear what the Bible's position is, as well as the Lord's position, on idolatry. So now that we've taken a deeper look into this slippery slope, how about taking a deeper dive into those storage lockers and garages? Let's dust off those unearthed idol wannabes from their resting places and donate them to an organization who knows someone who is in desperate need of your forgotten treasure. Look how wonderful this act would be; it helps us avoid potential idolatry and it helps those less fortunate than us. How about that old chair that you just dusted off, it may now give a young child the ability to get off the floor and sit comfortably at a desk.

I once had a closet full of brand new, very expensive, and much-sought-after golf shirts. I'm sad and embarrassed to say they started to become idols to me. I loved each and every shirt and just couldn't part with any of them. Fortunately, the Lord helped me through this. He led me to a family that fell are hard times, and of all things, it was shirts they needed. Thank you, Jesus!

I feel I must reiterate a crucial point; it really is okay to like your things, love your family, just be sure to never elevate the love of anything above our Heavenly Father.

Apples

How many times have we heard the old adage 'The apple does not fall far from the tree'? Good, bad, or indifferent, we use this simple but effective phrase to compare similar traits and or actions of a parent and their off-spring. It's an easy phrase to use, doesn't require much if any supporting information, and it allows us to immediately classify and label someone's life, 'He's just like his father.'

Rather than spending time on the attributes of the apple, I'd like to take a look at the attributes of the people, the actual fall from grace. In the Adam and Eve story, Adam tells God, 'The woman you gave me made me eat the apple.' Some of you may remember a comedian by the name of Flip Wilson; his famous line when caught doing something wrong was 'The Devil made me do it.' And today's modern spin is 'I was thrown under the bus.' No one wants to talk about the 'fall,' and sadly some only dwell on the apple, the Devil, and the bus.

In the Adam and Eve passages, the issue is not a half-eaten apple; it is a fall from grace. If this story happened in today's world, it would most probably go something like this:

- A committee would be formed to investigate
- Statements would be taken from the alleged perpetrators
- The investigative committee would attempt to determine the root cause of the actual incident
- What was the value of the apple in today's marketplace
- Any witnesses to the incident

After we weed out all the nonsense listed above, we should be left with one very obvious and succinct point: What was the root cause? The apple was merely a conveyance of the incident, a prop if you will; the one main issue was their failure to follow the one rule that God put into place, 'Do not eat from this tree.'

So, did the apple fall or did Adam and Eve and mankind fall?

The introduction of New Testament times has given us the ability to say, 'Yes, I was the one at fault, Lord please forgive me.' Yet as easy as that may seem, no one wants to talk about the 'fall' or who actually was at fault.

What makes us fall and what makes us want to avoid ownership and the responsibility of the fall? In today's corporate world, a fall can get you into trouble with the 'suits' on the top floor. At home, it can be patriarchal fear; 'Just wait until your father gets home.' So instead of owning up to our misdeeds, we have learned through life that it's sometimes better to look for a patsy to pin it on, a way out with minimal self-incrimination. Many of today's top executives wouldn't think of taking a position unless it comes with a 'golden parachute,' a get out of jail card if you will, that protects and rewards the doer of the misdeed, especially when things go horribly wrong. Unfortunately, the only person being fooled and cheated by this slanderous escape is the doer of the misdeed. The only knowledge gained from this misadventure is how to escape responsibility and how to completely avoid having to pay the penalty of default. If one took the time to dissect this type of lifestyle, it almost seems like it was garbage in and garbage out. Nothing learned, nothing gained, and deception at its best.

Job 36:5–12 'God is mighty, but does not despise men; He does not keep the wicked alive but gives the afflicted their rights. He does not take His eyes off the righteous; He enthrones them as kings and exalts them forever. But if men are bound in chains and held fast by cords of affliction, He tells them what they have done- that they have sinned arrogantly. He makes them listen to correction and commands them to repent of their evil. If they obey and serve Him, they will spend the rest of their days in prosperity and their years in contentment, but if they do not listen, they will perish by the sword and die without knowledge.'

Okay, I'll be the first to admit that the Job passage is a little scary. No, I take that back, it's quite scary, but as it usually does, the Old Testament calls it the way it sees it, no artificial sweeteners required. However, this same passage tells us that if we own up to our 'fall' and repent and seek the forgiveness of our Heavenly Father, He will reward us abundantly.

A very important fact to remember is that we have been given, through the grace of God, the gift of the Holy Spirit within each and every one of us. So, when we fall into a sinful situation, don't look around to see if anyone is watching, He is right there with you, waiting to see if you call upon your inner spirit for guidance, repentance, or if you are going to listen to the voice on the other shoulder, Satan, who is keen to tell you it's no big deal, it happens all the time, keep quiet and move on, you're in the clear. I can promise you this, if you make the wrong choice, it will be more than your wrong doings that will be going south.

What causes us to fall and how can we avoid falls? We need to start right off by stating that as Christians we are not perfect, but we are indeed forgiven. The best way to avoid most pitfalls is to start your day with an exchange of wills, His will for your will. Lord please direct me and give me the courage and strength to do the things you have set before me on this day. If your relationship is right with the Lord, it will most always be right with everyone and everything else. Time permitting, and it usually is, open your Bible and read a few passages, feed that inner spirit. Now you're spirit-filled and off to a great start. If you are faced with a decision that has the option of not being spiritually proper, go to Jesus in prayer as it is impossible to select evil as a choice when you are on your knees with the Lord.

Falling short on your spirituality can sadly be quite easy as our choices can sometimes lead us to a false sense of security. Deep within your heart you may realize you may be wrong but everything seems to have worked out well, no harm, no foul. We sadly sell ourselves and our spirituality short when we take this approach, as it eventually leads to more compromises and more erroneous justifications, which become the norm rather than the exception and ultimately saps our Godly spirit.

Proverbs 12: 1–3 'Whoever loves discipline, loves knowledge, but he who hates correction is stupid. A good man obtains favor from the Lord, but the Lord condemns a crafty man.'

Proverbs 12:19 'Truthful lips endure forever, but a lying tongue lasts only a moment.'

Discipline yourself so the Lord will not have to do it for you!!!!

Counterfeits and Confusion

It should be a well-known fact that Satan plants counterfeits among us to cause confusion, and truth be told, he is the colossus of confusion.

The definition of confusion is very simple, put three or more people in the same room with the objective of defending a hot topic. Conversely, the definition of counterfeit is one of the three people has the specific goal of alienating both of the other politicos. You're talking about the rising cost of gasoline, and all he wants to talk about how we should ban all luxury gas-guzzling cars.

As political pundits do, they have fun putting their comical spin on the politics of the day, and during these turbulent times, Satan must be feeling he has hit the all-time political jackpot. If you're looking for a good example of what I'm referring to, walk into a room and offer your personal opinion on the political events of the day. Instant combatant confusion, compliments of the Evil One himself. Politics not your thing, you can achieve the same results by tossing out a religious barb.

Now let's take a look at spiritual confusion and counterfeiting techniques. There are folks out there that will attempt to convince you that religion is designed to separate you from your money and then the age old non-believer's mantra: If God were truly good, why do bad things happen to good people? Now, the one thing they do not want to discuss is that each of us has been blessed with the gift of free will as that very salient point takes the onus off God and places it on you, diluting their ability to attack religion.

I don't subscribe or believe to the fact that we are living in Eden or Utopia; things are going to happen, and some will be not so nice or bad.

The one thing we all have in our favor is the ability to seek forgiveness for our transgressions. And, if one of our brothers is stumbling, we have the duty and obligation to pick him up. I also believe with all my heart that when bad things happen, our Lord feels an unimaginable pain that one of his flock has lost their way. No one likes to see a loved family member or friend depart this world before their time, but the reality of this is that it is his time, not ours.

Without free will, I believe we might as well be programmable robots, no individuality, a bland and mundane society sharing a single thought and purpose. While this may sound somewhat contradictory to my stance on confusion, we must allow others the ability to openly share their beliefs; it's not 'my way or the highway.' If this were the case, evangelizing would succumb to a quick and devastating death. The key is being able to quickly sort out who is the counterfeit in the mix and not allowing you to become swayed or influenced by their deceptive rhetoric. Being grounded in the Word can be very beneficial here. There is an old saying that if you do not believe in something, you will fall for anything. While we know that every-one has an opinion and I'm fairly sure most are well grounded in thought, you can take it to the bank that at least one person in the midst of the dis-cussion upheaval has been put there by Satan to 'stir the pot' in the name of passion and correctness. Buyers beware; Satan is the master peddler of deception and confusion.

One final thought: A discussion is an exchange of knowledge; an ar-gument is an exchange of ignorance.

There is a saving grace to our lives though, no matter how hard he tries, Satan cannot counterfeit spiritual fruit.

Proverbs 12:17 'A truthful witness gives honest testimony, but a false witness tells lies.'

Proverbs 14:25 'A truthful witness saves lives, but a false witness is deceitful.'

Matthew 7:15 'Watch out for false prophets. They come to you in sheep's clothing, but inwardly they are ferocious wolves.'

1 Timothy 6:20–21 ' . . . Turn away from godless chatter and the opposing ideas of what is falsely called knowledge, which some have professed and in so doing have wandered from the faith. Grace be with you.'

Proverbs 19:9 'A false witness will not go unpunished, and he who pours out lies will perish.'

I Woke up Dead this Morning

It's morning and you are now awake and starting to rub the Sandman's dust out of your eyes. There is a sense of emptiness permeating the air around you and you feel completely out of sync? Nothing in your life seems to be going right, and you seem to be in a cloud rather than basking in the bright sun. Sound familiar?

Okay, so you missed a few Sundays at church. I mean really, that's not such a big deal, right? Surely that cannot be the reason for the empty feelings? What about the promiscuous movies you have been staying up late to watch, can that be it? What, you no longer say grace before a meal in a restaurant!? Also, you just don't have that spiritual zing you used to have. Are you allowing the 'easy fix' thoughts and actions to rule your life or are you doing things the proper way, wholesome and with spiritual correctness? In other words, you need a healthy dose of 'what would Jesus do?'

Scenarios like those above can creep into anyone's life with such stealth that we are caught completely off guard until we are sometimes knee deep in the muck and mire. Now the question becomes how can we reverse this trend and bring the 'Son' light back into our lives?

Someone once told me that a little spiritual flossing can prevent moral decay. So how does one spiritually floss? The following are a few time-tested tips that are guaranteed to eliminate moral decay.

- Start your morning with an exchange of wills, His will for your will.
- During Morning Prayer, ask the Lord to guide you through the day.
- Open your Bible and read a few passages of any book.

- Having a little trouble with spiritual focus, purchase a WWJD bracelet.
- Attend church and Sunday school on a regular basis, be consistent.
- Stepped on one of Satan's banana peels, no biggie, ask Jesus for forgiveness.
- Each day thank Jesus for allowing you to enjoy another day in His creation.
- Finally, pray that the Spirit within you is always vibrant and active in your life.

Once you take these few steps, everything else will begin to take shape as you will start to feel like the old you again. It's the dawn of a new day, welcome back, you were missed!

1 Samuel 25:6 'Say to him: 'Long life to you! Good health to you and your household! And good health to all that is yours'!

3 John 1:2–4 'Dear friend, I pray that you may enjoy good health and that all may go well with you, even as your soul is getting along well. It gave me great joy to have some brothers come and tell me about your faithfulness to the truth and how you continue to walk in the truth. I have no greater joy than to hear my children are walking in the truth.'

Psalm 73: 4–5 'They have no struggles; their bodies are healthy and strong. They are free from the burdens common to man; they are not plagued by human ills.'

Psalm 25:4–5 'Show me your ways O Lord, teach me your paths; guide me in your truth and teach me, for you are God my Savior, and my hope is in you all day long.'

Which Gospel?

What gospels do we have today?

One is the gospel of non-believers. This is the gospel touted by atheists and those who simply have no religious affiliation and they do not have a religious interest in establishing one. I sometimes wonder if atheism is the lazy religion. If they claim there is no God or Supreme Being, does that mean they can do whatever they want as long as they don't get caught? Additionally, there is absolutely no requirements or obligations to be met, so it's game on for these folks. The definition of atheism is non-belief, skepticism, agnosticism, and a complete rejection of the existence of any type of deity.

Next, we have the gospel based on science. This gospel is structured around the fact that it was evolution and the Big Bang Theory that created the world and life as we know it today. Their main premise is that if it cannot be proven by a scientific method or hypothesis, it simply can't be true. Supporters of this gospel do not subscribe to a theistic creation but rather a naturalistic creation which can be supported by scientific fact. They are indeed passionate about discovering the truth, but only a truth that can be unequivocally supported on a proven hypothesis rather than spiritual faith.

And finally, we have the Holy Gospel. This gospel is supported by the Bible and by a very sincere belief in the deity of Jesus Christ, and is further supported by a deep and abiding faith in the message of the Holy Gospel. Christianity embraces the fact that one does not need to see indisputable proof to believe in something but rather they subscribe to a favorable action of faith within their hearts. The Holy Gospel is the backbone of Christianity, and it is the only known document that recounts creation from the beginning of time to the end of time.

There are many theories regarding the creation of the world and what lies ahead for mankind, and everyone must believe in something or you will fall for anything. Don't get caught with your spiritual knickers down. Satan is beckoning.

If you're in the market for a gospel, may I suggest you choose wisely and allow me to recommend the Holy Gospel, it is filled with rich blessings and an entrance ticket to eternal salvation with Jesus Christ, the Lord and author of our salvation.

Finally, always remember, the Holy Gospel does not need to be sold, it needs to be told!

Chapter Seven:

Fruits of the Spirit

A Few Personal (Tough) Questions to Myself

While I wrestle with my heart, perhaps you might want to think about tackling a few of these knee knockers yourself.

Question 1 – *Does my view of God come from man or God's word?*

This was a real eye opener for me.

Question 2 – *Do I care about God's reputation?*

Yes, I do, but sometimes I feel like I'm Peter, denying my relationship with the Lord, usually supported by a non-Christian act on my part.

Question 3 – *Is the purpose of prayer for God to hear me or for me to hear God?*

A close relationship with God allows for meaningful intercession and for me that means getting the ME out of Meaningful.

Question 4 – *Does my schedule reflect my desire to get to know God?*

It most certainly would if I stopped being a Christian Couch Potato.

Question 5 – *Do I ever pitch my tent near sin?*

I plead the fifth. No, I take that back, I have been known to have the proverbial foot on the banana peel.

Question 6 – *God is a God of His word; am I a man of my word?*

I would like to believe I am about 90 percent of the time. Now, is 90 percent good enough for God? I can answer that . . . NOT . . . I'm sure He would happily settle for an even 100 percent.

Question 7 – *Is a little sin much better than a big sin?*

I suppose if we didn't put values on sin and look at sin the way God does, we would never be able to live with ourselves.

I don't know about you, but I have had enough squirming, fidgeting, and sweating to last me for a while, so I'm bailing out now so I have enough energy left to get on my knees and ask for more help.

I Can't Wait to be a Child Again!

I took a beautiful trip down memory lane the other day; I have been so busy with work and life in general, that I haven't spent much time with my family, most specifically my daughters, Genese and Breanna.

I remembered when they were very young and I would come home from work and they would run to the door to meet me, they would take my coat, my briefcase, and then after a huge hello kiss, they would escort me to a chair and unloosen my tie. I loved these moments because no matter what had happened at work or on the way home, they washed away all of the day's woes and filled my day and my heart with a new warm glow, a love you can actually feel. Now it would only be fair to parents of young children if I didn't add a warning at this juncture; enjoy it while you can, it changes rapidly. Be brave though, the child-like love will return in the not too distant future, it only seems like it takes FOREVER.

The memories that will always stay in my mind and my heart were how genuinely happy they were to see me, the happiness that only a child can know before becoming influenced or even jaded by the 'world.' A love so pure, so full, so giving, completely uncompromised and so very beautiful, it staggers the mind. Remember those moments when you thought how wonderful it would be to be a child again, living in a world with only peace, love, and sheer joy from the time you wake up until it's time for your nightly bedtime prayers. They have not gone the way of your favorite childhood toy, just a distant memory; they are still very real, and Jesus is anxiously waiting to give those feelings back to you. It's not magic; it's called prayer and a sincere relationship with Him. Seek the blessings, and you will most definitely find them.

Well, we all are children of God, aren't we? The next time you're out for a drive or a walk, look up at the sky for a moment and think, Wow, one day I will be up there sitting right next to my heavenly Father! And guess what? He will be bursting with the excitement of a child that you are excited about the day you come home to Him. Hallelujah. Your heavenly Father, who was with you through all the trials and tribulations, the mistakes, the times you would not listen, the good and the bad times, the special moments of joy, every millisecond of your life, wants to have a heavenly feast in your honor because you've come home. The tears of joy will flow abundantly and eternally. We may be adults or think we are adults, but in the eyes of our Lord and Savior, we are and will always be; His children.

Have you ever heard someone say, 'Youth is wasted on the young'? I was a subscriber to that theory until I allowed my heart and mind to be opened by the love of Christ, and now my wife tells everyone I'm her biggest child.

Luke 16:31 The Parable of the Lost Son. 'My son, the father said, you are always with me and everything I have is yours. But we had to celebrate and be glad, because this brother of yours was dead and is alive again; he was lost and is found.'

Deuteronomy 14:1 'You are the children of the Lord your God.'

I don't know about the rest of you, but this adult is getting really excited about becoming a child again, and walking through the Gates of Heaven and seeing the out-stretched arms of my Lord, the incredible joy in His eyes and His face as I run to Him. Thanks be to God.

Are You a Biblical Expert?

Don't be too hasty in answering that question, you may be surprised.

Who is Jesus Christ?	(Our Lord and Savior)
What did He do?	(He died for our sins)
Where is He now?	(In our hearts and at the right hand of the Father)

If you were able to answer the above three questions, you are indeed a biblical expert because they are the only three things you will ever need to know. You have now mastered the 'Doctrine of Christianity.' Congratulations!

So now that you have all this knowledge, what are you going to do with it? I have a suggestion: Don't keep the faith, share it! Lead a Sunday school class, either children or adults, or attend one of the many great Christian Education classes offered at your church. You have so very much to offer. Remember, you're an expert now, become involved in an outreach program and do something! When you fail to share your knowledge with others, someone is most definitely going to miss a blessing and that person could very well be someone close to you.

If you still feel that you're not quite ready to serve, did you know that God equips those He calls? Need Proof?

Hebrews 13:20–21 'May the God of peace, who through the blood of the eternal, covenant brought back from the dead, our Lord Jesus, that great Sheppard of the sheep, equip you with everything good for doing his will, and may he work in us, what is pleasing to him, through Jesus Christ, to whom be glory forever and ever. Amen.'

2 Timothy 3:17 'So that the man of God may be thoroughly equipped for every good work.'

2 Corinthians 2:14 'But thanks be to God, who always leads us in triumphal procession in Christ and through us spreads everywhere the fragrance of the knowledge of him.'

I know it takes GUTS to take that first step, but I have a theory on GUTS.

> *G*od *U*plifts *T*he *S*ervant
> God uses the sanctified
> God uses the servant
> God equips those He calls
> Glory unto the Savior

I read somewhere that only 1 percent of the world reads the Bible and 99 percent of the world reads you. Now that we know so many folks out there are reading us, why not ensure we put our best spiritual foot forward and give that 99 percent a great reason to switch sides.

All that we have been blessed with, our talents, our skills and our time are a direct gift through the Grace of God and we must all remember that *the debt we owe to God is payable here on earth to others.*

Your reward in the service of Christ is not what you can get, but what you become.

So how about it, you biblical experts? Shall we all start making payments on a debt that is long overdue and turn that debt load into one of great spiritual 'interest'?

Conversations with God

I think we all know that conversations with the Lord should for the most part be reverent and spiritual, as in prayer. However, there are times when we just sort of blurt out, 'Lord I want, Lord, I need.' completely self-serving and definitely non-spiritual. So, with that thought in mind, I was wondering how The Lord might respond to some of those 'it's all about me' outbursts.

Gary: Lord, I would really like a new car.
The Lord: Funny, I don't remember you thanking me for the last car I gave you.

Gary: Lord, I'm excited about eternity; can you describe it for me?

The Lord: Sure, which one? (Ouch)

Gary: Lord, If only I could win the lottery.

The Lord: You can't handle the money I have already given you, what makes you think you can handle more?

Gary: I really don't like my boss; can you find him another job, away from me?

The Lord: Someone was not wearing their listening ears when I asked them to love thy neighbor.

Gary: Lord, my life is boring, it just plain stinks, and will it ever get any better?

The Lord: Let's talk and we'll see what we can do about it.

Gary: Lord, I wish I had more patience.

The Lord: Has anyone ever mentioned to you, 'Be careful what you wish for?'

Gary: Lord, nothing good ever seems to happen to me.

The Lord: Did I not send my Son down to you, to die for your sins, so that you can spend eternity at my side? Was that not good enough?

Gary: Lord, life is not fair; I hardly ever get my own way.

The Lord: If I didn't love you so much I would indeed let you have your own way.

Gary: Lord, how could I have been so stupid?

The Lord: Look who you listened to.

If any of the above sounds familiar, I suggest you immediately call home, Pray.

Fun Facts in the Bible You Probably Did Not Know!

It's time for a little levity and a few little-known passages (for fun only) that you have probably read in your Bible and didn't realize these were biblical 'firsts.'

1. The first recorded fast food.

Genesis 18:6–8 'So Abraham hurried into the tent to Sarah. Quick, he said, get three seahs of fine flour and knead it and bake some bread. Then he ran to the herd and selected a choice tender calf and gave it to a servant, who hurried to prepare it.'

2. The first car pool
Genesis 4:24 'After He drove the man out, He placed on the east side of the Garden, cherubim'

3. The first dishwasher
Mark 6:4 'And they observe many other traditions, such as the washing of cups, pitchers and kettles.'

4. The first 'Happy Meals'
Acts 14:17 . . . .'he provides you with plenty of food and fills your hearts with joy.'

5. The first catering company
2 Samuel 16:1 'He had a string of donkeys, saddled and loaded with two hundred loaves of bread, a hundred cakes of raisins, a hundred cakes of figs and a skin of wine.'

6. The first calorie counting
Daniel 10:3 'I ate no choice food, no meat or wine touched my lips and I used no lotions at all until the three weeks were over.'

7. The first beauty contest
1 Kings 1:3 'Then they searched throughout Israel for a beautiful woman and found Abishag, a Shunammite, and brought her to the king.'

8. The first UFOs
Jeremiah 10:10' Do not learn the ways of the nations or be terrified by signs in the sky, though the nations are terrified by them.'

9. The first rock and roll
Ezekiel 26:13 'I will put an end to your noisy songs and the music of your harps.'

10. The first recorded 'quacks'
Job 13:4 'You, however, smear me with lies; you are worthless physicians, all of you.'

So, What About All Those Acronyms?

As an ex-airline employee, my life was all about acronyms. I even used them in my personal life, but it wasn't until recently that I became hooked on biblical acronyms . . . so HML (Here's My List).

BIBLE: Basic Instructions Before Leaving Earth
GRACE: God's Reward At Christ's Expense
JOY: Jesus, Other and Yourself (Now that's a good Christian order)
FAITH: Forsaking All I Trust Him
FAITH: Favorable Action In The Heart
POP: Power of Prayer
WWJD: What Would Jesus Do
PUSH: Pray Until Something Happens
ASK: Ask, Seek, Knock (Matthew 7:7)
ACTS: Acknowledge, Contrition, Transformation, Supplication
ENVY: Every Nerve Viciously Yearning
HOPE: Helping Others Procure Eternity
GUTS: God Uplifts the Servant
JACOB: Just Accept Christ's Own Birthright
THE: This Hope Endures
END: Eternity Never Dies

What's Done in the Dark Will Come into the Light!

No one likes to get caught with their hand in the cookie jar, but life happens, and while we may believe we are slick enough to grab an Oreo without getting caught, justice will inevitably prevail as we will suffer betrayal by the trail of cookie crumbs down the front of our shirts.

We are a funny breed of humans. Whenever we do something wrong or stupid, we immediately look around to ensure no one has witnessed our colossal blunder. Once we have confirmed our blunder went unseen, we write it off as if it never happened. Our logic being 'no harm, no foul, no one was watching.' Sorry to say, my friends, that someone was indeed watching and His name is Jesus. Granted, Jesus may be thinking, 'Good grief, where did I go wrong with that one,' but He was indeed watching.

The old adage 'out of sight, out of mind' does not fit into the spiritual or Christian environment, and one day we may all have to own up to the likes of all those cookie thefts we so brilliantly lifted right out from under the watchful eyes of the cookie monitors.

If life were just about a jar of cookies, we would most probably have one foot near heaven's entrance, but unfortunately, life can sometimes be more treacherous than a cookie obtained by a five-finger discount.

You're driving home late at night and as you make your way into your parking complex, a misjudged turn by you causes a broken taillight on someone's car. The damage is small, and as you look around and survey the situation, you confirm that your car is fine and suddenly you come to the realization that no one has witnessed this minor mishap and you can safely get away with not getting caught.

You're in a store and you are admiring a beautiful piece of crystal which you have removed from the display shelf to get a closer look. When putting the object back onto the shelf, you inadvertently bang it against another valued treasure and a small piece of the crystal breaks off. You look around and see that there are no store clerks in the immediate area and no one saw what happened, so with great stealth, you slink away from the scene of the crime.

And what happens when we do get caught in a dumb act? We try to transfer the blame onto someone or something else. You're walking down the street and for no reason you trip, you immediately look down at the sidewalk as surely there was something there that caused the trip as it certainly wasn't a result of your impeccable walking stride.

Remember the car you hit and damaged its taillight assembly? Well, the apartment complex should know better than to put a parking slot so close to a turning area. It's their fault, not mine. The same holds true for the broken piece of crystal; if the retailer left enough space in between the objects on the shelf, the incident would have never happened.

Ever wonder why most burglaries happen at night and not in the light of day? Ever wonder why stores feel compelled to place security cameras and guards throughout their establishments? Ever wonder why most animals hunt at night? Ever wonder who tempted Judas to throw Christ under the bus?

The sad fact is that the Great Tempter, the Evil One himself, knows that while we do possess a reasonably good sense of right and wrong, if he provides a quick escape, an easy way out, chances are that in a moment of weakness we may succumb to compromising our values and we just might buy into the 'no one saw me do it' philosophy. After all, isn't this one of the best ploys in his evil bag of sinfulness? Get the Christian do-gooder to compromise his spirituality and take a walk on the dark side of life.

There is a certain amount of comfort and security when one is operating either solo or in a remote setting as one of two philosophies may come into play. The first being; many of life's rules do not apply as there is 'supposedly' no one around to judge our actions. Secondly, we are in a position to modify, adjust, and re-create existing rules to fit our immediate needs; again, no one is there to judge. It's almost as if we are invisible to our surroundings and can enjoy an incredible modicum of freedom. We can pull the tag off the pillow that says 'do not remove under penalty of law' or we cannot only touch wet paint, we can put an entire hand print on it if we so choose. Why? Because we can and no one will judge us for our actions. Sadly, once again we have entered the path of misguided thinking.

Unfortunately, these misguided worldly compromises or pretenses can creep into our spirituality which in turn may put us on a very dangerous path. It's okay to touch the wet paint when no one is looking and get away with it, but you cannot deny the commandments of the Lord, even if you believe you are in total obscurity. When combined, the veil of darkness and the feeling of obscurity can lure us into a very false sense of security and may even cause us to challenge existing beliefs that have been the mainstays of our spirituality. It is during times like this that we need to reach deep into our souls, calling upon the Holy Spirit for strength of conviction and 'lead us not into temptation but deliver us from prevailing evil. What is the saying; 'get behind me Satan.' I always try to rely on the acronym WWJD, 'What Would Jesus Do,' when I find myself in these situations. It always provides me with great spiritual clarity and a sound sense of purpose.

So what is the best way to avoid temptation or the beckoning of the dark side? Ensure that whatever you are about to say or do is the exact same course of action you would be taking if you were in front of the *20/20* investigative team cameras. When the cameras are not there, remember that there is still a very interested audience; you are always under the watchful and loving eyes of our Lord and Savior.

Job 34:22 'There is no dark place, no deep, shadow, where evil doers can hide.'

John 3:20 'Everyone who does evil hates the light, and will not come into the light for fear that his deeds will be exposed.'

Psalm 18:28 'You, O Lord keep my lamp burning; my God turns my darkness into light.'

Romans 2:19–23 'If you are convinced that you are a guide for the blind, a light for those who are in the dark, an instructor for the foolish, a teacher of infants, because you have in the law the embodiment of knowledge and truth – you, then, who teach others, do you not teach yourself? You who preach against stealing, do you steal? You who say that people should not commit adultery, do you commit adultery? You who abhor idols, do you rob temples? You who brag about the law, do you dishonor God by breaking the law?'

1 John 1: 5–7 'This is the message we have heard and declare to you: God is light; in him there is no darkness at all. If we claim to have fellowship with him yet walk in the darkness, we lie and do not live by the truth. But if we walk in the light, as he is the light, we have fellowship with one another, and the blood of Jesus, his Son, purifies us from all, sin.'

Paths

There are many paths we can take in our lives; some lead to goodness and some lead to depravity, so it should become self-evident that it is incumbent on each of us to choose wisely. Whenever I am faced with directional dilemmas and I am not sure which path I need to be on, I go to the Lord in prayer, seeking discernment and guidance.

As an avid hiker, one who has traversed many trails both domestically and internationally, I fully understand and appreciate the importance of sticking to the designated paths, no matter how tempting it may be to stray from the trail. The hiking trails or paths were designed to keep hikers as safe as possible and to keep them from falling prey to the many hidden or uncharted dangers that are lurking beyond the safety of the designated trail. The most common danger is becoming hopelessly lost in a vast wilderness, where every step takes you deeper and deeper into a dark abyss.

I believe our spiritual and worldly life to be very similar to hiking, there are many safe paths or trails available to us, but when we stray or we are lured from the safe path provided for us, we typically find ourselves facing a myriad of unpleasant circumstances.

Every good hiker will tell you that they never begin any adventure without proper preparation. Their backpacks always contain a map of the trail, an adequate amount of water, an energy bar or two, sun tan lotion and foul weather clothing for protection against the elements. Much like the hiker, we should be equipped with a trail map which in our case is our Bibles. Next, our water and energy bars are the spiritual enrichment that is our church family and our Sunday school education, which feeds the Holy Spirit within us. And finally, our sun tan lotion and foul weather gear are the prayers we offer to our Heavenly Father for protection and guidance. We are now clothed in the full armor of God, which will certainly serve to help keep us safe as we take on life's paths that will ultimately lead us to salvation.

Now that we have provided the necessary equipment by providing a solid educational experience for our children, which included being spiritually grounded in the Word of God, it doesn't stop there; parents also have the responsibility to lead by example thereby providing our children with two very safe 'paths' for life's journey.

And remember and be aware, even in the light of day, if you are not properly equipped, you may be hiking in darkness but you can avoid that unpleasantness by Son Light, letting Jesus be your guiding light through every phase of your life.

Psalm 16:11 'You have made known to me the path of life; you will fill me with joy in your presence, with eternal pleasures at your right hand.'

Psalm 23:3 'He guides me in paths of righteousness for his names sake.'

Proverbs 22:5 'In the paths of the wicked lie thorns and snares, but he who guards his soul stays far from them.'

Proverbs 15:24 'The path of life leads upward for the wise to keep him from going down to the grave.'

Psalm 109:105 'Your word is a lamp to my feet and a light for my path.'

Even if you're not prone to hiking, dust off those spiritual boots that take you through life, fill those backpacks with all the spiritual necessities and get on the path of righteousness, He is waiting for you at the end of the adventure.

Self-Control or Self-Indulgence

The nemesis to the inhabitants of the world, the ability to exercise that sometimes very elusive trait, simply but aptly named 'self-control.'

If I were a betting person, I would hazard to guess that we exercise the trait of self-control perhaps more than any other internal attribute. Here are just a few examples of the application of self-control.

- You're on a strict diet; you need to excise self-control when the dessert menu comes around.
- Someone has done something that makes you want to explode in a tirade at their stupidity but hopefully you choose self-control.
- When things don't go as we wish, we can sometimes use unsavory language to explain our frustration, when we should have been using self-control.

- The car in front of you in moving slower than the speed limit, as you move by to pass them, almost instinctively, you give them the 'ugly stare down' to ensure they know you are not happy with their driving skills or lack thereof, instead of exercising self-control.

These are just a random sampling of the many choices we make daily, from should we steal, tell falsehoods, curb impure thoughts or misbehavior, especially when we know better. Will I do what's right and pleasing in the eyes of the Lord?

Self-control should not be confused with Common Sense; while the two may be similar, there is a very distinct difference. One is based on the knowledge of right and wrong, and the other is based on what you believe your emotional needs and desires to be at the moment of choice.

Self-control also goes by the name of the Holy Spirit. That got your attention, didn't it? The Spirit within each of us is the barometer of good and not so good. I believe Self-control is similar to a muscle; it needs to be exercised on a regular basis or without that muscle tone, our choices and actions will be like the pattern of a shotgun spray, everywhere but centered. Your barometer needs a few things to ensure it is running properly. First, you need to summon the will to be in control. If you're not willing to make the right choices or if you're still centered on guilty pleasures over providence; then self-control in your life will be random and inconsistent. Next you need to talk to Jesus in prayer on a very consistent basis, asking Him for the strength, determination, and the courage to avoid temptation. Ask and you shall receive. When I am being tempted on something, I like to bring out that old but effective acronym, WWJD; 'what would Jesus do.'

There's someone else out there who also wants to be in control of your decision-making processes and you know who I am referring to—the Evil One, Satan. His goal is to take advantage of our weaknesses, to justify wrong over right and make our non-spiritual choices seem reasonable and palatable, as opposed to our harboring any feelings of guilt.

There is an old Chinese Proverb that states, 'When things go wrong, don't go with them.' The only reason I know this is because it was the saying inside my fortune cookie with last night's dinner. Once again, the Lord moves in mysterious ways.

Proverbs 25:28 'Like a city whose walls are broken down is a man who lacks self-control'

Titus 2:11–13 'For the grace of God that brings salvation has appeared to all men. It teaches us to say no to ungodliness and worldly passions, and to live self-controlled upright and godly lives in this present age, while we wait for the blessed hope—the glorious appearing of our great God and Savior, Jesus Christ.'

1 Peter 1:13 'Therefore prepare your minds for action; be self-controlled, set your hope fully on the grace to be given you when Jesus is revealed.'

Matthew 23:25–26 'Woe to you, teachers of the law and Pharisees, you hypocrites! You clean the outside of the cup and dish, but inside they are full of greed and self-indulgence. Blind Pharisees, first clean the inside of the cup and dish and then the outside also will be clean.'

The above Matthew passage should be very clear: Once our inner soul, our inner being is clean, our outer being will be noticeably clean as well. Then, when we profess who we claim to be, as well as the perception of others who look to us for guidance and leadership, we not only become a beacon of hope to our own inner peace but a beacon of hope to others as well. Keep that window to your soul squeaky clean and your days will be filled with endless 'Son Light.'

Courage

The on-line dictionary defines courage as 'bravery, guts, nerve, daring and valor.' While these are all good definitions, I still like what John Wayne once said, 'It's being scared to death but saddling up anyway.'

Our Bibles are filled with courageous men and women throughout every book. Let's briefly look at a few.

Abraham – Lead and feed thousands of Israelites through the desert.

Daniel – Walked fearlessly in a lion's den.

Paul – In every town he set foot, there was always someone waiting to harm him.

Ruth – Traded the safety of a trip back home to stay and protect Naomi.

These are just a few of the many acts or bravery and courage by God's children, all of whom knew deep in their hearts that God would never leave their side.

When I think about courage, I believe that courage and faith are blood brothers, maternal twins, 'frick and frack,' ham and cheese; you can't have one without the other.

When you summon the courage to tackle the seemingly impossible, while the task before you might be very ominous, you most probably have faith in your innate ability, knowledge of the fact that the task may be perilous and most important of all, faith in knowing that God is with you, every single step, no matter where the task may lead you.

Courage is more than the physicality of a dangerous task; courage is also having the strength of conviction to stand up for your beliefs, especially when others around you do not share that same opinion. In today's peer-pressure world, courage plays a daily role in what we say and do.

You're at a crowded party of your peers, someone whispers to you, 'The hosts are not Christian people, so if the topic of religion comes up, don't say anything.' Well, sure enough, someone offends the name of God and now it's decision time. If you say something, you may run the risk of being ostracized by your peer groups, and if you don't say something, you're showing the world you're a milquetoast Christian, one who doesn't have the courage and gumption to defend one's beliefs. And worse yet, someone may lose a blessing by your silence. A tough decision indeed and with a lot at stake. It's during times like these that we need to offer up a quick silent prayer asking for discernment; Lord, should I become involved and if so, grant me the courage and the words in my heart and on my lips that will bring your glory to this situation.

Courage can also be as simple as saying grace in a public restaurant, knowing some people may snicker at your faithful act. My feeling on prayer in a restaurant is that by me initiating the pre-meal blessing, perhaps a nearby patron may be thinking, I need to be doing that as well.

Matthew 14:27 'But Jesus immediately said to them: "Take courage! It is I. Don't be afraid."'

Acts 4:13 'When they saw the courage of Peter and John and realized that they were unschooled, ordinary men, they were astonished and they took note that these men had been with Jesus.'

Acts 23:11 'The following night the Lord stood near Paul and said, 'Take courage. As you have testified about me in Jerusalem, so you must also testify in Rome.'

1 Corinthians 16:13 'Be on your guard; stand firm in the faith; be men of courage; be strong.'

Hebrews 3:6 'But Christ is faithful as a son over God's house. And we are his house, if we hold on to our courage and the hope of which we boast.'

1 Chronicles 28:20 'David also said to Solomon his son, "Be strong and courageous, and do the work. Do not be afraid or discouraged, for the Lord God is with you."'

I was particularly fond of these passages as each one depicted a call from Jesus to 'take courage,' be defenders of the Lord your God or made it known to us that; 'the Lord God is with you.'

So like John Wayne, 'saddle up in the name of courage,' pack your Bible in your saddle bag, and invite the Lord to ride along with you. You'll both be glad you did.

I'm Completely Stressed Out!
There are so many events in today's world that can easily upset us—April 15th, political news, unplanned large bills, weather damage to our homes,

the in-laws are on their way to your home for two weeks, and the list can go on and on. Now for the moment of truth: Have you ever realized that most of everything that upsets us has absolutely no eternal significance! Who knew?

That being said, why then do we plug into life's resounding dilemmas and all the associated nonsense that goes along with it, when we know that we are about to get cranked? While I'm no physician, I do believe that every time we get upset, the stress factor has to somewhat diminish our overall longevity. Stress is by no means a healthy emotion, and I'm sure there is a medical website out there that can quantify the vast number of people that have succumbed to stress related situations.

Did you know that stress is another of the Evil One's ploys to move us away from Jesus? When we get mad or stressed out, what happens? We don't think or say rational things, we can lash out at people for no reason and we are prone to using some unsavory expletives. Does any of this sound Christian-like? Of course not, it's Satan at his best again, causing yet another stumble in our faith.

Unfortunately, in the heat of the moment, we do not stop to consider the protection of our spirituality; we're more concerned about the ugly issue at hand. Okay, so it's April 15th and we have to pay this year, we will survive and months later it's all forgotten. An unplanned bill arrives, yes, it's a frustrating moment but is the bill marked pay or die? Your home gets damaged by a storm, okay, at least you have a home to repair, thank the Lord that the storm didn't completely take away your house. You'll notice I'm skipping the in-law scenario, that one always gets me in trouble. LOL.

I have a friend that is a huge football fan, but it's hard for him to watch a game that his team is playing in because the pressure associated with the fact that his team may lose becomes far too difficult for him to handle. I'm a sports fan and I have my favorite teams, but when I watch a game, I want to enjoy the game. Win, lose, or draw, it's always fun when you can walk away saying, 'Wow, that was a great game.' Some sports fanatics will openly admit that the games they most enjoy are the games their team is not participating in.

My youngest daughter, Breanna, lived and breathed soccer and my wife, Cathy, and I would attend every game as dutiful parents. I'll never forget one particular game as long as I live. One of my daughter's teammates was the daughter of a very talented and well-known basketball star. At halftime, her parents were screaming at her in front of the entire bleacher section because she didn't score a goal. I guess they felt she wasn't upholding the star power of family tradition. My heart went out to this poor child who was in tears and I'm sure very embarrassed.

My favorite players and coaches are those that display a consistent modicum of control regardless of what may be happening or not happening on the field.

Okay, before I digress any further, the heart of the matter is 'God-centered control.' When God resides in your heart, when you are filled with the Holy Spirit, it's very difficult to be anything other than Christian like. Need help, just say to yourself; 'what would Jesus say and/or do'? You cannot profess to be a solid Christian and then act like an out of control maniac when things are not going your way. It is times like these when our spirituality should immediately take over and keep us firmly focused on God. Remember, a totally secure man does not to bring down others to build him up.

When Moses was denied entry into the Promised Land after leading countless thousands of Israelites for forty years in the desert, he had every right to be ticked off, yet his God-centered life allowed him to graciously accept the Lord's wishes. I believe he knew there was another Promised Land waiting for him.

Proverbs 30:33 'For as churning the milk produces butter, and as twisting the nose produces blood, so stirring up anger produces strife.'

Proverbs 29:11 'A fool gives full vent to his anger, but a wise man keeps himself under control.'

Proverbs 16:29 'A wise man's heart guides his mouth, and his lips promote instruction.'

Store this final tidbit into the chamber of your heart that's marked open in case of stress: 'Worry does not empty tomorrow of its difficulty, worry empties today of its strength and peace.'

So, get out and enjoy every moment and know that if God brings you to it, He will bring you through it. Stress is an emotion for amateurs, not spiritual warriors such as you.

Work, it's a Four-Letter Word

When we think of the word work, I'm pretty sure the first thing that comes to mind is our home away from home, that sweatshop where we toil a minimum of eight hours per day, a minimum of five days per week, for that piece of paper that's supposed to make it all worthwhile, the paycheck!

Work for some can be a very enjoyable experience and sadly for others it can sometimes be a miserable experience, and for those that fall into the 'miserable' category, I may have a solution for you.

We have our five-days-a-week hard hat or wool suit corporate job which provides a monetary reward. Then we have our seven-days-per-week job, spirituality. We should be in the Word daily, and at some point during the week, we should be trading in our hard hat for our spiritual hat. Let's take a look at the benefits of each. We can start and/or end each day with reading a few lines form our Bible, we can attend and/or lead a Sunday School class, we can volunteer at a shelter, there are numerous 'jobs' that are just waiting for someone with your skill set and your time and talent.

Five days per week: financial reward, food, clothing, entertainment, and a host of purchased items we really didn't need. No argument here, all these things are very important to our daily lives. Also no argument, all items in this category are temporary. You cannot take them with you and they are all on loan from our Lord and Savior. You may bring home the bacon but rest assured He will bring home your soul.

Seven days per week: heavenly reward, spiritual food, promised clothing that will never wear out, a great feeling of peace and love. What reward could ever top eternal salvation, what clothier could ever produce a garment equal to that woven by the Lord and who else can promise you an eternity of love. All items in this category are most definitely eternal.

When you work for the Lord, your inner Spirit starts brimming with peace, you'll feel it I promise. You can feel the warm glow of the Lord around and within you as you begin to help others less fortunate than yourself, or visit some folks in a nursing home or bring food to a food bank or collection station. On Sunday, attend church; perhaps you can fellowship with other Christians in your congregation and soak in a great sermon. This kind of you work is from the heart and not from the timecard.

Remember that warm glow you felt inside when you helped an elderly person across a busy intersection, that young lost child in the store that you comforted until the child was reunited with the parents? Now couple this with a good dollop of spirituality and see what happens. How about, 'Lord, may there always be someone to help this lady cross these busy streets.' When someone you knew was suffering, you asked, 'May I pray with you or for you?' How about the lost child? Your prayer was 'Lord, please calm her aching heart until we can locate the parents.' These are certainly all feel-good moments, but without sincere spirituality, they all boil down to 'It's all about me' and for the accolades to follow. The only reward we should keep our eye on is the reward in heaven, because down here we are just doing the work that the Lord has set in front of us.

Okay, I promised you that I had a solution for your five-day miseries. While you may not have realized it at the time, all the sincere work you have been doing for the Lord, reading your Bible as often as you can, if only for a few moments each day, and offering prayers for direction in your life, just washed away an ocean of misery and now you walk around with a spiritual glow about you. The five-day job is not that awful any longer, because now you have been looking for the good things in the job and not what you perceive to be bad. And guess what, the new you may very well be contagious, seeing your transformation will most certainly influence others who want happiness and salvation. Who said things couldn't change? Who knows, you might even wind up saying grace in the lunchroom!

I know you have heard the saying 'Life is short, so make the best of it.' Unless we've won the lottery or inherited an obscene amount of money, we all have to work, so why not make it a positive experience, a partnership between you and the Lord. Start tomorrow with a promise, I'm going to find two really neat things about my job and then I'm going to thank the Lord for being my co-worker. Shake off the despair you once felt for your work environment and replace it with the knowledge that if the Lord has brought you to it, He will guide and protect you through it. Really and truly I tell you, in truth and in biblical fact; we all work for a higher power than the suit on the twenty-fifth floor.

Colossians 3:23–24 'Whatever you do, work at it with all your heart, as working for the Lord, not for men, since you know that you will receive an inheritance from the Lord as a reward. It is the Lord Christ you are serving.

1 Corinthians 3:9 'For we are God's fellow workers, you are God's field, God's building.

Hebrews 6:10 'God is not unjust; he will not forget your work and the love you have shown him as you have helped his people and continue to help them.'

Use It or Lose It

You may have guessed by now that I enjoy writing, especially these spiritual missives and if I do say so myself, I give it my best and I hope I'm providing a ray of Son light to some of my readers.

During the past three months, I have been actively involved in leading a Sunday school program entitled 'The Story.' The Story is His Story, our Story, and it truly is a wonderful trip through the Bible. Many of you have heard me relate to the fact that when your spiritual meter rises keep a close eye over your shoulder for Satan, he truly hates it when you're on target with the Lord's work.

Recently, my nemesis Satan has stepped up his satanically infused opposition in my life, creating roadblocks and filling my available time with nonsense to keep me away from the keyboard and I'm embarrassed to say that he did have a few minor victories here.

Knowing my struggle with time management, a very smart lady, whom I'll call Cathy, my very smart wife, said to me, 'The Lord gave you the gift of writing, and if you do not get back to writing, He may take that gift away and give it to someone else who will use it.' Wow, those few but to-the-point words struck a chord deep in my heart and soul, shouting, 'Gary, ignore the nonsense and foolishness that Satan has placed in your path, pray for better time management, and pray for the Lord to keep your eyes on His goal, so get back to doing what you love; writing.'

We all have busy lives and it is easy to get sidetracked from time to time, but left unchecked, before you know it your thinking to yourself, Wow, where did all that time go. Each of us know what our gifts are, volunteering within the church or community, mentoring some, being a prayer warrior, writing, leading, or teaching or whatever you have been blessed with and called upon by the Lord to accomplish.

So, my friends, if you have found like myself, some valuable time has slipped away, recharge those spiritual batteries, go to the Lord for protection and direction, and get back to serving with singleness and gladness of heart, those things you do so well in the eyes of your Heavenly Father, He will love to say welcome back my child, I have missed you.

An excellent example of someone who lost sight of his blessings comes out of the Old Testament, our friend Solomon. You may recall that he was offered a wish by the Lord and his wish was not 'more wishes,' not for 'riches,' he simply wanted wisdom. Our Heavenly Father was pleased with his desire and blessed him with wisdom and understanding that still transcends all the ages. Solomon's wisdom was so great that people traveled from across the globe to learn from his wisdom and hear firsthand the pearls of wisdom he uttered consistently on all facets of life. If you want a sample of his wisdom—which by the way, applies today as much as it did when it was first written—open your Bible to Proverbs and you will be amazed. Now, guess who could not stand it that someone was spreading truth and fairness and gathering throngs of people to listen and accept these teaching as a way of life. You're right it was Satan, who flooded Solomon's life with many women, over 700 Royal Wives and over 300 concubines, distracting him away from his blessing of wisdom and ultimately away from his Lord by falling prey to many of the foreign gods the women of his life brought into his heart, mind, and boudoir. A great gift suffered an even greater fall; another victory for Satan, as he distracted Solomon from his gift that led him along the path of spiritual destruction.

Proverbs 10:4 'Lazy hands make a man poor, but diligent hands bring wealth.'

Romans 12:7–8 'If it is serving, let him serve; if it is teaching, let him teach, if it is encouraging, let him encourage, if it is contributing to the needs of others, let him give generously, if it is leadership, let him govern diligently, if it is showing mercy, let him do it cheerfully.'

The above Romans passage truly pulls together the entire premise of our responsibilities and covers all aspects of our gifts. Each of us has been blessed with specific talents and we are required to use those talents or for sure they will wither away. So, as we opened this missive, 'Use it or Lose It' the choice is yours, but remember who will claim victory on any and all unused and tarnished talents.

Spiritual couch potatoes may end up in the deep fryer.

Leave the Door Open . . .

Words spoken in anger can have devastating effects on those in the line of fire, and unfortunately, since this is not Oz, the directive 'Pay no attention to the man behind the curtain,' not only failed to work in the movie, it's even less effective in real-life scenarios.

If you ever ask my wife, Cathy, what is one of her most favorite things to do, she would immediately tell you, 'That's easy, it's Chapel,' as she loves teaching the school children about God. On one occasion, she was charged with the topic of how angry words, once spewed out, can never be taken back. She invited two children to come forward from their pews and handed them each a tube of toothpaste. She had two plastic sheets on the floor and challenged both students to get as much toothpaste out of the tubes as they could. Both children squeezed their little hearts out and at the end there was little if any toothpaste left in the tubes. Both children were quite proud of how well they did in emptying their respective tubes. After acknowledging what a terrific job they did, she then directed them to put all the toothpaste back into the tubes. After a quizzical pause, they simultaneously answered her, 'Mrs. Villani, that's impossible, we can't put the toothpaste back into the tubes.' She then lovingly acknowledged that impossibility and proceeded to tell the children it is the same with harsh words, like the toothpaste, once the words have been spoken, they cannot be taken back or put back.

I would venture to guess that verbal arguments have caused more discontent among people than any other combatant interchange. The deadly war of words almost always leads to a permanent damage of relationships, because we argue to win. If someone hurts us, we instinctively want to return the favor of hurt.

2 Timothy 2:23–24 'Don't have anything to do with foolish and stupid arguments, because you know they produce quarrels. And the Lord's servant must not quarrel; instead, he must be kind to everyone, able to teach, not resentful.'

How many times after a reconcilable argument have we uttered the words; 'I'm so sorry, it was stupid argument.' And better yet, how many times have we said, 'I can't even remember what we were arguing about.' What is it that makes us go for the jugular vein when we enter into an argument? We're not mean by nature, so what makes us turn into this ugly carnivore that thirsts to win at any cost?

While in a discussion on the pitfalls of arguments, someone said to me, 'Why can't we just leave the door open?' They went on to say that whenever we find ourselves being drawn into an ensuing argument, first try to avoid the argument through early recognition that the majority of all arguments usually end in a lose-lose scenario. So, if we really need to put our two cents into an argument, why can't we simply 'leave the door open,' leave a safe exit to graciously withdraw from the interchange, even if it means the other person feels they have clearly dominated the war or words. If you back yourself into a corner during an argument, you allow Satan to take over your mind and heart and he is only interested in one thing, win at all cost, no matter how ugly it may get, beat the other person into submission. Chalk one up for the dark side.

I had an aunt and uncle that unfortunately entered into a horrible argument, and it still hurts me to this day to say that it caused a rift between them that lasted over twenty-five years. Not one word was ever exchanged between the two of them right up until their deaths. How very sad for them both and for those who were caught in the middle. I asked my mom one day, what could have been so important that it would end in hate and tragically, not one relative could recall what the issue was that drove a spike between the two. Why couldn't either one of them just leave the door open? I loved both but found myself avoiding them for fear that one of them would think I was taking sides. End result: Shame on me and shame on my youthful ignorance.

Sarcastically, I could ask, 'Are their Olympic medals awarded for the most hurtful argument?' And if you feel you may have some hanging in your closet, please consult your Lord for guidance on recycling the medals for love and forgiveness. Trust me, you do not want to go down the path my aunt and uncle chose.

I truly believe, and you may feel the same, that most arguments have absolutely no earthly or spiritual significance whatsoever, so ask yourself that simple little phrase that was on so many wrist bands that we wore: 'I'm about to enter into an argument, what would Jesus do?' And if you find yourself caught up in the moment and drawn into an argument, offer a prayer to the Lord for a safe exit; He knows your heart and it is good.

I have a thought. Why not channel the energy we would have spent into trying to beat someone down into a spiritual event where we are trying to lift someone up? What is the greatest commandment? 'Love thy Neighbor'!

I wonder how arguments would go if the combatants had to get on their knees before exchanging hurtful barbs.

New Social Disease on the Rise

Brothers, Sisters, and Friends everywhere, please be cautiously aware of a new social disease growing daily in our communities and perhaps even in our homes. This disorder, when left unattended, could reach epic proportions and unfortunately it hasn't even remotely piqued the interest of the Surgeon General of the United States.

This new disease has been appropriately dubbed the 'ation' disease (pronounced 'a shun') and is nondiscriminatory to all those it will attack. Let me give you a brief explanation of the symptoms in the hope that should you become infected, you will be able to take preventive measures (prayer) before it completely consumes you and perhaps even those around you.

The first symptom is easily recognized, it's called . . . **'Procrastination.'**
The next symptom has always been tried and true. . . . **'Justification'**
Once these take hold, you're a prime candidate for . . . **'Non–Creation'**
Finally, the dreaded and most vicious blow is delivered . . . **'Stagnation'**

Let me explain how this works.

Procrastination—You're mentally struggling with the knowledge that an old friend has become ill and what if anything should you or could you do. You really care about Friendly Freddy, but after all, he is retired and unlike yourself, he has significantly more time on his hands than you do. Your life on the other hand is extremely busy, packed to the hilt and you barely have time for your own family, so how could you possibly take on or find time for one more life event to participate in.

Justification- Freddy has lots of friends and family, why aren't they doing something to help; I can barely support my own needs. I also heard that he has a very lucrative retirement plan.

Non-Creation—I've decided that I'm going to help my friend . . . the first chance I get. First chances have great intentions but are typically as elusive as time itself and after an all too long hiatus; they become a distant blur on the radar screen of your life. If I may be blunt, absolutely nothing happens.

Stagnation—Months later you're talking to mutual friends and the question arises; 'Hey, whatever happened to our old friend Freddy, I've heard he was quite sick and his prognosis did not sound very positive. Next someone else adds what we never want to hear; oh, didn't you hear, Freddy . . . You can finish this story however you wish.

What happens next is disease transference. We catch the 'shoulda, coulda, woulda' malady. I should have sent flowers. I could have stopped at the hospital on my way home, if only just for a few minutes. I would have come to see him sooner if I knew how sick he really was. Unfortunately, all too often, we are left to carry the burden of a self-professed prophesy; 'I'm a good person, I really wanted to be there for my friend, time just got away from me.'

Sometimes a compassionate thought or feeling can be influenced by obligations we self-create, such as 'what if I'm asked for financial assistance' or 'will Freddy expect to see me on a regular basis until he recovers.' Care to guess who is putting those little gems in your head?

I can't help but wonder if the mental anguish we just self-inflicted upon ourselves could have been easily avoided by the simple act of sitting down and writing our dear friend a note wishing him a speedy recovery and letting him know that he was in our thoughts and our prayers. I have a suspicion that a note of this nature would have meant the world to Freddy, as he strikes me as a guy who truly cares about his friends and their wellbeing.

Ephesians 4:32 'Be kind and compassionate to one another.'

1 Peter 3:8 'Finally, all of you, live in harmony with one another, be sympathetic, be compassionate and humble . . . because to this you were called so that you may inherit a blessing'

Colossians 3:17 'And whatever you do, whether in word or deed, do it all in the name of the Lord Jesus, giving thanks to God the Father through him.'

However, fear not, my friends, as dreadful and debilitating as this disease may have seemed, through the grace of God there is a cure and it's called prayer. That Bible you own, the one that is sitting close at hand, it is filled with many wonderful prescriptions prepared especially for you by your Lord and Savior. Welcome back to Spiritual Wellness and cast the 'Ation' disease in the trash can where it belongs.

P.S. Freddy is doing much better now; he had the 'Great Physician' by his side throughout his illness.

So What's the Problem?

Someone once told me that at the heart of every problem, there is a problem of the heart. If we subscribe to this theory, then we must subscribe to the following account. When it becomes time for Jesus to measure our worth, I don't believe He will put His tape measure around our wallets, our checkbooks, or our heads. I honestly believe He will put the tape around our hearts.

Throughout time we have written songs of the heart, we've heard of heart ache and heart break and we have been led to believe that some folks just plain don't have a heart. Really, what's the big deal about hearts anyway? They pump blood throughout our bodies which in turn enables us to survive and it's a simple matter of life support. After all, the heart is just a human organ, it doesn't have a brain, it can't reason, it just pumps away day after day. A heart doesn't even have a soul or feelings . . . or does it?

Let's take a moment to look at a few heart-related issues. When we experience heartache, does that mean our heart is actually experiencing pain or does this mass of muscle somehow know something has upset our inner peace? What about heartbreak; we know our heart doesn't actually break, so why do we use this analogy? Could it somehow be that our hearts know when we are in distress? Keeping with our journey into the heart of things, why do we use the symbol of a heart to express our love? Are we giving way too much credit to this phenomenon of the heart, or is there really something there?

I believe the heart is one of God's greatest gifts. And yes, the brain is good as well, it allows us to reason, achieve complex solutions to problems, and recall eons of data, and it may even get you the secret recipe to Colonel Sanders' chicken, but the one thing it lacks is a sense of feeling. Our brains are like computers; they can instantaneously tabulate numbers, dig deep into history data banks for an infinite number of inquiries, but when was the last time you saw the response on your computer screen that said, 'Thank you for using me today, it was great serving you and by the way, I love you'?

While the Lord has blessed us with vital organs that enable us to get physically and emotionally through each day, we need to look beyond the physically apparent. The Lord also blessed us with a 'soul and spirit,' which supersedes the physical and emotional ties we routinely assign to the organ we call a heart. Spiritual heart and soul are the peanut butter and jelly of heaven. Now, who hasn't grown up on PB and J?

A spirit-filled heart has many chambers; in some of the chambers we lock away the loving memories of friends and family lost, in another chamber resides the Holy Spirit, and yet in other chambers we store the treasures of love. A spiritually filled, heartfelt love is about as close as we will ever come to an agape love until we join or Savior in our heavenly home.

Throughout the pages of our Bibles we see the heart in action. Moses led the Israelites for 40 years in the desert, which took a lot of heart. The Christian hater and persecutor Saul went from heartless to a heart filled with love for Jesus, the disciples left their families and their lives to follow Jesus, which took miles of heart. In each incident, they followed their hearts not their minds.

Matthew 5:8 'Blessed are the pure in heart, for they will see God.'

Jeremiah 24:7 'I will give them a heart to know me, that I am the Lord. They will be my people and I will be their God, for they will return to me with all their heart.'

1 Samuel 16:7 'But the Lord said to Samuel, 'Do not consider his appearance of his height, for I have rejected him. The Lord does not look at the things man looks at. Man looks at the outward appearance, but the Lord looks at the heart.'

By now I hope you have seen that and that you believe that our Lord speaks to us through the heart, a place where we share our love for one another, a place of honor and humility. The world can taint our brain with nonsense, but a spirit-filled heart will remain true and faithful.

Some folks say that the depravity of man begins in the heart. Sin begins unseen, but in the end, it is obvious to everybody. Conversely, a spirit-filled heart that feeds off the 'Word' and does not feast on worldly sustenance. A spirit-filled heart is eternal; a worldly heart lives for the moment. If you feel that warm glow in your heart may be dimming a little and you may need some spiritual repair, call upon the best in the business, Jesus. I'm pretty sure that before you can say 'Thank you, Jesus,' after a few minutes of prayerful meditation, that warm and loving glow will return to your heart. Remember, if home is where the heart is, then the heart is where Jesus is. Please keep the welcome mat to your heart visible, the doors of your heart open and invite the Lord to reside within you.

I opened this missive referring to a problem of the heart and now I will add the second part to that statement. Are there any doors or chambers in your heart that have not been opened? Unless your heart changes, your character and your conduct will not change. You can quickly and easily determine where your heart is by asking yourself the following question, When God dwells in your heart, does He feel at home?

Misguided Kudos

Do you suppose and I do not mean maliciously or intentionally, we can give our thanks and credit to the wrong benefactor?

Let's see if any of these little pearls of wisdom ring a bell.

- I always wake up before the alarm, I have an internal clock.
- Something told me I shouldn't have done that.
- My ESP always keeps me on track; I think it runs in our family.
- Mary's premonitions are always right on target, she's awesome.
- Bill never gets lost, it's like he has a built in GPS

While it's nice to think we possess these wonderful traits and we may even believe they have been handed down from generations past and perhaps some of us actually believe we are gifted beyond our Internal Ego System. But wait, do you think there just may be another answer?

Personally, I do not possess any of the super traits listed above; however, I have experienced many of them over the years. No, I'm not trying to confuse you, it's simply my belief that the spiritual gift that has kept me from many random and dumb acts and the Lord knows I've made my share, mostly due to my lack of consistent listening skills, is the one who unconditionally loves me and resides within me always, the Holy Spirit.

When I awake before the alarm, instead of applauding and feeding my self-imposed wonderfulness, I think I need to be shooting a quick arrow up saying 'Thank you, Lord for the gift of the Spirit who watches over me.' Personally, I also need to add, 'Lord, if my spirit comes to you asking for a change of venue, please quickly tug on my heart strings and help me to appreciate His presence within me.'

It so easy to give credit to made-up entities. I mean really, do you know of anyone who has swallowed a clock? Do you know a Mary whose premonitions are always eerily correct? If so, let's talk with her before we buy the next super Lotto ticket. My absolute favorite, and I know many of us have muttered this more than once in our lives, 'Something told me I shouldn't have done that.' People, it's not a something, it's not magical, it's not something cooked up in the laboratory at Hogwarts by our friends Harry, Ronald, and Herminie; it's the Holy Spirit, the Beautiful and Loving gift from God. Say Thank You! Lord!

We are all familiar with the two angels sitting on our shoulders, one offering good and the other offering misguided advice. Do you really believe there are two little angelic and not so angelic little people sitting on your shoulders or are we once again experiencing the love and protection of the spirit?

Some folks may be thinking, 'Hey Gary, wait just a darn minute, if what you're saying is true, then why am I always either in trouble or making wrong decisions?' Great question, and I am *Very* familiar with the reason why. It's because like me, we don't always listen to our inner spirit,

240

but rather we become mislead by what we think is the popular decision or an internal desire that sometimes borders on insatiable. To put in other words, been there, done that and I truly do not want any more T-sheets to remind me that I put personal desire over a righteous act.

Because we are human, we need to ensure we are feeding the spirit within us on a very regular basis. Read your Bible, attend a Sunday school class and offer prayers for direction. Why do we need to do this, it's because we not only 'leak' but as the Disciple Matthew tells us:

Matthew 26:41 'The spirit is willing but the body is weak.'

Ephesians 1:13–14 'And you also included in Christ, when you heard the word of truth, the gospel of your salvation. Having believed, you were marked in him with a seal, the promised Holy Spirit, who is a deposit guaranteeing our inheritance, until the redemption of those who are God's possession—to the praise of His glory.'

Romans 8:26 'In the same way, the spirit helps us in our weakness. We do not know what we ought to pray for, but the Spirit Himself intercedes for us with groans that words cannot express.'

So, give your thanks to where it belongs, aim those praises of thanksgiving upward and thank your Heavenly Father for the incredible gift of the Holy Spirit. And by the way, the Spirit was not a temporary gift; it was an eternal gift, one that is with you 24/7/365. Who else can make that claim, that guarantee?

So once again I say . . . .Thank Him for the Gift of the Spirit and stop giving secular accolades to made up figments of an over active imagination and keep those arrows aimed high, you'll be glad you did.

Hallelujah and Thanks Be to God. Amen, My Brothers and Sisters in Christ.

Don't Mess With God's Kids
Once again, the Nichols family has provided me with another wonderful pearl of wisdom. Several months ago, my friend Willie Nichols related to me, 'People should learn not to mess with God's children.' Well, that

thought remained with me and on my heart, so now it's time to put this pearl to paper.

Throughout biblical history there are numerous stories whereby the Lord has protected His people from enemies and warring factions determined to remove God's people from the face of the earth.

When Moses was leading the Israelites from captivity in Egypt, the Pharaoh had a change of heart and led his army out after the fleeing Israelites with one goal in mind, kill every last one of them. God parted the waters of a sea as an escape route for his people and when the Pharaohs army pursued them, they became the casualty of war; the entire army was swallowed up by the returning sea walls. Don't mess with God's kids!

During the forty-year exodus of the Israelites to the Promised Land, numerous foreign lands had to be traversed and the owners of these properties sent armies out to defend their homelands. While seemingly always dramatically outnumbered, the Lord always blessed his chosen people with stunning victories. Don't mess with God's kids!

Joshua 24:17 'It was the Lord our God himself who brought us and our fathers up out of Egypt, from the land of slavery, and performed those great signs before our eyes. He protected us on our entire journey and among all the nations through which we travelled.'

When three young men of God, Shadrach, Meshach and Abednego, men who were spiritually strong indeed but not physically strong enough to take on a king's guard for refusing to praise King Nebuchadnezzar over the God of Israel, the King had the men thrown into a fiery furnace. The ensuing flames were so hot merely standing near the furnace would cause items to melt from the heat emanating from this massive inferno. To the King's dismay, after sending the young men to their death, he witnessed them walking around within the blazing furnace, completely unscathed by the ferocious flames. Don't mess with God's kids!

Psalm 41:1–2 'The Lord is He who has regard for the weak; the Lord delivers him in time of trouble. The Lord will protect him and preserve his life; he will bless him in the land and not surrender him to his foes.'

While there are numerous similar events throughout the Bible, the point should be very clear; God loves and protects His children. Thanks be to God!

Now that it's very clear God protects His kids, what then, if any, are our responsibilities here on earth to assist God in the protection of His children? Our Lord has tasked each of us with the responsibility to 'raise up the children of God' and to protect those who cannot protect themselves. We accomplish this by ensuring several things; one that they are spiritually strong and grounded in the Word and secondly by instilling in one another that a spiritual journey is not a solo event, one must always bring others with them.

Okay, so how do we go about this task? Pull out your spiritual tool box and if you do not own one, it may be time to create one. To be successful, you must ensure your toolbox contains the following;

Humility: We are all equal in God's eyes, no one is better that the other. Treat everyone with respect and dignity. No one stands as tall as when they stoop to either help a child or fellow human being in need.

A Bible: The Word of God contains all that one will ever need to know in serving and pleasing the Lord. It is the basic instructions of life, the one book whereby the author is always with you on every page, from beginning to end.

Faith: All things are possible when one has an abiding faith in God. Faith does not believe that God can, it knows that God will. Faith begins in the heart and directs the mind in all matters. Faith looks beyond all obstacles.

Love: Love is the strongest of all gifts, love your neighbor, love your enemies, and turn from hatred to understanding and forgiveness.

Hope: There is always hope for every event or situation, it simply comes down to how our collective hearts wish to view, see, and interpret what is present before us. Remember, there are only two possible views to any life event, yours and the world's. Choose wisely.

Charity: Share the gifts you have been blessed with as he who dies with the most 'stuff' will not guarantee you a seat at the table. Everything we own is on loan, it is a gift from God and He expects us of us to share the abundance He has blessed us with.

Example: Most people will take your example far more seriously than your word. Guard against falling into the trap 'do as I say, not as I do.'

Okay, our toolboxes are equipped with everything we need, but there is still one very important element remaining and that is you. If your spirit is not willing, if your heart does not believe in what you are about to do, or you feel compelled or forced into this path, you might want to consider putting the toolbox back on the shelf. However, before you do, may I offer something that will definitely remedy this feeling, 'prayer'? Find a quiet spot, get down on your knees and go to your Lord and Savior and ask for guidance, strength of conviction and the will to be a good and faithful servant. I can pretty much guarantee that after a good heart to heart with your Heavenly Father; you will be amazed about your new direction and focus in your life.

So, now pick up that toolbox, don the full armor of God, feel the excitement of the Holy Spirit within you and hit that spiritual trail, both you and the Lord will be glad you did.

It was the Christian Thing to Do!
Sometimes we can get so caught up in the issue at hand and our own agenda that we can step on our Christianity.

Recently, I led myself to believe that I uncovered a scam cleverly designed to get myself and a few of my neighbors to switch from our existing exterminating company to a competitor's company. Actually, it was my wife that figured it out twenty-four hours before I did, but I was there for the actual ruse so I sort of took credit. I became so involved into the alleged scam that my collective thoughts were on the loyalty to my existing service company and not much else.

Well, now the embarrassing part of the story. First, a little background information. Friday afternoon, a young man came to my door wearing the ID badge of our current exterminating company and asked if I was happy with the pricing structure of the service we receive. He then asked what was I currently paying. I provided the information, and he stated he would be back tomorrow if he could lower the cost. I called my wife who immediately said, 'Why do you think our company would hire someone to walk around asking these questions? They have our phone contact.' Hmmmm? Well, sure enough, a young man shows up the next day wearing the ID badge of a different exterminating company and offered me a lower price for his service; ironically, it was just a few dollars less than my existing contract. After making sure the young man at out front door, whom I immediately tagged as the perpetrator, knew that I was fully satisfied with my current service provider, I had a pretty good idea on what was going on. I then proceeded to boldly and proudly announce that I was very content with our existing service and was not interested in switching companies. Score one for my super sleuthing abilities. How dare they use a false ID badge to extract information from me! I should add at this juncture, how dumb on my part to divulge the information to begin with.

The young man politely said fine and then stated that he has been walking around all day and wanted to know if he could use our bathroom. I am ashamed to say that I told him that the bathroom was occupied when indeed it was not. I took the position that he was a scammer and why should I allow someone who tried to pull a fast one on me use my bathroom. After about ten minutes of reflective guilt, I finally came to the realization that the young man was only doing what he was being paid to do. Next, putting all that aside, I was finally hit smack between my supposedly Christian eyes. The Spirit within me tugged at my spiritual heart strings proclaiming; 'Gary, I'm disappointed with you. You know the Christian thing to do was to allow the young man to use the bathroom.'

I tried to console my guilt feelings by thinking, 'My daughters and maybe even my wife would not be happy with me by letting a stranger into our home to use the bathroom,' but the Spirit within was spot on. I had the opportunity to reach out to one in need and I turned my back on the offer of relief. Adding insult to injury, my wife and daughters were disappointed in my poor judgment by not allowing the young man in. I became so conflicted by my careless Christianity that I immediately sat right down at my computer so that I might share my stumble of faith in the hope that it may help others in a similar situation.

I allowed Satan to stand next to me at my front door, directly adjacent to a plaque on the wall that says 'This house believes' while I became judge and jury, the young man was guilty as charged. Satan had me defending our existing exterminator as if I was a major stockholder.

Once I came to my Christian senses, I offered prayers to the Lord seeking forgiveness for my lacking hospitality to one in need and prayed that another house along his appointed route would be more gracious than I was.

Ephesians 4:32 'Be kind and compassionate to one another, forgiving each other, just as Christ God forgave you.'

Psalm 119:77 'Let your compassion come to me that I may live, for your law is my delight.'

2 Kings 13:23 'But the Lord was gracious to them and had compassion and showed concern for them because of his covenant with Abraham, Isaac and Jacob.'

1 Peter 3:8–9 'Finally, all of you, live in harmony with one another; be sympathetic. Love as brothers, be compassionate and humble. Do not repay evil with evil, or insult with insult, but with blessing, because to this you were called so that you may inherit a blessing.'

Chapter Eight:

Grace

Who is the Richest Person in the World?

The answer to that question is not Bill Gates or some oil-laden Sheik. The answer to that question is quite simple; it could very well be you and it doesn't matter if you're flipping burgers at Mickey D's or if you're the CEO of your own company.

Okay, so how is this possible, you ask? Once you realize and accept that all that you have, money, possessions and 'stuff' is a gift from the Grace of God and that it truly all belongs to Him, you will become the richest person in the world. When the Lord measures your wealth, He doesn't put his tape measure around your checkbook or the overabundance of stuff you have amassed, He puts the tape around your heart. Fort Knox has nothing compared to the amount of rich blessing and love that can be held in your heart.

'Easier said than done' is the thought going through your mind right now because we are all so attached to 'our stuff.' We need to take heed, though, 'stuff' is temporary, it can burn, it can break or it can simply wither away with time, but the richness of heaven is forever, forever eternal.

2 Corinthians 8:9 'For you know the grace of our Lord Jesus Christ, though He was rich, yet for your sakes He became poor, so that you, through His poverty *might become rich.*'

2 Corinthians 9:11 '*You will be made rich* in every way so that you can be generous on every occasion, and through us your generosity will result in thanksgiving to God.'

James 2:5 'Listen, my dear brothers. Has not God chosen those who are poor in the eyes of the world to be rich in faith and *to inherit the kingdom* He promised those who love Him'?

Still need more proof? Look around you—your spouse, your children, your church, and your Bible, all riches beyond our comprehension, but riches still the same. We are given riches we certainly did not richly deserve.

Let me paraphrase those three verses above one more time. '*So that you might become rich,*' '*You will be made rich,*' and '*Inherit the Kingdom,*'

The Lord said it, I believe it and that's enough for me. Amen!

P.S. The next time you're on your knees in prayer, remember to thank Him for making you the richest person in the world because you're going to inherit a kingdom. How cool is that!

Outlook versus Up Look

Webster defines outlook as: 'The prospect for the future.'

The Bible defines up look as: 'Keeping your focus consistently on the Lord.'

It is so easy to get these two basic functions confused. We have, on one hand, the earthly outlook. What's the market going to do? Should I save for the future or should I spend it all now? He's a cheery person, he must have a great outlook on life, and so it goes on. On the other hand, we have our spiritual up look, our knowledge in the fact that our future is undeniably tied to our Lord and Savior. Our spiritual focus must always be directed to Jesus, He is our undeniable guarantee of eternity, a prepaid ticket into our heavenly home.

I love the story where Jesus asks Peter to get out of the boat and walk across the water to the Lord. We all know what happens, he's doing just fine as long as his eyes are on the Lord, but the minute he looks down at the water, he sinks immediately into the abyss. I can't answer for most of you, but as for myself, I completely subscribe to this anomaly. It doesn't matter what task I have undertaken, one that is relatively easy or relatively hard, the minute I take my eyes and focus away from the Lord, I can guarantee with great certainty that somewhere along the line my project is apt to derail. Perhaps this can be considered another clear case of Outlook versus Up Look.

Speaking of deep waters and outlook, the Lord does not bring us into deep waters to drown us but rather to cleanse us and to strengthen our faith. So, I have changed my outlook on most things now and try to keep my focus in an upward direction as often as I can. It's certainly not easy with all the distractions out there, but it truly does bring great rewards.

Someone shared a story about a minister travelling back home from aboard, and it very accurately depicts a clear loss of heavenly focus.

A minister and his wife were returning to the USA after spending twenty-five years abroad spreading the Gospel of the Lord. Prior to boarding their ship home, they noticed a large military band and many dignitaries hovering about the main boarding area. The minister immediately thought the band was for him, celebrating his great work for the past twenty-five years. To his great sadness, he quickly learned that the band was for the President of the United States who was also a passenger on the same ship. Upon arriving home in the USA, another band and yet another disappointment: No one from the minister's church was there to welcome him home. Noticing his sadness, his wife suggested he go to church and talk with the Lord. A short time later the minister burst from the church as happy as if there were three military bands on the dock to welcome him home. He thanked his wife and said, 'I now know why no one was here to welcome us home; it's because we're not home yet.'

Whether the story is true or not, I think it's very evident what happened here; the minister took his eyes and focus briefly away from the Lord and directed it upon himself. The great work of the past twenty-five years was for God and His people, and like Peter's episode on the water, the minister had an all about me event moment instead of being grateful to God for the ability to do the work that he was called to do. It's one thing to accept kudos, and it is yet another to solicit them, especially on your own behalf.

We are human, and like the minister, we enjoy knowing that our work has been appreciated and recognized. When we have successfully completed the work God has set before us, whether we are aware of it at the time or not, I'm pretty sure the Lord is smiling down at us and saying; 'Well done, good and faithful servant.'

Revelation 19:11 'I saw Heaven standing open and there before me was a white horse, whose rider is called Faithful and True.'

Psalm 25:15 'My eyes are ever on the Lord, for only he will release my feet from the snare.'

Proverbs 3:7 'Do not be wise in your own eyes, fear the Lord and shun evil.'

Proverbs 17:24 'A discerning man keeps wisdom in view, but a fool's eyes wander to the ends of the earth.'

Lord, Is This a *Test*?

How many times have we either uttered or thought about that phrase? How do we respond? 'Lord, there is no way I can do this,' or my personal favorite, 'Lord, why me?'

I have a few thoughts on this subject that I would like to share.

- God does not bring us into deep water to drown us but rather to cleanse us, to help us grow in Him.
- God does not keep us from trials, He keeps us through trials.
- Choice not chance determines our destiny; today's trials are tomorrow's testimonials.
- A faith that cannot be tested is a faith that cannot be trusted.

- The Lord will strengthen those whose hearts are fully committed to Him.

Getting the message yet?

If God brings you to it . . .

He will bring you through it . . .

        Happy Moments   –   Praise God

        Difficult Moments   –   Seek God

        Quiet Moments   –   Worship God

        Painful Moments   –   Trust God

        Every Moment   –   Thank God

John 14:1 'Do not let your hearts be troubled, trust in God, trust also in Me.'

Psalm 9:9 'The Lord is a refuge for the oppressed, a stronghold in times of trouble.'

God will test us to bring out our best.

Satan will test us to bring out our worst.

Remember, even when you're down, the right direction is still up!

Momma or Papa, What's in a Name?

I truly never wanted to address the gender issue of God as I instinctively knew that whatever I attempted to say, I would wind up alienating fifty per-cent of my readership; yet having made that claim, my wife has suggested that I do indeed make the attempt. That point in itself should indicate to all that once again, I'm skating on a very thin layer of gender-infused ice. Even my dog, Heidi, who sits by my side for all my written entries, looked at me with that facial expression that needs no words, 'You're on your own here, dude,' as she gracefully pranced over to my wife's lap. Obviously even for me, who always seems to be the last to catch on to even the most obvious point, knew this was not a good sign.

God is God, and while I'm not completely foolish enough to tackle the gender issue in less than two pages of dialogue, I will acknowledge that God becomes who we need, when we need God. The admonition is not as confusing as it sounds. I believe God is genderless and becomes man or woman or friend based on what our need may be at that specific moment in time.

When we were children and perhaps even today, we go to our earthly mothers for one kind of support and our earthly Fathers for yet another. When we need the nurturing love of a mother figure, I believe God comes to us in a maternal fashion. When we need the strength and courage of a father figure, I believe that God comes to us as a paternal figure. Before I get myself in trouble here, ladies, I honestly believe (a man who lives with a wife, two daughters, and a female dog) that you are equally as strong as any man, but I'm speaking strictly from a Biblical point of view.

In an attempt to seek gender salvation here (and remember I said I really did not want to go here, knowing I would take on the wrath and indignation of men all around the world), God is, as I believe it, a unisex being, capable to being whatever gender is required at a specific point in time. Wow, there it is, I said it. So, what happens next, will I get global hate mail from some or kudos from others? Either way, it does not matter; I call the shots the way I see them.

Okay, so now that I have made this wild declaration about God, where do we go from here? Actually, we go nowhere. Every person is entitled to their own opinion and description of God. Look at how many ways television and movies have depicted Him over the years. Which brings us to the million-dollar question; does it really matter what the gender of our Lord is? Let me offer a small amount of help here . . . NO, it doesn't.

What we really need to be thankful for is that God is love.

To quote Steve Martin, here's a wild and crazy thought. The Old Testament was without a doubt, male-dominated, women were (sorry, girls) a necessary byproduct and needed to stay home to cook, clean, and make babies. Ooh, I'm going to pay for that one.

But wait, we're now in New Testament times and life has taken on a whole new direction. Women and Men are equal. Hopefully that gets me off the hook. (P.S. notice that I listed women first.)

How fortunate are we that we have a God who can be what we need to soothe our aching and broken hearts? A God that can relate to both men and women, a God that can offer the appropriate solace that truly can be gender specific.

Without attempting to be crass, men and women view certain events in a completely different manner. Most men come across as the bull in the china shop as opposed to most women who have a much gentler spirit and outlook. Most guys operate on the concept of shoot first and ask questions later but much to our chagrin, the majority of women want to know 'What was the underlying cause of the incident, so it will not happen again.' Sorry, guys, we can't argue with that theology.

Titus 3:9 'But avoid foolish controversies and genealogies and arguments and quarrels about the law, because these are unprofitable and useless.'

Genesis 1:2 'Now the earth was formless and empty, darkness was over the surface of the deep, and the Spirit of God was hovering over the waters.'

Our Lord and Savior is Omnipotent, a God who is all powerful, invincible, and supreme, so, knowing this, for what reason would we need to challenge and clarify the gender of God? Are we in some way challenging God's authority, audaciously claiming that one gender is better than another? Yes, Jesus came to our world from the holy trinity of God in the form of man, but since we know there is a trinity, can you or I safely and unequivocally make a gender claim? Careful, my friends, we are swimming in very dangerous waters, and as such, it's now time for me to swim to the safety of the shore.

It's the Ugliest of Words

Hate. It not only sounds ugly, but the mere inclusion of the word in any circumstance immediately congers up unwholesome thoughts and reeks of evil. Hatred can absolutely consume your thoughts, your actions, and your life. It is without a doubt, a relentless cancer in its pursuit of your spiritual soul and perhaps it may even attack your physical being as well.

What happens in life that can cause a rational human being to absolutely loathe something so deeply, they feel compelled to apply an evilness to the matter—hate.

Okay, I understand that there are different levels of dislike. Anyone who knows me can testify to the fact that I do not like beets, can't even be at the same table if they are present. Do I hate them? No, I simply prefer not to make them a part of my dinner fare. Have you ever found yourself saying, 'Let's not go to the ball game, I just *hate* all that traffic when it's time to leave.' No one really enjoys traffic, but do you really hate it? Come on people, it's only traffic. I seriously doubt your life will immediately be subjected to a violent tailspin because you had to spend another thirty minutes to get home. It may be a slight inconvenience, but does it seriously awaken hateful thoughts within your soul?

On a more serious note, someone has harmed or intends to harm a loved one. If indeed the unthinkable happens, the Evil One begins screaming in your ear, you want and need hateful revenge, demand it! This situation may be the hardest one you will ever address in your lifetime. Someone has taken a loved one away from you. Yes, it's easy to immediately slip into a world of hate, but that will only interfere with the healing process that is being extended to you by a loving Father who also shares your heartache. While you may feel that your world has almost ended, your Heavenly Fathers pain has doubled. Not only does He feel the pain of your loss, He also feels the pain and loss of the perpetrator; who while operating with obvious evil intentions is still a child of God. We must believe that God loves all His children and when one falls from grace, out of the fold, His greatest joy is when He can get a lost soul back home.

You may be thinking the same as I am at the moment: 'Sure, Gary, it's easy to say all this because you're not the one feeling the pain.' You are absolutely correct, and my hope and prayer is that if I'm ever in that place, Jesus will reach down into my aching soul, and give me the strength I need and bless me with a forgiving heart. Our hopes and prayers are that we may never get to this unpleasant place in life, but should it happen, always remember that Jesus is standing right next to you and there is a real chance that some of the tears being shed are His as well.

If you feel so inclined that you really need to hate something, there is an acceptable hate; you may and should hate evil, but just evil. Avoid as best you can, applying the word hate to the daily maladies and inconveniences that are simply a part of life as we know it on this big blue marble, our temporary home.

Psalm 97:10 'Let those who love the Lord Hate evil, for he guards the lives of his faithful ones and delivers them from the hand of evil.'

1 John2:9 'Anyone who claims to be in the light but hates his brother is still in the darkness.'

Romans 12:9 'Love must be sincere, hate what is evil; cling to what is good.'

Luke 6:27 'But I tell you who hear me; Love your enemies, do good to those who hate you.'

Leviticus 19:17–18 'Do not hate your brother in your heart. Rebuke your neighbor frankly so you will not share in his guilt. Do not seek revenge or bear a grudge against one of your people, but love your neighbor as yourself. I am the Lord.'

May the Peace of the Lord be Always with You.
What exactly is peace and where do you find it? Webster defines peace as 'a state of quiet or tranquility, calm quietness, repose and the absence of strife.'

Ask a group of folks what peace means, and you'll probably hear such things as: a remote island in the Caribbean, an empty nest, retirement from my insane job, soaking in a hot bath tub surrounded by scented candles and soft music, or a few minutes to myself completely away from everyone. This list could go on and on, but I think you get the picture.

All the explanations of peace above define peace as the 'world' sees and understands peace; a worldly view that fits comfortably into our hectic lives and offers us a safe haven from the trials and tribulations of Life, right?

Wrong, all those tranquil moments are only a 'temporary haven' and not a ticket into 'permanent heaven.' If you are having trouble finding peace, use this four-step plan to a guaranteed attainment of everlasting peace:

Step 1 – No Christ

Step 2 – No Peace

Step 3 – Know Christ

Step 4 – Know Peace

So, what is peace and where can we find it? You guessed it, in the Bible and developing a relationship with Jesus Christ. Get to know Him; He has so much He wants to share with you.

Proverbs 14:30 'A heart at peace gives life to the body.'

2 Thessalonians 3:16 'Now may the Lord of peace himself give you peace at all times.'

Romans 1:7 'Grace and Peace to you from God our father and from the Lord Jesus Christ.'

Remember that wildly hectic moment at work, everything was going down the tubes fast; panic was not only in the air, it was very contagious and everyone was losing their cool? Then out of the corner of your eye, you spot a colleague who is in complete control of his/her emotions, not even a bead of corporate sweat was dripping from his/her forehead. Your first thought was 'Wow, look at the person, how calm, cool and collected they are; I want some of whatever he/she has.' A peaceful soul is a contagious soul.

Guess what, they didn't get it from Daniel Webster's Book. Biblical Peace is the assurance that, in the presence of God, all will be well. Peace be with you!

Woe is Me

Poor me, nothing seems to go my way. I'm always tired, no one offers to help me at work or at home, the weather is terrible and everything I touch doesn't seem to work. Why me, Lord?

Any of the above sound familiar? You can't fib here, we are all guilty of complaining at one time or another and some more than others, right?

So here is my spiritual thought on complaining: When we complain, are we being ungrateful, we know better than God what is best for us? Sadly, sometimes we unknowingly or dare I say knowingly, believe we know what is best for us and fail to seek His guidance. When our best laid plans start to go south and any moment will burst into flames, we cannot blame God for any plans or actions that He has not been consulted on, and it's all on us.

What happens when we attempt problem resolution on our own, we usually have a 50/50 chance on the outcome right? Unfortunately, when we tally life's score cards and learn that in many of our decisions we were spot on, we begin to think and feel a dangerous and superior attitude; I am the master of handling disaster, just look at my track record. This is the entrance to the slippery slope; this is where we begin setting ourselves up for a huge fall, both worldly and spiritually. There is a grand old saying which I just love and use often: 'If God truly wanted to punish us, He would let us have our own way.' What is it about us that after a few victories we begin to think we are invincible? We are the best of the best and can adequately handle anything that life throws our way. Don't be shocked when the bottom of your plan falls off.

Yes, it's wonderful to be self-confident and very talented, but another quick question is required here. Exactly who do you think provided those esteemed talents that you hang your hat on? I sincerely hope your answer is God and not The University of the Wonderful. Learning institutions are necessary and an educational must for some; however, who do you think blessed you with the finances to attend this buttress of brilliance? Let me help again: God!

Tell me if you have ever heard something along these lines. 'Lord, I love the new Ford you blessed me with but I really wanted the Jaguar.' I'm betting He knew within a few short weeks I most probably would have killed myself while stretching the legs of that power machine. Lord, how come I never win the lottery; I've heard that some people have won it more than once. Lord I have repeatedly asked for a promotion and still nothing.

Complaining, Complaining, and Complaining. Thank goodness God does not tire of our relentless nonsense and still calls us His children.

My parents had a sign hanging in our basement back in New Jersey and the wisdom of that sign has remained with me forever. It read, 'I complained about having no shoes until I met a man who had no feet.'

In our defense, the media has quite a bit to do with our complaining. Every time you buy something, two weeks later there is a bigger and better mousetrap being offered and now a most recent purchase is bordering on being passé.

God has blessed us with so many gifts, and if we stopped to count them, trust me, we would never complain again. Need some thoughts; a home, a family, the ability to wake up each day, a career, sunrises and sunsets, food on our tables, transportation, clothing and if I continue this will turn into an encyclopedia of blessings.

My family and I spent several summer vacations as volunteers at a magical place called Give Kids the World Village, in Kissimmee, Florida, a haven of fun for Make a Wish candidates. The village hosts a Disney-like atmosphere for children who are dying of a terminal disease. Entrance to the village must be confirmed by a physician that the guest is suffering from a terminal illness. It only took a few short hours for our entire family to recognize the very positive attitude of the children and their parents. Talk about getting our socks jerked up in a hurry. Each of us quickly realized we did not have one single thing going on in our lives to complain about.

Someone once told me that everything we complain about has absolutely no eternal significance. That being the case, then why do we waste an inordinate amount of time complaining? Remember the last time you complained, what about the time before that? What about the complaints from a month ago? Can't even recall what they were, can you?

Thank your Heavenly Father for all the blessings of this life and when adversity hits, don't complain, accept it, learn from it, and move on. Besides, if you do this, people will stop running away from you when they see you coming. LOL.

Philippians 2:14–15 'Do everything without complaining or arguing, so that you may become blameless and pure children of God in a crooked and depraved generation in which you shine like the stars in the universe.'

Mark11:22–23 'Have faith in God, Jesus answered. I tell you the truth, if anyone says to this mountain, Go throw yourself into the sea and does not doubt in his heart but believes that what he says will happen, it will be done for him.'

Guts, Grace, and Glory

In life Christians will receive God's Grace; in death Christians will receive God's Glory! I think after a statement like that we most definitely need a Heartfelt Hallelujah.

If everything the Lord called on us to do was easy, I wonder how much we would learn from the experience and would there be any significant spiritual growth? Sometimes it takes 'GUTS' to step up to the spiritual plate. The acronym for the word 'guts' pretty much sums it all up: God Uplifts The Servant. God will always equip those He calls. We see this throughout the Bible, but most notably in the calling of the disciples and the power granted them through the Holy Spirit. Looking for another great example of 'guts,' open your Bibles to The Book of Acts and follow the disciple Paul. When you're finished, I'm sure you will feel the same as many others; no, I do not want to go on a vacation with Paul and I'm sure glad I live in the times of the New Testament. If every task or event in our lives were accomplished with little or no effort, I wonder what our sense of self-worth and our core values would be like. No victories to celebrate, no moments of triumph, no blessings to be felt, everything is simply taken for granted. Please do not be afraid to answer His call, reach deep down into your soul and summon the 'guts' and the Lord will provide.

Genesis 26:24 'Do not be afraid, for I am with you.'

2 Samuel 26:33 'It is God who arms me with strength and makes my way perfect.'

Psalm 73:26 'My flesh and my heart may fail, but God is the strength of my heart.'

We have all been blessed by our Lord with 'Grace.' Once again, an acronym explains it best: 'God's Reward at Christ's Expense.' When Jesus died on that tree, it wasn't long after He took his last breath, until the gift of 'grace' was bestowed upon God's children, all of humanity. The indwelling of the Holy Spirit came upon us and death no longer held its mortal grip on us. Thanks be to God! Through God's grace we have received many blessings—our spouses, our family and friends, all that we own, which by the way is just on loan, our jobs, our faith, our church, the food that sustains us, free will, and each and every breath we take. The list goes on and on, but as you can see, we are blessed through His grace. God's grace is a gift that should be embraced, treasured, applied and we should be ever thankful for this wonderful blessing. What makes this gift so special is the simple fact that we do not deserve it, we certainly did not earn it and it came to us through an incredible act of love? The next time you're in prayerful conversation with the Lord, remember to thank Him for the gift of grace.

Romans 3:24 'And are justified freely by His grace through the redemption that came by Christ Jesus.'

Romans 12:3 'For by the grace given me I say to every one of you: Do not think of yourself more highly that you ought, but rather think of yourself with sober judgment, in accordance with the measure of faith God had given you.'

Ephesians 3:7 'I became a servant of this gospel by the gift of God's grace given me through the working of his power.'

Glory be to the Father. Finishing with a final acronym, glory is 'God Loves Our Righteous Yearning.' Our desires should always focus on our Lord and Savior, the path to heaven, the way home provided to us by the Lord. Ponder if you will the fact that God wants and I'm sure yearns for every one of His children to come home and spend eternity at His side. When I think about His waiting up for me, it stirs the spiritual goose bumps within my soul. Wholesome earthly desires can be a good and a necessary staple in our lives, as long as they do not become obsessive or border on idolatry or prevent us from walking in the ways of the Lord. The end result of a fruitful Christian life has but one result, to dwell in the house of the Lord forever.

Psalm 26:8 'I love the house where you live O Lord, the place where your glory dwells.'

Psalm 108:5 'Be exalted, O God above the heavens and let your glory be over all the earth.'

John 14:2 'In my Father's house are many rooms; if it were not so, I would have told you. I am going there to prepare a place for you.'

The Lord has blessed us with many gifts, none of which we have either earned or deserve, yet His loving heart is bigger than our sinful nature. We know that the crucifixion of Christ removed deaths hold on us and then guaranteed an eternal existence within the heavenly home He has prepared for us. So, my brothers and sisters in Christ, rejoice in the knowledge that the Lord Christ is standing at the entrance gate to heaven and on your arrival, you will immediately recognize Him, He will be the one with the heartwarming smile and greeting that goes something like this: 'Welcome home, my child.'

In closing, I have chosen to paraphrase a line from my Sunday Church Service which proclaims; Walk in His ways, Delight in His will, to the honor and glory of His holy name. Amen.

P.S. The entrance fee to heaven is very affordable; just be clothed in the righteousness of God!

But It's such a Small Word

It's only three small letters long but it packs a hard spiritual punch and gets our shorts twisted in trouble more than we care to admit, but it's only three small letters: s-i-n.

Sin is a very interesting character flaw of Christians and Non-Christians alike. Why do we struggle so with sin? Perhaps it's because the word of God is like a spotlight; it reveals our sin, and let's face it, no one wants to look bad in front of fellow earthlings whether they are believers or not.

Although the word is very small, let's take a moment to dissect the effects of sin.

We truly are unique living organisms; we will always find an easier way, a better way, or a way out when the need arises. No one can be as creative as one in need. Here's a fairly common scenario; I am planning to tell a small white lie to my boss, it's only a small lie, it's not like I killed someone for goodness sakes.

So, what just happened above, a small lie to a boss, perhaps, but consider the following:

- It was a premeditated lie; the deception was planned long before it happened. (sin)
- The actual lie itself takes place. (sin)
- Anyone else in on the lie will now stumble because of your lie. (sin)
- A companion may be called upon to add credibility to the lie, there goes yet another lie. (sin)
- You may be called upon to repeat your transgression, so the lie lives on. (sin)
- And finally, we become a victim of the lie as well because we have just lied to ourselves thinking it's okay to tell small lies. (sin)

Didn't see that coming, did you? It all seemed so small and insignificant at the time.

Ah, the sliding scales of justice. As long as we classify the lie as a small white lie, we can live with that. Since we have failed to take into consideration that the lie was 'planned' or premeditated, which makes the lie more of a felony than a misdemeanor and that there are the others who were dragged into our deception, our small white lie has taken on a life of its own as it grows bigger and bigger. People, it's no longer a small lie, it's becoming a huge deception, a dark and ugly win for the Evil One and if we are honest with ourselves, it has to hit the bad side of our sliding scale. But will it, after all, we are still human and we need to believe that as long as we make little sins, life will be okay and we're pretty sure we will still get our ticket punched for heaven. The problem with this ideology is that if it were only one small sin and we sought forgiveness, yes, all would be good. However, one small sin leads to another and another and so it goes, down the slippery slope of evil.

I hate to cast aspersions on those who own a sliding scale of justice for sin, where the values placed on sin change according to the mood of the sinner, but here is a truth you must understand. Sin is not judged through the eyes of man; it is judged through the eyes of God. God alone decides judgment, no one else. Love and Judgment are the two sides of the same coin.

Here are a few sayings that should be committed to memory and called upon when sin is looming on the horizon.

- Man is not sinless but does sin less as he believes and trusts in Jesus.
- The Bible will keep you from sin or sin will keep you from the Bible.
- Some people run from the truth because it exposes their sin.,
- If we fail to trust God, Satan will bring out the worst in us.

The hard truth is that God does not have a sliding scale; in His eyes, sin is sin and that seems to justify why we find it necessary to possess a sliding scale. Maybe we should change the name from sliding scale to a 'feel better scale.' The truth of the matter is that if we sin, we need to seek forgiveness; we need to pray for direction and ask the Lord to protect you with the full armor of God. In case you miss His response, the armor can be found in your Bible, Ephesians 6, The Armor of God. My suggestion is that you make that armor part of your daily spiritual wardrobe. With Satan roaming around, we need all the protection we can get

John 8:34 'I tell you the truth, everyone who sins is a slave to sin.'

Psalm 119:113 'Direct my footsteps according to your word, let no sin rule over me.'

Proverbs 14:9 'Fools mock at making amends for sin, but goodwill is found among the upright.'

Romans 6:14 'For sin shall not be your master, because you are not under law but under grace.'

Okay, you're ready to go out and face the world head on. One final thought, discipline yourself so God won't have to do it for you.

2 Corinthians 13:14 'May the grace of the Lord Jesus Christ, and the love of God, and the fellowship of the Holy Spirit be with you all.'

God Bless!

When You're Having a Bad Day . . .

. . . think of your Friends and Family members, perhaps even those who are no longer with us, take in a sunrise or sunset, view the multitude of stars in the sky, the magnificent landscape around you and I'm pretty sure your day will get significantly better. Amen, Brothers and Sisters!

We humans are funny folks, we have a great tendency to major in the minor, we become self-absorbed over truly trivial issues. Need some proof;

'Oh my, I'm so old.' If you are old, don't complain about it; you have been blessed by the Lord, thank Him.

'I really hate getting up in the morning' Guess what, I'll bet there are many bedridden folks out there who dream of the day when they will be able to get out of their beds at any hour of the day. You may want to consider shooting an arrow of thanksgiving to the Lord that He has given you the power to get up every morning, so don't complain, thank Him for yet another day.

'I'm so bored, there's nothing to do.' I have an idea, how about reading the Bible? It's the only book you will ever read where the author is with you the entire time you're reading it and it will be as though you are sitting at His feet and being fed. Now tell me that doesn't give you spiritual goose bumps.

Okay, I think the point has been made; therefore, we need to look at everything that comes our way as either a blessing and/or a spiritual learning experience and we should rejoice in the blessing of these God given gifts. I know you're probably saying to yourself, 'This guy is off his rocker, he is saying that an unpleasant situation is a gift.' Absolutely I am!

Remember the time when someone in your circle of friends announced, 'Boy, am I in a pickle'? After listening to their sad lament, you announce, 'Hey, man, I was in that same pickle jar two years ago and I can offer some very helpful advice so you wouldn't have to go through what I did.' Your past dilemma just became someone's blessing. And quite frankly, life is too short to make all the mistakes yourself; we must rely on others to help us or to learn from.

When we run into a difficult situation, what typically happens? We seek solace and resolution from our Heavenly Father. Next, we learn to rely upon God, knowing that if He brought me to it, He will bring me through it. We offer up our prayers for guidance as we repent for our short comings and the faithful are rewarded as they emerge a much stronger servant of the Lord. Now, in addition to the resolution blessings from your life event, you have now learned how to minister to others who may be struggling with the same issues that brought turmoil into your world. Have you ever noticed that when you reflect back on the trials and tribulations of your life, and take a close look at the score card, you'll find that the blessings have far outweighed the problems? And even better, the insurmountable problems of the past are not that intimidating any longer.

I honestly believe the gift here, albeit disguised as a lesson, is simply that many a life that is marred by accident is truly being shaped by providence. Thank you, Jesus!

When we look back at some of the great Biblical Moments, we see the Lord's hand in directing Moses, Paul, Daniel, Ester, Jeremiah, and Ezra, just to name a few. Do you think that whenever these fine servants were in trouble, the Lord simply waved a wand and whoosh, life is good again? Had that been the case, there would have been nothing to be learned or gained from the experience, just another blessing that sadly went by the wayside along with a misdirected hearty pat on the back for us. Reread the names in this paragraph, do you see a pattern here? They all possess the same common denominator; they trusted in the belief that God was not the way out of trouble; God was the way to triumph through trouble.

Have you noticed that in today's society we can be quick to step up to the podium when life is good, and we love to revel in all the accolades being lavished on us? Conversely, when the news is not so good, forget about the podium, we cannot even be found within the building. Another round of blessings that will be missed by others because in our value system, we have determined what is and what is not a blessing. I sometimes feel that it is all about the perks and rewards, much of which we claim as our own personal achievement, with divine intervention playing an almost non-existent part. Some of us are fortunate enough take many sponsored business trips where we rack up those precious miles and then have the gall to seek praise and envy from those who do not fly as often. Yep, it took me a whole year of flying but I'm cashing in my miles and my wife and I are going to Hawaii and the best part is, it's not going to cost me a penny. I wonder if Fred Flyer here ever stopped to consider that on the day he was born, Jesus had already prepared him for the job and those miles were in his account long before Fred even got that job. Sorry to let the air out of his Executive Platinum Balloon, but perhaps it would have resonated significantly more on a spiritual level had old Fred shared the blessing rather than the hot air.

A wise man once shared with me a nugget of wisdom that still prevails today: When we peel back the onion of life, the reality of it all is that in the final analysis, most of everything that upsets us has absolutely no eternal significance.

One final note . . . Know It and Show It. Give all the glory to whom it belongs and be ever thankful for all the blessings of this life and don't be shy about sharing with others how much you have been blessed. Thank You Jesus!

Man's Best Friends

On more occasions than I can count, I recall hearing folks ask if their pets will make it to heaven. Now, what I'm about to say in these passages is completely my own personal feelings, and there is no scriptural evidence to refer to on this matter other than passages of love.

If you're a pet lover ,you will completely understand where I'm coming from on this matter, and if you're not a lover of animals, you'll probably be thinking that I have missed my last six therapy sessions and need immediate help, or if you're a hardcore evangelist, you're probably thinking an exorcism is in order for such blasphemy. Either way, that's okay.

Pets come in a wide variety of species, and most people's attitude toward their pets is equally as wide and varied. Some people feel they are simply a domesticated animal, some feel they are work animals used for hunting, bomb sniffing, and such. Finally, there are those people like my family and myself, who whole-heartedly believe our pets are loving members of our family unit.

I truly believe that when I get to heaven, my Lord and Savior will be standing there to welcome me and standing right beside Him, with their tails wagging with heavenly joy, will be Jazz and Shawna, two beautiful dogs, members of my family that have since passed. Now it's time to share why I believe this is so. As I'm typing away, my faithful companion and family member Heidi, an adorable lapdog, is sitting by my side, almost as if she's encouraging me to write.

We should all agree that our Lord loves us beyond our limited human understanding and comprehension, an agape love that is so great it is not only hard to explain but sometimes hard to believe, especially knowing we do not deserve such a love but are ever so grateful for it. He has repeatedly told us in the Bible that we will never fall from His grasp, a very comforting fact that in of itself should humble us. We should also all agree that the Lord looks at us not by our deeds or our outward appearance, but He sees us inwardly, through our hearts.

Knowing how very much our Lord loves us, I have to ask myself why He would give us the supreme joy of allowing us to take our pets into our homes and our hearts only as a temporary measure and when it's over, never to see them again. Not my Lord. It is my personal belief that my Lord, who is so loving and caring, will always take care of His faithful.

When I come home after a hard day at the office, Heidi, our little lap dog, has been patiently waiting at the front window for my arrival runs to me, tail wagging ever so joyfully, and as I walk through the door, proceeds to lovingly shower me with welcome home kisses. Now if I can only teach my wife, Cathy, that welcome home routine. Only kidding, I get kisses there as well.

If I'm sad, Heidi senses it and she will do everything in her power to cheer me up. She offers more kisses, gets her favorite toy so we can play or sometimes she will curl up against me, look at me with loving eyes that say, 'Daddy, I'm here if you need me.' This little maneuver of hers becomes especially endearing when I'm lying on the couch watching TV. She will jump up on the couch—yes, she's allowed—snuggle her head under my chin as she lies next to me as if to say, 'You can take a nap, I'll protect you while you're sleeping' What Heidi lacks in size, she has been compensated in love and devotion. This beautiful gift from God warms my heart every time I look at her. She provides countless hours of love and affection to our entire family and her whole reason for being seems to be nothing short of bringing us constant joy.

A final thought, and perhaps one of the most important qualities in your pets, especially dogs, is good old tried and true, unyielding, unequivocal, undeniable 'Loyalty.' They possess a love and loyalty that is completely untainted by the world; they don't have to think about being loyal because it's in their nature. As humans, we should only be so lucky to possess a loyalty that cannot be tempted or tampered with by anyone. Recently, I was watching the local evening news when a story broke that just tore at the strings of my heart. There was a fire in one of our neighborhoods and it unfortunately completely gutted a home. The residents of the home, a young man, an elderly gentleman and his pet dog, praise be to God where rescued before the home burned to the ground. The young man was spared any injuries but the elderly man received burns on about twenty five percent of his body and was transported to the hospital. The newscast, when televising the aftermath of the fire, had an indelible sight that will remain with me forever. There, standing tall on his hind legs, sitting in front of the home he just lost, was the elderly man's dog, standing guard and waiting for his companion to return. Neighbors tried to provide water and feed the dog, but the dog could not be swayed from his post. This beautiful act of love, devotion and loyalty is bringing tears back to my eyes as I relate this story to you. My prayers that evening and for many evenings to come were for the elderly man and his faithful companion, 'Please, Lord, let your loving hands be upon them, offering healing, protection and reuniting these loyal friends back together.'

My God does not build that kind of love and devotion for it to be discarded at a later time and date. I know in my heart, that even before their time on earth ends, God has already prepared a place in heaven for this gentleman and his faithful friend, a place where they can spend an eternity standing shoulder to shoulder on the threshold of their new heavenly home.

I think I have given you an ample view into my heart regarding our beloved pets and you're starting to understand that a loving God does not provide anything on a temporary basis, every gift has eternal significance.

There are people who genuinely believe when they leave this world, they will see their friends and loved ones in heaven. A most beautiful thought and that being the case, I know in my heart that ALL members of my family will be there as well.

Recently I read a feature story on MSN where a woman was taking her cat to the vet to be euthanized due to a serious irreconcilable illness. On the way to the vet's office, her cat, who was sitting next to her in the car, reached out and held her hand, which seemed to say, 'It's okay.' Now, you can call it blasphemy, hierocracy, or lunacy, but in my heart of hearts, I truly believe those two souls will meet again in heaven.

When my daughters, Genese and Breanna, were toddlers, we watched what seemed like well over one hundred times, a video that was a great favorite of theirs, a Disney movie entitled *All Good Dogs Go to Heaven*. So, in closing I will take the liberty of saying, if Disney said it, I believe it and it's good enough for me. Amen!

P.S. If all of the above has still not convinced you, take a closer look at the word 'dog'; when spelled backwards, it spells 'God.'

And Jesus Wept

One of the many glimpses we see throughout the Bible of the humanness of Jesus comes to us in the Book of John when Jesus hears that His lifelong friend Lazarus has died.

John 11:32–35 'When Mary reached the place where Jesus was and saw Him, she fell at His knees and said, "Lord, if you had been here, my brother would not have died." When Jesus saw her weeping, and the Jews who had come along with her were also weeping, He was deeply moved in spirit and troubled. "Where have you laid him?" he asked. "Come and see Lord," they replied. Jesus wept.'

Remember, the verse in John 11:35—'Jesus wept'—is the shortest verse in the Bible but it also speaks volumes and we will refer back to it later on.

Recent events around the world—terrorist acts, the slaughter of innocent people, hatred, fear, grief, pain, and this heinous list unfortunately can go on—often make me wonder if what's falling from the sky is actual rain or the tears of our Lord. He certainly has every reason to be upset with us, but most fortunately for you and me, His love and forgiveness transcend far beyond our human comprehension. Before you accuse me of being a heretic or falling off a theological limb, remember I prefaced my comments by saying, 'It makes *me* wonder.'

I fully understand our Heavenly Father is greater than anything we can imagine, but I also know how very much He loves us and that fact can sometimes make it hard to differentiate between an earthly love and a heavenly agape love. Case in point; we know that if we disappoint a loved one, it can cause a tearful reaction and while we don't mean to disappoint anyone, life happens and we are, after all, only human. We are the children of our Heavenly Father, and what parent doesn't want the absolute best for their children?

So, philosophically, let's say it rains tears, how then can we turn that sorrow into brilliant rays of 'Son' Shine? There are many ways to experience this, but a great start is; Love thy Neighbor, read your Bible, talk to your Father in heartfelt prayer and accept Jesus Christ as your Lord and Savior. I can feel those warm rays gloriously beaming down already.

When we truly believe that 'Real Joy comes when we value what God values,' we will never go spiritually astray, our hearts and minds will always be in the right place. A joyful heart is not only pleasing to God but to all those around you and provides great joy and comfort to those in need. When God instructed us to 'Love thy Neighbor,' He was not just referring to the folks that live in our either side of our home or in our neighborhoods, He was referring to the world as our neighbors. The single most important commandment, 'Love Thy Neighbor,' should always remain at the forefront of our Christian walk.

If we stop to do a little soul searching, how many times do you think we have looked at someone and immediately decided 'I don't like him or her'? What prompted this dislike? Did they look at us wrong? Perhaps they don't fit the mold of the type of folks we want to associate with. Maybe it's the way they talk or act. Whatever the reason, we are making a biased judgment or a prejudiced view of God's children. It doesn't sound very nice when it's put that way.

It's hard to love or for that matter even like someone who has committed an egregious act, but in the eyes of our Lord, sin is sin, regardless of the magnitude we arbitrarily assign to it. Knowing that we are all guilty of sin at one time or another, we are called to offer forgiveness, no matter how hard it may be, to those we dub as the offenders of our beliefs. So, direct your heavenly arrow (prayer) which can be as simple yet poignant as the prayer Jesus offered in His darkest hour to His Heavenly Father on our behalf.

Luke 23:34' 'Father forgive them for they do not know what they are doing.'

Colossians 2:13–16 'Bear with each other and forgive whatever grievances you may have against one another. Forgive as the Lord forgave you. And over all these virtues put on love, which binds them all together in perfect unity. Let the peace of Christ rule in your hearts, since as members of one body you were called to peace. And be thankful. Let the word of Christ dwell in you richly as you teach and admonish one another with all wisdom.'

Luke 6:37 'Do not judge and you will not be judged, do not condemn and you will not be condemned. Forgive, and you will be forgiven.'

Forgiveness is not an easy task; it's not a switch you can turn on and off, so the best advice I can give you is to pray to the Lord, seek discernment and strength to make the tough calls of forgiveness and then feel the love of the Lord.

One last point to ponder: God does not make junk. The defects can be removed. The removing agent is one basic ingredient, the power of prayer. Try it!

And who knows, once you have forgiveness in your heart, that moisture that falls from above, the moisture I referred to earlier as possible tears may actually be a Shower of Joy mixed with a generous amount of Son Shine. Thanks be to God!

Saving Grace or Saving Face

When we are involved in sin, are we more concerned about saving grace or saving face? A little humility may be in order here; we need to face the cold hard fact that no one likes getting caught with their hand in the cookie jar. In my house, the crumbs on my shirt or the crumbs on the floor shine the spotlight of guilt on me every time. One would think by now I would have learned to hide or cleanup the incriminating evidence.

Cookie Crumbs should be everyone's worst case scenario, but unfortunately, they take a back seat to sin and we all know that sin is not as easily swept under the rug. The humorous part of this parody is that we believe we have become the master of the cover up. Wrong, the only ones we are fooling are ourselves, the Lord's sin finding vacuum cleaner reaches under the carpet of our feeble attempt at camouflage and into our 'out of sight out of mind' secret silos of sin.

Let's assume sin begets guilt, so the next logical assumption should be; guilt keeps us limping in the dark but grace keeps us walking in the light. And Son Light, my Brothers and Sisters, is exactly where our Lord wants us to be. Much like the story of creation, God loved to walk in the garden with Adam and Eve and here we are thousands of years later and nothing has changed, He is still thrilled to spend time with each and every one of us, day in and day out. This thought alone should evoke an immediate Thank You, Lord.

While we were created in His image, the sin of the Garden of Eden will forever remain a part of our lives, but herein again is yet another display of His love; He gave us a path to seek forgiveness with the ultimate destination of salvation.

Some of us ease our guilt by reasoning 'Hey, I'm only human.' Yes, we are indeed only human, but that does not give us the right to whip out the 'get out of jail free card' whenever it's convenient to do so. In our humanly state of being, we have become the absolute masters of the fine art of justification. When in a sinful pinch, we can justify almost any act or deed—good, bad, or indifferent. Why, because it helps soothe our troubled souls. Unfortunately, this is just another cover up, another distraction from what we truly know deep in our hearts what needs to be done; seek His forgiveness through prayer. We cheat ourselves through prayerlessness. While our choices can take us out of God's will, they can never take us out of God's reach.

What keeps us from acknowledging our sins and bring the hide and seek sin game to a complete halt? Do we suffer from embarrassment; everyone thinks I'm such a good Christian and I don't want them to think otherwise? Perhaps it's an open declaration of our weaknesses; no one likes their shortcomings exposed for the entire world to see? Whatever the reason, we need to redirect our spiritual energies from the ground up, getting on our knees in prayer, looking up to heaven, acknowledge our sin, not bury it somewhere in a dark corner of our soul but out into the light of His forgiveness.

Grace: God's Reward At Christ's Expense. Don't waste such a beautiful gift that came at such a high cost, the blood of our Savior. Remember our Lord spilled His own blood rather than ours. Our doing can never be worth more than His dying!

Ephesians 2:4–5 'But because of His great love for us, God, who is rich in mercy, made us alive with Christ even when we were dead in transgressions, it is by grace you have been saved.'

Romans 3:22–24 'This righteousness from God comes through faith, in Jesus Christ to all who believe. There is no difference for all have sinned and fall short of the glory of God, and are justified freely by his grace through the redemption that came by Christ Jesus.'

Ephesians 2:8 'For it is by grace you have been saved, through faith, and this not from yourselves, it is the gift of God.'

You have only two choices that I can see: You can save face, a temporary fix or you can save your eternal life through grace. Please choose wisely.

And now for the good news; your Heavenly Father is waiting at the gate for your arrival home; He will be the one with the huge smile and the open arms.

How Far Do You Reach?

I'm told that the spiritual reach of a Christian should far exceed their grasp. Now, having said that, let's look at a few everyday opportunities that are indeed within our reach.

The neighbor across the street just had five yards of mulch dumped in his driveway, an imposing task for any DIY (Do It Yourself) person to tackle. Do we stand safely and obscurely behind the curtains and think, 'Wow, it's going to take Bill all day to move that mulch,' or do we step out of our safe haven, walk across the street with shovel in hand, and offer Bill some neighborly assistance?

Your church or child's school is attempting to build some props for a play they are about to put on, but either your keen observations or the bewildered builders scratching their heads quickly tell you they do not have the slightest clue how to begin the project. While simple construction is your forte, it's your day off and you were really looking forward to chilling out and watching football games for most of the afternoon. Do you decide that it's not going to kill you to miss a little football and offer your expertise, or do you think, 'I'm sure sooner or later they will figure out how to build the props' and walk away from reaching out to those in need?

Finally, you're in a huge department store, one famously known for having a skeleton sales force, and you see an apparent customer with the deer-in-the-headlights look on their face as they stand in the aisle of the store looking obviously frustrated. It's obvious they are looking for something but are clueless to its location. Do you continue on your own shopping quest—after all, you not an employee of the store—or do you stop and offer guidance or at the very least, offer to locate a salesperson for them?

The examples above were certainly indicative of how our physical reach can help ease the struggle of those in need. Now, let's take a look at the flip side, spiritual assistance to those in need.

You learn through a reputable grapevine, that a family in the congregation at your church is struggling with their spirituality and may be planning to pack it in, church is not working for them. Our options are several. We can approach the family and ask if they are okay or in need of any assistance, or we can contact the pastor to ensure he is aware of their struggles, or we can take the approach that it's very prudent to keep our nose out of their issues.

While there are many similar scenarios we can bring to light, the fact of the matter is very clear; we are compelled by the same standards and actions of our Lord and Savior when He walked the face of His creation. We are to reach out and help those in need.

In the examples we looked at, the physical effort we needed to expend in offering help to those in need was minimal at best. So, we had to give up a few hours of the idiot box, take a few hours out of our day or simply ask if someone needed help. Other than the calories from helping with the mulch, which we probably needed to burn anyway, everything else was a minimal effort on our part.

How very fortunate are we that the Lord continually reaches out to help each and every one of us, day in and day out, 24/7/365, and while there are times I'm sure we did not truly deserve His help, it was there nonetheless.

Another way to reach out to those in need is through prayer. We all know that life is by no means perfect, and therefore, we all know of someone who would benefit from our petitions on their behalf. By the way, His reach is significantly further than anything we will ever face, and that in of itself should give us the incentive to exercise our earthly spiritual reach. And yet the Lord has given us, through prayer, the ability to extend our spiritual reach directly to His very being, because He loves us so very much.

Psalm 33:20–22 'We wait in hope for the Lord; he is our help and our shield. In him our hearts rejoice, for we trust in his holy name. May your unfailing love rest upon us O Lord even as we put our hope in you.'

Leviticus 25:35 'If one of your countrymen becomes poor and is unable to support himself among you, help him as you would, an alien or a temporary resident, so he can continue to live among you.'

The Passion of a Pastor

A Tribute to Father Chuck Woehler

My dear friend, mentor and pastor, the Rev. Chuck Woehler has been in the ministry for well over 40 years and he has spent the last 27 years as the Pastor of St. Thomas Episcopal Church in San Antonio, Texas. My family and I believe that an appropriate ending to this book would be a heartfelt tribute to a man of God, who served his church with the grace, heart and righteousness of a true servant of the Lord.

Father Chuck, please know that my entire family has been blessed by your ministry and your friendship and we will always cherish the great times, the adventures and the moments we have shared together and most assuredly by the St. Thomas Family you have welcomed us into.

Approximately 20 plus years ago when we walked through the St. Thomas doors, we felt like this was going to be our church. As we sat in the sanctuary and listened to an impassioned sermon delivered by you, the die was cast for the Villani' family, we wanted to be a part of this church family, a church that many in the congregation now lovingly refer to as; 'The House that Chuck built. Thank you Lord!

Over the years, we have watched with great pride in the direction you have taken St. Thomas, how you have unceasingly cared for, ministered to and prayed for the congregants of our church. Most notable over these years was that every member of St. Thomas always and we truly mean always, took priority over your own personal needs, time and desires. It was never even a debatable issue, your flock came first.

One of our greatest memories comes during a baptism, when we watch the heartfelt joy on your face when you welcome a new member into the family of Christ.

We can't even begin to imagine the number of lives you have touched over the past 27 years of your ministry at St. Thomas, the faith and direction you have so generously, unselfishly and lovingly offered to anyone who graced the doors of our church. We also believe it's very safe to say that many of the people and souls that have been captured through grace by Father Chuck Woehler now have a confirmed seat on their journey to their heavenly home.

And finally, we love our friend very much and we wish that your retirement may be as richly blessed as the many lives you have so richly blessed over your 27 years at St. Thomas. May the peace of the Lord be always with you!

Gary, Cathy, Genese, Breanna and Heidi Villani

My Praise and Thanksgiving Offering...

Lord, I praise you and thank you for bringing me, Cathy, Genese, and Breanna into the St. Thomas Church Family.

Lord, thank you so very much for Father Chuck, my Pastor, my mentor and my friend, who has spent countless hours going over my type written drafts, correcting spelling, grammar and the occasional spiritual blunder.

Lord, I praise you and thank you for filling my heart and my mind with the desire to write this book and for the recall of this material so that I may share it with others.

Lord, I thank you for expanding my time so that I was able to complete the task that you set before me.

Lord, I praise you and thank you for all the truly wonderful believers and participants in every Sunday school class that I have led and for allowing me to grow so very much from their wisdom, their sharing and their experiences. I have been truly blessed.

Lord, I thank you for the support and patience of my family as I typed long into the night.

Lord, I thank you for so graciously blessing me with the desire, the ability and the opportunities to lead Christians in the study of your Word.

Lord, I thank you for my friends Steve and Debbie Zito, who, by their walk in life, were living examples of faith and trust in God.

Lord, I thank you for my friend Willie Nichols who patiently and faithfully read every written page of this book and provided me with the encouragement and the confidence to pursue this task to the finish. And Lord, a special thank you to Mrs. Verma Nichols, Willies Mom, who provided many wonderful pearls of wisdom that grace some of the pages of my work.

Lord, a heartfelt and grateful thank you for my good friend Joe Bodak, who graciously afforded me many hiking adventures around the world. It was on each and every hiking adventure, I was able to seek solace and inspiration to write as I enjoyed the beauty and splendor of the Lords magnificent creation.

Heavenly Father, I praise you as The Great I AM and The Most Holy of Holy's. I thank you for your mercy, your grace and your patience with me, none of which I deserve. Father it is my prayer that all who read the book that we have written together, will grow closer to you and that they will take at least more step closer to their eternal home with you. All this I ask in the name of your Son, our Savior, Jesus Christ.

Amen.